South Africa:
A Botched Civilization?

*Racial Conflict and Identity in
Selected South African Novels*

Jane Davis

University Press of America, Inc.
Lanham • New York • London

Copyright © 1997 by
University Press of America,® Inc.
4720 Boston Way
Lanham, Maryland 20706

3 Henrietta Street
London, WC2E 8LU England

All rights reserved
Printed in the United States of America
British Cataloging in Publication Information Available

Library of Congress Cataloging-in-Publication Data

Jane Davis
South Africa : a botched civilization? : racial conflict and identity in
selected South African novels / Jane Davis.
p. cm.
Includes bibliographical references and index.
1. South African fiction (English)--History and criticism. 2. Literature
and society--South Africa--History--20th century. 3. Social conflict in
literature. 4. Race relations in literature. 5. Group identity in
literature. 6. Blacks in literature. 7. Whites in literature. I. Title.
PR9362.5.D38 1996   823--dc21   96-36986 CIP

ISBN 0-7618-0604-0 (cloth: alk. ppr.)
ISBN 0-7618-0605-9 (pbk: alk. ppr.)

∞™ The paper used in this publication meets the minimum
requirements of American National Standard for information
Sciences—Permanence of Paper for Printed Library Materials,
ANSI Z39.48—1984

Dedicated to J. Congress Mbata who
sacrificed much to transform South Africa;
"His life was [noble] and the elements so
mixed in him that nature might stand up
and say to all the world,
'This was a man.'"

Contents

Preface	vii
Acknowledgments	xi
Introduction	
Racial Conflict, Identity and Mythology	xiii

Chapter 1
    The "Nigger in Them": Sarah Gertrude Millin's
    Ideology of "Blood" in *God's Stepchildren* (1924)   1

Chapter 2
    "The Ways of Whitefolks" II: White Sterility in Gordimer's
    A World of Strangers (1958) and La Guma's *Time of the
    Butcherbird* (1979)   39

Chapter 3
    In the Grasp of White Primitives: The Fight for Humanity in
    Andre Brink's *A Dry White Season* (1984)   69

Chapter 4
    Abrahams' *The Path of Thunder* (1948) and Fugard's *Tsotsi*
    (1980): Cross-Currents with African American Literature   107

Chapter 5
    Coming of Age: Lynn Freed's *Home Ground* (1986) and
    Toeckey Jones's *Go Well, Stay Well* (1979)   145

Conclusion
    The Deep Shadow   163

Bibliography	177
Index	181

Preface

Transitions. That would be an excellent first word to open my book. Of course, such decisions are central as we writers often spend needlessly long hours on the search for our own "Call me Ishmael." "He wrote and wrote. . . . He'd say, 'I'm working on these transitions but new riffs keep occurring to me'." "Just recently Ralph told me that I would be getting the book soon, and I know he had been working on it every day, but that he was having trouble with what he termed 'transitions'."

The complications of "transitions," which Ralph Ellison's colleagues recall above as plaguing his completion of his second novel, are certainly something with which this writer can empathize. For while no one would be so condescending or stupid as to have as his or her main response to this book the use I make of 'therefore' of 'nevertheless,' — transitions in the Comp. 101 sense — transitions, in the sense of the "new riffs" that plagued Ellison, certainly confront any writer on South Africa. And for this reason, I must clarify certain issues concerning my perspective on "transitions" and related issues from the outset.

"There is no white man who can write my book." These words from the Jamaican poet Claude McKay capture — both elliptically and essentially — my perspective on the transitions which have occurred in South Africa over the period during which this book was conceived, researched, and written. While it is a stupendous development that in the course of less that a decade South Africa has gone from being in a state of emergency to having Nelson Mandela as president, on many of the following pages, you will find my view of fundamental change in South Africa to seem somewhat skeptical. My view is colored — and the pun is intended — by living in a society where *de facto* racism and segregation shape the lives of many Blacks. Hence, my view of progress in racial relations and economic opportunities for Blacks is best summed up by Derrick Bell's *Faces at the Bottom of the Well*, where Bell makes clear that racial progress is not the relay race many misguided souls would like to believe where each generation picks up the baton and goes further towards 'winning' than the last. Rather, progress is a matter of constant diligence where a 'finish line' does not exist, and those who think or feel that the transformation of society is something that does not take their continued involvement and vigilance in confronting inevitable setbacks are merely looking for a resting place where they can live with their comforting illusions. Moreover, in judging these ideas, consider Mandela's words in his acceptance of the Nobel Prize:

> We live with the hope that . . . South Africa will be a microcosm of the new world that is striving to be born. This must be a world of democracy and respect for human rights; a world freed from the horrors of poverty, hunger, deprivation and ignorance.

Behind such goals lies the need for land redistribution and increased economic opportunities for Blacks, among other things. So before the world starts celebrating 'freedom' in South Africa, we need to realize that, as Bell points out, the attainment and maintenance of freedom is a struggle; in the words of a song, "Freedom isn't free." Thus, before we absolve ourselves of the need to care about South Africa, we need to realize that the struggle for the ideals that Mandela discussed in his Nobel speech will never give us such an absolution; nor should we want it.

Having used the word "we," I should clarify how this book is written against a certain ideology. First, much of this book is written with a belief best explained in Gunnar Myrdal's groundbreaking study of racism, *An American Dilemma*: that racism against Blacks has been the manifestation of a "white problem"—psychological problems which I explore in several chapters. And here, I know someone will wonder, "What has *An American Dilemma* got to do with South Africa?" My sources include works on racism in and outside of South Africa because many works discuss certain psychological features of racism that are represented in South Africa, America, and other societies. Hence, theories of the psychology of racism and bigotry will be applied to the South African literature under discussion which best exemplifies them.

The topic of white racism is another area in which this book is written against a certain ideology: an ideology that recoils from frank talk about racism. Hence, I expect that my discussion of sterility and moral bankruptcy in racist whites will provoke in some readers a discomfort that is best summed up by Lani Guinier: that many feel "that the remedy for racism is that we just stop talking about race." My answer is that creative tension and even creative conflict are much

Preface

more productive than suppression. If a nonracial society is ever to have a glimmer of hope, it will only come after we process the manifestations and effects of racism. I hope that this book is at least a small contribution to that process.

Two final points are important before the reader goes on to the rest of the book. First, the theoreticians used in this book do not necessarily constitute the 'greatest hits' of current post-colonial critical theory. They do constitute writers whom I have found most relevant on the topics under discussion. In addition, the books under discussion range primarily from works published from the late 1940s to the mid 1980s. Again, I have focused on novels I have found most relevant to the topics under discussion, primarily the construction of identity in a racist society. Rest assured that I am thoroughly familiar with current South African literature — but broadening the scope of this book would make it into a different project. Contemporary South African literature of the 1990s and liberation is certainly a timely topic — it is simply not the main focus of this work. Finally, I would like to point out that I discuss Sarah Gertrude Millin's 1920s' novel *God's Stepchildren* not to use her as a 'strawman' or model of obsolete racism. Discerning readers will know that her work is an example of many timeless psychological features of racism. Hence, though Millin is certainly the epitome of late 19th and early 20th century racist theories, she is more than the antique that J.M. Coetzee judges her to be — many of her racist ideas are both timely and timeless — and that is part of our collective tragedy.

"I'm working on these transitions but new riffs keep occurring to me." Me, too, Ralph; would that they were of the Comp. 101 kind.

Acknowledgments

J. Congress Mbata is the first person whom I must thank. Congress, whom I knew all too briefly in his final years, was my colleague at the Africana Center at Cornell University. Congress Mbata was history in the flesh, for he had contributed much to black liberation in South Africa (he had been, for example, the very first secretary of the A. N. C. Youth League when Nelson Mandela was its president). Moreover, what was most inspiring about Congress was that though he had endured much hardship as a result of his dedication to equality and justice in South Africa, no finer and truer gentleman could be found on God's earth. Congress possessed the grace of a true visionary and revolutionary. His spirit lives on not only in those who knew him and admired him; but also in the lives of those who have benefited and will benefit from the stalwart courage of Congress and people like him. Congress, your spirit spurred me on during the difficult times in the course of this book; this book is for you.

I also must thank the National Endowment for the Humanities for opportunities which stimulated me to conceive of this book. This book would never have been conceived if I had not been fortunate enough to be a participant in a National Endowment for the Humanities Summer Institute on post-colonial literature directed by Albert Wertheim at Indiana University. Furthermore, I was lucky enough to participate in a National Endowment for the Humanities Summer Seminar at the University of California at Berkeley, Race and Slavery in American Literature, directed by Eric J. Sundquist. This seminar raised many theoretical questions which were to become central in my research on South Africa. To the N.E.H. and to Al and Eric, I owe my deepest gratitude.

Another major opportunity that deeply affected my work and my life was my two years as a Mellon postdoctoral teaching and research fellow in the Africana Center at Cornell University. Cornell provided magnificent library resources as well as excellent students on whom to 'test' my ideas. Moreover, in addition to giving me the opportunity to have Congress Mbata as a colleague, the African Center provided me with other colleagues whose intellectual prowess had an impact on my work. Specifically, I want to thank Locksley Edmundson for letting me sit in on his stimulating summer class on South Africa; and James

Acknowledgments

Turner, whose intellectual sharpness and knowledge of issues concerning the connection between race, power and identity inspired me to think further about these issues. Finally, Tom Weissinger, director of the library in the Africana Center, provided needed assistance in helping me find sources and introducing me to certain works which have become an essential part of my research and teaching. In sum, without the Africana Studies and Research Center, this book probably would not exist.

Other colleagues made needed and positive contributions to this work. Chris GoGwilt, my colleague at Fordham University, gave a careful and perceptive critique of the manuscript. Moreover, his insight and humanity have been an oasis in the desert. Also, Lupenga Mphande of the Ohio State University gave important suggestions concerning the manuscript. And Paula Backscheider, then of the University of Rochester, listened to and critiqued many of my ideas in the developmental stages of the study. In addition, without Paula, I would never have known about Al Wertheim's N.E.H. Institute, without which this work would not exist and my life would be vastly different. Each of these individuals has enriched my work and my life.

Deep thanks must go to those who helped with the research or preparation of this manuscript. First, Liza Garnes gave invaluable research assistance as a summer exchange student at Cornell from Princeton University. At different times, Sheila Towner of the Africana Center and Siga Jagne of Spelman College did much of the laborious typing of this work. Bill Mottolese also contributed much time and effort to the preparation of this manuscript. I am also deeply indebted to Dorothea Thorne, who as a visiting student at the University of Rochester, when I was teaching there, showed me a great deal about South Africa and was a living example of the courage displayed by those who have struggled for liberation from oppression.

Words cannot express my gratitude to my family and to my mother for reading and making suggestions on the manuscript. Finally, Sandy, Danny, Julie, Amalia, Emma, and Zach: you have provided unknowingly the spiritual milk which has helped sustain me. To all of these, I give eternal thanks.

Introduction

Racial Conflict, Identity and Mythology

> Upon the man with the black skin there is projected the evil which the [racist] white man refuses to acknowledge as part of his own nature, and the black man becomes the scapegoat of the white. Unlike the traditional scapegoat, however, he cannot be sent into the wilderness, out of sight and out of mind, so to speak, but must remain a constant reminder and therefore, a constant object of hostility within [a racist] white community.
>
> I.D. MacCrone
> *Race Attitudes in South Africa*

I.

"The problem of the twentieth century is the problem of the color line — the relation of the darker to the lighter races of men in Asia and Africa, in America and the islands of the sea."[1] These words were written by W.E.B. DuBois at the beginning of the twentieth century in *The Souls of Black Folk.*

A sea of humanity — nearly 200,000 people by some estimates — awaited the arrival of Nelson Mandela in Harlem in June of 1990, nearly half a year after his release from prison. As I stood in the teeming crowd, we were all awash with anticipation. People sat on ledges in front of the top of buildings, stood on the raised islands in the street facing the Adam Clayton Powell State Office Building, crowded down on the street with less than an inch of space between people. The day, while a harbinger of future South African liberation, was that and more. For me, the appearance of Mandela in Harlem was also a stimulus for reflection. The past was alive; rejuvenated by the appearance of yet another Black hero in the community through which Black giants have walked: the late Congressman Adam Clayton Powell; Malcolm X; Langston Hughes; and untold, unknown others. Mandela would cite some of the great Black heroes when he spoke. I stared at him; I stared at the sky, a sky that Franz Fanon had once said was filled with an oppressive "white song" which deafened the world to the songs of Blacks.[2] Here, today, the song of Blacks filled the air.

Introduction

The singers were both Mandela and the unseen Black heroes, including his late comrade, J. Congress Mbata, with whom he has walked; those in whose footsteps he walks; and those, even yet unborn, for whom he helps to pave the way. And what were some of the words of the song Mandela sang, the song which filled the air, seeming to rid it of the oppressive "white song"? While seemingly silenced, the "white song" was responded to by Mandela in the words he chose at a key point in his speech. Again courageous Blacks of the past were present as Mandela quoted: "The problem of the twentieth century is the problem of the color-line."

II.

One of my key goals in this book is to focus on the ramifications of "the problem of the twentieth century" as depicted in certain South African novels, primarily of the era of apartheid. My quest to a degree is similar to the one Toni Morrison identifies in her study of white American literature, *Playing in the Dark*: "I began to see how the literature I revered, the literature I loathed, behaved in its encounter with racial ideology. . . . Yes, I wanted to identify those moments when . . . literature was complicit in the fabrication of racism, but equally important, I wanted to see when literature exploded and undermined it."[3] Toni Morrison's statements in her critical work helps to explain many of my own central goals in my study of South African fiction. More specifically, I am concerned with writers' representations of the effect of racial conflict on the identities of the oppressor and the oppressed. In the novels under discussion, racial conflict and its impact on identity are revealed in a variety of ways.

For example, it is interesting to look at racial and identity conflicts among the Black characters in certain South African and American fictional works. A comparison of the following sets is especially useful: "Of the Coming of John" from W.E.B. DuBois' *The Souls of Black Folk*, Langston Hughes's "Home" from *The Ways of White Folks* and *The Path of Thunder* by South African writer Peter Abrahams; and Athol Fugard's *Tsotsi* and Richard Wright's *Native Son*. These works yield a comparison of modes of identity of Black characters who are in conflict with society, and, at times, with themselves. These conflicts

Introduction

make evident a comparison of types of identity of Black characters who try to assert themselves against the white racist notion that they have a predetermined 'place' and should never attempt to move beyond it. All of them do. And all of them die. Yet, the writers are stressing at least two central points: the homicidal lengths to which some whites will go to retain their superior status in racist societies; and that regardless of the danger, many oppressed people would rather 'die on their feet than live on their knees.' In direct opposition to the works discussed above is Sarah Gertrude Millin's *God's Stepchildren*, in which the white racist novelist herself is at war with miscegenation in general, with Blacks and with people of mixed Black and white heritage in particular. In this novel, one sees the power of a member of a dominant group to define identity and its development when non-whites are at the hands of a bigoted white artist. Clearly, *God's Stepchildren* has an agenda: to define so-called 'Coloreds' and the whites who intermarry as befouled beings.[4] The novel reveals, therefore, how a white bigoted author can use the power to define a different — and to her, abhorred — racial group as having no point of entry into the dominant culture. Moreover, as Millin argues for separation of the races, she makes ever so obvious that separate is inherently unequal, as the 'Coloreds' are depicted as having no culture other than an abysmal, poverty-stricken one, as is shown when the 'Colored' Barry decides to return to his 'Colored' roots. Furthermore, racial conflict in Millin's novel is deeply tied to the issue of identity, both in terms of how Millin defines "Coloredness" in the novel and in how the 'Colored' characters are at war within themselves, wanting to realize their "whites status [and] white hopes."[5]

In opposition to Millin, both Nadine Gordimer, especially in *A World of Strangers*, and Alex La Guma, in *Time of the Butcherbird* depict how a racist system befouls white identity. Both of these authors depict, among other things, that the South African system of white domination gives rise to a race of whites who share two things — active or passive support of the racist status quo and a psychological and moral bankruptcy of identity. In *Time of the Butcherbird*, for instance, Maisie and Edgar Stopes' choices to try to be above the racial turmoil of which they are actually in the midst results in their being mindless, empty characters whose triviality of thought and action regarding South African racism La Guma obviously detests. Though

Introduction

Edgar — and the Afrikaner politician Hannes Muellen — is killed by the Black Shilling Murile who shows one way in which Blacks may grow spiritually richer in rebellion, by acting as a butcherbird and getting rid of whites who act as parasites towards Blacks, no white character undergoes an equivalent transformation. Thus, whites are faced with personal complicity in keeping things as they are (as is Maisie's role in thinking of protecting herself from racial conflicts as being like a mere James Bond movie). La Guma shows the whites who populate *Time of the Butcherbird* to be barren souls in a volatile situation.

Similarly, many of Gordimer's novels throughout her career are also populated by sterile white characters. Whether it be the heroine's in-laws in *The Late Bourgeois World* or the people in the store, as well as Ann, the white woman having an affair with a Black man, in *Occasion for Loving*, Gordimer's characterizations of many whites emphasize their sterility. There is this description of the racist shop assistant, for example, from *Occasion for Loving*:

> The assistant was a little gray-skinned woman without breasts or lips or eyebrows, but whose head of hair, distinct from the rest of her, was fresh from the hairdresser's, elaborately swirled and curled, stiff and brilliant yellow.[6]

The woman's racism is almost immediately shown after this unsavory description. Thus, Gordimer uses description, as well as characterization, to show the sterility of those who are either blatantly racist or who are part of a careless minority which ultimately upholds racism. Clearly, when Gordimer makes such descriptions, it is not merely to have a backdrop for the main action. Such passages show, in fact, that she is populating some of her novels with the sort of sterile persons who contribute, thinkingly or unthinkingly, to prejudice and exploitation. In contrast, therefore, to Millin, both Gordimer and La Guma show in their characterizations that one's facing or not facing the racial conflict of South Africa greatly determines the quality of one's identity.

Afrikaner writer Andre Brink's *A Dry White Season* goes beyond Gordimer's depiction of sterility in *A World of Strangers* and makes more of a blanket condemnation of different facets of white South African society of the apartheid era than does La Guma in *Time of the*

Introduction

Butcherbird. In Brink's novel, which concerns a white man's search for justice for a Black man and his son, both of whom die in detention, racist Afrikanderdom is blatantly condemned as a totalitarian institution. Ben du Toit, the Afrikaner protagonist, is progressively crushed by his family, by the religious system, by police, by a member of the medical profession, and by the legal system as he learns more of the truth about how these systems operate. In this novel, though the interracial conflict is central, it takes a back seat to Brink's concern with an innocent white's (Ben's) intraracial conflict with the apartheid system. Most importantly, this conflict also goes to the heart of Ben's identity as a Afrikaner. As Ben tries to find the truth of the two Black men's deaths, other Afrikaners, including members of almost every aspect of Afrikaner establishment, cause him to wonder if he is an Afrikaner in the sense of the word as defined by the dominant group itself. In facing this issue, Ben's thoughts of his identity are greatly shaped by the interracial and intraracial conflicts he must face as a result of questioning, rather that merely supporting, and being, a part of the dominant group which upholds Afrikaner-devised apartheid.

Still, however dramatic, and however much Brink's novel shows the lengths to which white South African society has gone to keep racial equality at bay, defeat is not the message of central South African literature of the apartheid era. Later novels such as Gordimer's *July's People* and *A Sport of Nature*, in addition to Yvonne Burgess' *The Strike*, among others, show the endurance of the struggle against white racist rule. Moreover, in this light, it is important to see how relationships on a personal level can happen even in the midst of racial conflict. In Lynn Freed's *Home Ground* and Toeckey Jones' *Go Well, Stay Well*, the important issue of interracial friendships in the midst of a situation of racial conflict is depicted. Both white female protagonists, Ruth in Home Ground and Candy in Go Well, Stay Well, are in conflict with themselves regarding their feeling for Blacks. Moreover, as a result of this conflict, the protagonists find themselves in their relationships with Blacks on a journey which will either expand or contract their consciousness and broaden or restrict their identities in relation to how they reflect a racially oppressive system. In addition, both books raise the question of whether there can be a deep and meaningful development of white identity that can lead to interracial relationships that are more than "a slender stream at best."[7]

Introduction

As the works under discussion show, the impact of racial conflict on identity is major. From white 'superiority' to white sterility to Black rebellion to Black-white relationships, the consciousness of the characters impacts upon the authors' portrayal of whether there can be a meaningful development of identity under a racist system. The complexities of these issues will be explored in this study.

III.

Having given in the preceding pages a brief discussion of the major themes and chapters of this study, I would like now to focus on some of the larger issues involved in the aforementioned topics in order to lay a foundation for the succeeding chapters.

As Bill Derman writes in " Race and Class, Society and Biology: Problems in the Analysis of South Africa," "The "race" question should be understood as socially constructed race and racism, and not "race" as a natural or biological category."[8] What Derman is pointing out is that racism is not founded on the (purported) innate differences between races that racists like to claim gives authority to their ideas of white supremacy, but that racist ideology is a man-made fiction of distorted myth. Derman's analysis is especially relevant to Millin's *God's Stepchildren*, which is a quintessential expression of a racist ideology. Millin's racist argument is diagnosed accurately by recalling some of Franz Fanon's ideas on racism in *Black Skin, White Masks*. For instance, in Millin's fear of the Black presence in South African society and her call for strict segregation, "It is in his corporeality that the Negro is attacked. It is as a concrete personality that he is lynched. It is as an actual being that he is a threat" (163). Moreover, in Millin's hyper-vigilance in arguing against mixed marriages, the "[s]exual anxiety . . . predominant" in "Negrophobic women," as Fanon states it, is clear (158). Millin actually believed in and, in her writings, endorsed what Peter Abrahams so eloquently denounces in *The Path of Thunder*: that all people of Black heritage, including "[t]he educated Negro, [are] the slave of the spontaneous and cosmic Negro myth" (Fanon 14). This "Negro myth" is the racist ideology and all its defenses concerning alleged Black inferiority to whites and white supremacy over all who are not white. "[T]he myth of the Negro, the idea of the Negro" in the minds of racists has too often attempted to define Black's 'place' in

Introduction

this world (Fanon, 204). My hope is that this study breaks down and exposes racist myths, particularly in my analysis of how several novelists have attempted to perform the aforementioned tasks. In such an ideology as that represented by Millin, which is only one part of the timeless ideology of racism, as Fanon writes:

> The Negro is a toy in the white man's hands so, in order to shatter the hellish cycle, he explodes. I cannot go to a film without seeing myself. I wait for me. In the interval, just before the film starts, I wait for me. The people in the theater are watching me, examining me, waiting for me. A Negro groom is going to appear. My heart makes my head swim. The crippled veteran of the Pacific war says to my brother [in the film *Home of the Brave*], "Resign yourself to your color the way I got used to my stump; we're both victims." Nevertheless, with all my strength I refuse to accept that amputation. I feel in myself a soul as immense as the world, truly a soul as deep as the deepest to expand without limit. I am a master and I am advised to adopt the humility of a cripple.(140)

Fanon further elaborates on the ideology of racism and its effect on both white and Black identities:

> The white man wants the world; he wants it for himself alone. He finds himself predestined master of this world. He enslaves it. An acquisitive relation is established between the world and him. But there exist other values that fit only my forms. Like a magician, I robbed the white man of "a certain world," forever lost to him and his. When that happened, the white man must have been rocked backward by a force that he could not identify, so little used as he is to such reactions. . . . The white man had the anguished feeling that I was escaping from him and that I was taking something with me. He went through my pockets. He thrust probes into the last circumvolution of my brain. Everywhere he found only the obvious. So it was obvious I had a secret. (128)

What, one might ask, is this "secret"? This, clearly, is a huge question with multiple answers. Within the parameters of this literary study, Fanon again might be used to indicate the role of the writers who attempt to protest against and combat racism. With an urgency which is especially appropriate when applied to South African racism, with its history of violence and injustice, Fanon asks: "In this world,

Introduction

which is already trying to disappear, do I have to pose the problem of black truth?" (228). This is certainly the task of the anti-apartheid — i.e., anti-racist — writers under discussion: to counter the age-old racism of South Africa, with its ideologies of confines on both non-whites and on white dissidents. What such writers present is a multiplicity of truths which, as one will realize reading this study, overwhelm the life-negating ideology of racism.

Before proceeding, I wish to emphasize my methodology in my analysis of the literature under discussion. As you have just seen, with my use of Fanon and Derman, in my work it is central that one include some of that body of essential literature in fields other than literary criticism which illuminate the topics under discussion. I am not suggesting that one must superimpose 'predigested' material onto a literary analysis. Rather, while my main critical technique is rigorous textual analysis, it would be highly negligent — and ignorant— for me to exclude certain analyses from such fields as psychology, sociology or history, for example, which clarify the central implications of the issues raised in the fiction. Hence, I incorporate such writers as anthropologist Franz Boas and such works as Leonard Thompson's *The Political Mythology of Apartheid* and I.D. MacCrone's timeless and timely psychological classic, *Race Attitudes in South Africa*.

IV.

Directly related to the above discussion of methodology is the role of myth in my analysis of South African literature and the connection of this topic to the impact of racial conflict on identity. "[M]yth is above all a cultural force."[9] This idea by Bronislaw Malinowski captures my understanding of how much South African literature functions, the literature I discuss being primary examples. But what sort of myths are exemplified by this literature? Here, it is central to define or clarify my use of the term myth as it pertains to literature about racism — and certainly, by extension to racism itself. In applying and/or creating a definition of the term "myth" as it is analyzed in this work, the absolute best and most relevant source is Leonard Thompson's *The Political Mythology of Apartheid*. Thompson begins by stating the most fundamental aspects of his use of the word "myth": "By a political myth I mean a tale told about the past to legitimize or discredit a

Introduction

regime; and by political mythology, a cluster of such myths that reinforce one another."[10] Quoting form the 1976 Supplement to the Oxford English Dictionary, Thompson reinforces and expands upon the above definition of myth as "a tale which is told to justify some aspect of social order or of human experience"(8). Certainly, in the political arena, one might say that (logically or illogically speaking), apartheid was "justified" by racism. Similarly, in literature, the ideas of fiction work to either reinforce or argue against the central mythology of white South Africa, which has been racism. In this regard, it is necessary to distinguish between the literary myths under discussion in this work. Clearly, Sarah Gertrude Millin's racist *God's Stepchildren* is a conservative myth in that it argues for the conservation of racial division and for the belief in white superiority to other races. Hence, Millin's novel may even be conservative to the point of anticipating the ultimate conservation of white power and privilege: apartheid. (This point should answer the argument that Millin's racial philosophy relatively early in her adulthood seems at odds with her later support of apartheid — a point made by her biographer Martin Rubin in *Sarah Gertrude Millin*.) In contrast to Millin, however, the other South African authors, La Guma, Gordimer, Abrahams, Fugard, Jones and Freed, represent a central distinction in how the term mythology should be understood. For as Thompson writes in *The Political Mythology of Apartheid*, "Reacting against the racist order and ideology, the subject peoples have been creating a liberatory mythology" (242-43). In my study, we might add dissidents with "the subject peoples" in creating alternative myths; for, in reality, Black and white (and other races) who disagreed with the dominant mythology of racism are 'subjected' to it — albeit to vastly differing degrees. In any case, these are the two opposing mythologies my study focuses on: what I term 'oppressive mythology' — i.e., that which upholds racism; and to borrow Thompson's term, "liberatory mythology" written by writers who wish to expose and critique the human toll exacted by the politics and culture of racism in South Africa. Hence, understanding the literature under discussion as representing, in Millin's work, oppressive myths and, except for Millin, offering liberatory counter-myths, is central to one's reading of this book. To state it differently, against the oppressive political myths of South African racism, to quote Thompson, "Racial myths are created and propagated by . . . opponents of a regime, to discredit it or promote its downfall"(4). This clash is what I will examine on the literary

Introduction

front— the clash between oppressive myths of racism against the liberatory myths of the opponents of racism — clearly this critic included, in the latter group, as I am the organizing mind (or organizing principle) of this study. Thus, my goal is to expand upon the purpose of myth as Henry Tudor discusses it in a passage analyzing Malinowski's belief that myth "function[s] to prevent rather than promote structural change" in societies.[11] The key to my study is to examine how fiction writers, principally novelists, either uphold and further create oppressive myths, thus arguing against a change in the structure of South African racial policy while under white rule that might result in racial equality; or how they write answers to and critiques of oppressive myths exactly in order to "promote change" — certainly a change in the conscious or unconscious acceptance of racism as the norm — in a racist society and in the perceptions of that society in readers throughout the world.

In the context of my inventive adoption of Thompson's work on political myths to a discussion of literature as an embodiment and/or critique of political myths, it is important to understand how one might evaluate the validity of myths, especially those which constitute a "racist mythology" (13). As Thompson writes, one of the criteria for assessing the veracity of myths is examining and deciding "[I]f a myth is compatible with the evidence. . . . If it distorts the evidence, it fails the test and is bad history — and to that extent an implausible myth" (12). The central myth I am concerned with in this study of South African literature is the bedrock ideology of white South African life: racism. I.D. MacCrone's *Race Attitudes in South Africa* offers, perhaps, the best analysis of racism as a set of psychological assumptions (leading to racist actions). For our purposes, it is more accurate to say that MacCrone makes clear that racism is a set of "implausible myths," to borrow Thompson's term; thus constituting an implausible mythology. Not to belabor my point by attempting an exhaustive definition of racism (which would make up volumes), I will choose two examples from MacCrone's work which offer striking aspects of racist myths. For instance, MacCrone writes:

> The [racist] white sees a member of that [Black] race not as an individual like himself, but as a representative of an alien group, whose most striking characteristics are an inferiority in intelligence and knowledge, an inferiority in standard of living and occupation, a tendency towards violent and criminal practices, a behavior which

Introduction

is childish and often ridiculous, in short, the opposite of all those qualities which form the image of which the white man has in his mind when he thinks of his own group.[12]

Moreover, in a passage which illuminates the racist need for simplistic stereotyping of other races (which will be discussed in the chapter on *God's Stepchildren*) MacCrone clarifies how even evidence counter to the stereotype may simply evoke more racist myths. MacCrone speaks of the racist white's inability to tolerate any overlapping which may blur the distinction of a clear-cut and emotionally satisfying and pragmatically convenient division.

> Educated and civilized men of color are an anomaly which threatens the existing basis of distinction, and as such are more likely to become the object of hostility. They are not true to type, since they fail to conform to the stereotype of the black man which exists in the white man's mind and which controls behavior. For the same reason, the 'half-caste' who belongs to neither of the two mutually exclusive groups, membership of which is determined at birth, finds himself occupying a precarious intermediate position between the two groups. His very existence is an offense to the white man, not only on account of the infection of the taint of 'black' blood but also because he upsets the existing caste system based upon the palpable difference in skin color. Since in the case of the 'colored' person that difference is not so obvious, it tends to excite conflicting tendencies which confuse and irritate the white man. (291-92)

As Thompson writes, the implausible myth of the racist ideology of the apartheid era is clear: "To legitimize the policy of apartheid . . . the mythology presents the African inhabitants as a totally distinct subspecies of humanity" (29). Of central importance, considering Thompson's exposure of the irrational nature of racist myths is that, as Ernest Cassirer points out in *The Myth of the State*, in the creation of political myths—particularly, "implausible" political myths —

> [N]othing is left to chance; every step is well prepared and premeditated. It is this strange combination that is one of the most striking features of our political myths. Myth has always been described as the result of an unconscious activity and as a free product of imagination. But here we find myth according to plan. The new political myths do not grow up freely; they are not wild fruits of an exuberant imagination. They are artificial things fabricated by very

Introduction

skillful and cunning artisans. It has been reserved for the twentieth century, our own great technical age, to develop a new technique of myth. Henceforth myths can be manufactured in the same sense and according to the same methods as any modern weapon as machine guns or airplanes.[13]

In the creation of implausible myths, language is essential. In words that will prove highly relevant to our discussion of South Africa, Cassirer writes:

> The first step that had to be taken was a change in the function of language . . . the magic word has a predominant and overwhelming influence. It does not describe things or relations of things; it tries to produce effects and to change the course of nature. . . . The magician, or sorcerer alone [is] able to govern the magic word. But in his hands it becomes a most powerful weapon. Nothing can resist its force. . . . Curiously enough all this recurs in our modern world. If we study our modern political myths and the use that has been made of them we find in them, to our great surprise, not only a transvaluation of all our ethical values but also a transformation of human speech. The magic word takes precedence over the semantic word. (355-56)

Examples of this phenomenon during apartheid abounded. David Harrison writes of the difficulty facing a writer on South Africa who confronts "magic words":

> What has not been possible to avoid are the changing names of the government ministry which deals with Black South Africans. It has evolved from the Ministry of Native Affairs to Bantu Affairs to Plural Relations. Now it has become the Ministry of Co-operation and Development. Perhaps the best comment on it all came from Percy Qoboza, editor of *The World*. In 1977 his newspaper was shut down and he was detained without trial for five months. When he was released he said: "Let no one tell me there has been no change in South Africa. I went into gaol a Bantu and came out a Plural." Harrison later writes that "The Native Labor Act of 1953 even redefined the term 'employee,' specially to exclude all Blacks" (214).[14]

Thus, one sees the power of "magic words" to create and define reality.

Cassirer's ideas on language and "magic words" are nowhere more relevant than when applied to the question of the reform of the South

Introduction

African racist system. The word "apartheid" was disowned for several years by the Nationalist government, as if disowning a word equals a change in reality. Joseph Lelyveld's Pulitzer Prize winning *Move Your Shadow* alerted readers to such duplicity:

> In South Africa, the essential question about reform is whether it aims at eliminating, or simply renovating, the racial system. If reform can be deduced from narrowed political participation, centralization of power, duplicity, and deceit, then apartheid has always been a reform movement. And, in fact, it has always presented itself as one. No one needs to teach the Afrikaner politician that words can be weapons. Their grasp of that point is the reason they are forever renaming things, inventing new euphemisms for old realities. The "native reserves" became "Bantustans." Then they became "Homelands." Then they become "national states." The level of human misery within their borders rose in the process. The level of "purposeful blindness" rose, too.[15]

And, in fact, South Africa does prove a minefield for writers; for instance, the term 'Colored' is considered offensive by many designated as such; yet it is sometimes necessary for a writer to use it to denote the system of racial stratification at the heart of South African racism. Putting the word in quotation marks is one attempt to resolve the difficulty. Still, simultaneously, one is reminded of the power of words and the destructive, calculated 'magic' they perform. Hence, the issue of language plays an important role in the life of the South African racist system. However much the nationalist South African government changed and softened their rhetoric on apartheid, during the 1990s even after its demise, one must recognize the following: the fact is that "The political mythology that legitimized the South African social order [before and during apartheid] rests on a core assumption about humanity. The core assumption is that races are the fundamental divisions of humanity and that different races possess inherently different cultural as well as physical qualities" (Thompson 69). Hence, even the 'reformed' or 'post-release of Mandela' South Africa still had as one of its central myths both white supremacy and, as Thompson's chapter is entitled, the myth of "Inassimilable Races." Moreover, soon after Mandela's release, President F. W. De Klerk told Ted Koppel in a Nightline interview that he simultaneously believed in "one person-one vote" and in contorted doubletalk, that the votes of whites

Introduction

should count more than the votes of the Black majority. Hence, a new (and failed) myth: Yes to 'one person-one vote'; no to the concept of each person's vote having equal weight. Though this sham was never put into effect, the distortion and contortion of reality, to create "implausible myths" are facts to which the public must be highly vigilant when studying the nature and consequences of apartheid.

Another implausible myth is best summed up by people's acceptance of a racist-created identity for Blacks. Derman's article makes clear the significance of such beliefs. As Derman writes:

> The coverage of the uprising beginning at Soweto in June of 1976 provides a significant occasion to examine some of the ways in which media coverage reinforces the confusion between biological and socially-constructed "races." In addition there are broader issues involved. As we might recall, great publicity was given to conflict between Africans in Soweto in August and September 1976. The media emphasized the alleged Zulu tribal opposition to the Soweto students. An analysis of the selective nature of media coverage reveals many of the problems involved: first, great credence was given to the South African government claim of a vast groundswell of Zulu opposition to the series of strikes organized by Soweto students after their earlier demonstrations had been met by police gas, night-sticks, bullets and imprisonment. Little attention was paid to the propaganda value for the South African government of giving headlines to the "Zulu" response rather that to the sufferings and deaths of literally hundreds of protesting students. Second, the media neglected to discuss the strategy of the South African government to create and maintain divisions between black South Africans. The South African government works continuously to prevent class unity, but the foreign press can never find classes, only tribes. What was and is remarkable is that black South Africans created unity despite all efforts to divide them. Third, the North American media supports racism by defining the conflict tribally and racially, and then by asking why are not all black South Africans united, seeking a false unity. Indeed, if we remember all those French who cooperated with the Nazis during World War II, the Quislings in Norway, fifth columnists in England and the United States, etc., we also should expect to find similar collaborators among non-whites in South Africa. But that is no more remarkable than divisions within any nation and does not support the South African government propaganda that black South Africans are organized on a "tribal basis." (Derman, 290)

Introduction

The logical conclusion of such racist assumptions and representations of Blacks is clear in the following analysis by Derman:

> What would be defined as national pride, cultural identity, nationalism, class solidarity, or rural-urban conflict anywhere else in the world is reduced to tribal issues in South Africa. In my view, such reporting directly serves the interests of the South African government. It deflects outrage against the murders, assassinations, imprisonments, and the overwhelming poverty of black South Africans by pretending that black South Africans themselves are ambivalent about apartheid. This type of racial reporting leads readers to believe that if black South Africans are so divided and if they cannot achieve unity, it would be prudent to withhold normal and material support for them. If is clear that black South Africans are not divided in opposition to apartheid, but they can be divided on how to express that opposition. (291)

My hope is that the following study will make one question 'implausible,' oppressive myths, thus illuminating readers, in a 'liberatory' way, to the plausibility — the truth — entailed in the 'liberatory' works under discussion.

V.

As I have indicated, psychological studies on racism certainly illuminate how the fictional portrayals of racism are representative of ideas that are borne out by such works as MacCrone's book and *Prejudice*, edited by Thomas F. Pettigrew. MacCrone's book, for instance, is also especially enlightening when applied to Andre Brink's *A Dry White Season*, as Brink's novel deals, to a great extent, with the group pressure by Afrikaners to have uniformity in upholding white domination — a uniformity which attempts to squelch individual conscience and will that deviate from the norm on questions of race.

The group vs. the individual is an essential aspect of Brink's work, and MacCrone certainly contributes a central explanation of group thought in the development and perpetuation of racism. MacCrone writes, for instance, on factors that often contribute to the development of potentially racist attitudes: "At the level of attitudes, the individual is necessarily conscious of self in relation to other selves, for social attitudes represent the final differentiation brought about by a psycho-

Introduction

social environment in the individual as a member of a social group or society" (141). As innocuous as this may sound, it is especially ominous as an analysis of a society whose politics have been based for centuries on white domination and which was ruled from 1948 to 1994 by the Afrikaner Nationalist Party, which ushered in the age of apartheid. Moreover, the research of MacCrone's study (published a decade before the 1948 election) unveiled the uniformity of racial thought among those who internalize the white group's dominant racist ideology as a part of their own identity. Such an idea is borne out by MacCrone's statement that one essential aspect of racial attitudes in his study of South Africa is embodied in the fact that for many an individual "the group itself has become a part of the individual through his identification with it" (249). The danger of this phenomenon when one is discussing a society whose government and daily life were ruled by racism should be clear. Brink's *A Dry White Season* certainly powerfully dramatizes the danger of blind loyalty to a group system of racism To focus on a central idea in Brink's novel, this white group identity — an identity based on racist myths — can enslave an entire society, the individual, the group, and the 'out-groups'— chaining them all to a life ruled by racism.

MacCrone's ideas on group unity as a fixation of racism clearly can be understood to illuminate Brink's thesis in *A Dry White Season* that a white person who dissented from South Africa's racist policies and ideology could be subjected to ostracism and societal and police pressure. The pressure and ostracism which Brink depicts clearly portray apartheid-upholding Afrikaners as members of a herd who would punish fellow Afrikaners who disagree with the status-quo as traitors to the herd. Brink's novel depicts this oppressive enforcement of group identity which will brook no dissent from the prevailing Afrikaner brotherhood of racism. Indeed it is central to understand that Brink is not writing merely of an isolated and fictional incident but of a social and psychological reality. As MacCrone writes:

> The greater and more intense the group feeling, that is, the stronger the identification between members of a group, the greater is the strength of prejudice against the alien group and against those who are not members of one's own group . . . there can be little doubt about the existence of that principle of group psychology according to which the feeling for one's own group and the feeling against

Introduction

some other group tend to wax and wane in direct proportion to one another. (249)

The Afrikaner preoccupation with group identity as the chosen people to possess South Africa is well documented in T. Dunbar Moodie's *The Rise of Afrikanerdom* and David Harrison's *The White Tribe of Africa*. It is also a central element in both Brink's novel and Alex La Guma's *Time of the Butcherbird*.

To elaborate on this point, I will refer to a few passages from Moodie's book which states that in the 19th and early 20th centuries, "Oppression by British overlords and harassment by Black hordes could . . . be understood as an honor to be accepted and glorified for its own sake as the seal of God's election"[16]; especially, since in South Africa's white mythology "the sacred history is made up of two cycles of suffering and death — the Great Trek [to attempt to escape British rule — an attempted escape which entailed, of course, infringement on Blacks' land] and the Anglo-Boer War" (12). Though many South African whites may argue that this particular view of white election is dated, those very people may be singing a different song with the same meaning. To clarify, if white racism remains intact and supported, consciously or unconsciously, by many whites, those whites still are clinging to the implausible myth of 'election' as the chosen—i.e., privileged and powerful — people of South Africa. Thus, white group identity founded on racism has been and will continue to be a hindrance to actualizing racial equality in South Africa — a point borne out in both fiction and non-fiction. This final point is forecast by MacCrone in his study, showing the classic relevance of his work. He writes:

> A good deal of hostility, without a doubt, finds an outlet in the relations of members of the same group to one another if only in the form of competition, rivalry, and mutual criticism. But there are limits beyond which this intra-group hostility may not go. For one thing, it must remain within the limits prescribed by the recognized laws and conventions of the group, so that, in the form of legalized or socially approved behavior, it remains under control. As soon as it goes beyond these carefully circumscribed limits and becomes an internal threat to the unity and security of the group, it is severely and drastically curtailed either by the deterrent of social disapproval or by the forceful infliction of punishment, by depriving the individual of his liberty and, in extreme cases, of life itself. (250-51)

Introduction

To apply this important passage to Brink is to understand the significance of Brink's portrayal of group pressure on his dissident protagonist. The comment Brink is making in this aspect of the novel is a warning to society that if Afrikaners or, more generally, whites of various ethnic groups, define themselves as a rigid, repressed, racist white group, they will stamp out those members of the group who rebel against their racist restrictions. Hence, MacCrone's ideas illuminate the devastating consequences of the acceptance of racism as a group more of which Brink's novel is a representation.

VI.

I wish now to discuss more explicitly my understanding of my role as a literary critic in the present study.

The following passage from Cassirer's *The Myth of the State* is central not only in illuminating how one can fight against oppressive myths but also in inspiring one to understand what the role of the literary critic can be if one substitutes the word 'criticism' for 'philosophy.' Cassirer writes:

> It is beyond the power of philosophy to destroy the political myths. A myth is in a sense invulnerable. It is impervious to rational arguments; it cannot be refuted by syllogisms. But philosophy can do us another important service. It can make us understand the adversary. In order to fight an enemy you must know him. That is one of the first principles of a sound strategy. To know him means not only to know his defects and weaknesses; it means to know his strength. All of us have been liable to underestimate this strength. When we first heard of political myths we found them so absurd and incongruous, so fantastic and ludicrous that we could hardly be prevailed upon to take them seriously. By now it has become clear to all of as that this was a great mistake. We should not commit the same error a second time. We should carefully study the origin, the structure, the methods, the techniques of political myths. We should see the adversary face to face in order to know how to combat him. (373)

These same important works can be performed incisively by the literary critic, in analyzing oppressive myths, and by examining the protest literature under discussion, as it attacks such myths. In sum,

Introduction

Cassirer's words capture my intentions in examining the novels I discuss in this study.

In addition, Franz Fanon, in *Black Skin, White Masks*, articulates both the need to destroy white racist myths about Blacks and to pay attention to Blacks' ideas about Blacks. These ideas are indicated in a passage alluded to earlier; as Fanon writes: "All around me the white man, above the sky, tears at its navel, the earth rasps under its feet, and there is a white song, a white song. All this whiteness that burns me" (114). This "white song" can be readily heard in the fact that literary criticism has paid far more attention to white South African writers than to their equally complex Black colleagues. Moreover, this work is intended to give analyses to central works and ideas by non-white South African writers especially vis-a-vis the question of the representation of the identities of Blacks, whites in South African literature, and those of Black and white heritage. Moreover, another aspect of the "white song" of racist politics and of some of the literature, is what I allude to earlier as "the Negro myth," to borrow Fanon's phrase (151). In explaining this "myth," it is central to remember Fanon's words regarding white racists' perceptions of Blacks: "The Negro is a phobogenic object, a stimulus to anxiety" (151). This fear is a central part of the racist myths of white supremacy and of unassimilable races. Both Black and white writers have received primary exposure. While it is central to analyze how writers have attempted to disrupt the "white song" which oppresses and attempt to define those who are not white, I am especially proud to give non-white writers, particularly Alex La Guma and Peter Abrahams, their due in the discussion of representations of identity in South African literature.

With the exception of Millin's *God's Stepchildren*, the literature under analysis implicitly or explicitly fights and protests against racist mythology. Perhaps what this branch of South African literature expresses is best articulated in the vision W.E.B. DuBois expresses in *The Souls of Black Folk*:

> I have seen a land right merry with the sun, where children sing and rolling hills lie like passioned women wanton with harvest. And there in the King's Highway sat and sits a figure veiled and bowed, by which the traveler's footsteps hasten as they go. Three centuries though has been the raising and unveiling of that bowed human heart,

Introduction

and now behold a new century for the duty and the deed. The problem of the twentieth century is the problem of the color-line (239).

" . . . and now behold a new century." As we reach the turn of the century, it is tragic to think that DuBois' words may be adapted for a new century. Though changes in South African politics have been great, if the racist myths and oppressive realities they reinforce are not analyzed, understood and dismantled — as most of the novels under discussion attempt to do — we will fail to learn valuable lessons from South Africa's long racial nightmare. And thus, as we celebrate the dawn of the new century, if we do not perform "the duty and the deed" — in writing, in teaching, and, most centrally, in daily life — we will not be able to dismantle fully the ridiculous myths of racism. More importantly, we will fail to understand how and why "the problem of the twentieth century" has been the problem of bigotry.

Notes

1. W.E.B DuBois, *The Souls of Black Folk* in *Three Negro Classics*, ed.,John Hope Franklin (New York: Avon Books, 1965), 221.
2. Franz Fanon, *Black Skin, White Masks*, trans. Charles Lam Markham (New York: Grove Press, 1967), 114.
3. Toni Morrison, *Playing in the Dark* (Cambridge: Harvard University Press, 192), 16.
4. Throughout this work, the word 'Colored' will be used with single quotation marks, as it is a word many South Africans find offensive but it also conveys something of the specificity of the former South African government's policy under apartheid of racial categorization. It is also my feeling that the racial designation 'Black' should always be capitalized.
5. Sarah Gertrude Millin, *God's Stepchildren* (Johannesburg: A.D. Donker, 1986), 163.
6. Nadine Gordimer, *Occasion for Loving* (London: Virago Press, 1983), 257.
7. Charles W. Chesnutt, *The Marrow of Tradition* (Ann Arbor: University of Michigan Press, 1979), 194.
8. Bill Derman, "Race and Class, Society and Biology: Problems in the Analysis of South Africa" in *Southern Africa: Society, Economy and Liberation*, eds. David Wiley and Allen Isaacman (East Lansing: Michigan State University 1981), 286.
9. Bronislaw Malinowski, *Myth in Primitive Psychology* (London: Kegan Paul, Trenck, Trubner and Co., Ltd, 1926), 118.
10. Leonard Thompson, *The Political Mythology of Apartheid* (New Have: Yale University Press, 1985), 1.
11. Henry Tudor, *Political Myth* (New York: Praeger Publishers, 1972), 50.
12. I.D. MacCrone, *Race Attitudes in South Africa* (New York: Oxford University Press, 1937), 263.
13. Ernst Cassirer, *The Myth of the State* (Garden City, New York: Doubleday and Company, Inc., 1955), 354.
14. David Harrison, *The White Tribe of Africa* (Berkeley: University of California Press, 1981), 7.
15. Joseph Lelyveld, *Move Your Shadow* (New York: Penguin Books, 1986), 69.
16. T. Dunbar Moodie, *The Rise of Afrikanerdom* (Berkeley: University of California Press, 1975), 13.

> "There died a myriad,
> And of the best, among them,
> For an old bitch gone in the teeth,
> For a botched civilization."
>
> Ezra Pound,
> "Hugh Selwyn Mauberley"

> "But the spirit of the lion says, "I will."
>
> Nietzsche,
> *Thus Spoke Zarathustra*

> "Even if they kill me I won't die."
>
> Mbulelo Mzamane,
> *The Children of Soweto*

> "Why write this book? . . . Well? Well, I reply quite calmly that there are too many idiots in this world. And having said it, I have the burden of proving it.
>
> Frantz Fanon,
> *Black Skin, White Masks*

Chapter 1

The "Nigger in Them": Sarah Gertrude Millin's Poetics of "Blood" in *God's Stepchildren* (1924)

> The prude, whether man or woman, is more likely to be found displaying an intolerant or hostile attitude towards the native, since the very obsession with sex against which prudishness is a reaction formation may be expected to lead to such a result.
>
> I.D. MacCrone, *Race Attitudes in South Africa*

Of central importance in the discussion of the impact of racial conflict on identity is an analysis of Sarah Gertrude Millin's 1920s novel *God's Stepchildren*. Millin's work is important and intriguing because it is an indisputably racist novel. (Indeed, ironically for its Jewish author, the novel became much admired in Nazi Germany.) In fact, *God's Stepchildren* is a veritable catalogue of racist myths about Blacks, about 'Coloreds' and about whites who believe in racial equality. More importantly, Millin's novel contains many components of racism discussed in such studies as I.D. MacCrone's *Race Attitudes in South Africa* and *Prejudice*, edited by Thomas F. Pettigrew, et al. Furthermore, Peter Abrahams, in *Return to Goli*, points out some of the significance of Millin's racist novel. As Abrahams states, *God's*

Stepchildren is one of those works which helped make "the cult of blood respectable as a literary commodity. From then onwards, one could write about 'white blood' and 'black blood' and, presumably, 'brown blood' without fear of being thought moronic."[1] It is this "moronic" aspect of Millin's myth of race that bears out R. F. A. Hoernle's statement that "In truth, 'race' functions in modern political thinking not as a pure scientific concept, but as an emotional symbol."[2] An application of Hoernle's idea to Millin's novel makes evident how race can function in modern literature.

In the novel, Millin's white racism clearly impacts upon her depiction of mixed-race and Black characters. In this regard, one sees the power of racism to define its targets in a distorted manner in the media — in this case, in literature. This form of literary power — expressed in Millin's portrayals of non-whites — is a clear illustration of the definition of power as "the ability to define phenomena and, in turn, make it act in a desired manner."[3] In the case of Millin's novel, the phenomena are the non-white characters, who are typed as inferior to whites in a number of ways (especially mentally and intellectually) and are "made" by the novelist, "to act in a desired"— inferior — way. In addition, the catalyst behind this form of literary power has the qualities of racism as critiqued by cultural anthropologist Franz Boas. Summarizing the psychology of arguments for white supremacy, Boas states:

> [W]e like to support our emotional attitude toward the so-called inferior races by pursu[ing] a line of thought like this: since the aptitude of the European is the highest, his physical and mental type is also highest, and every deviation from the white type necessarily represents a lower feature.[4]

Boas critiques this irrational "reasoning" (4) as being, in fact, a self-absorbed "unproven assumption" (5). Thus, the identities of the Black and 'Colored' characters are the products of the racist author's conflict with them, as Millin clearly believes in white superiority over people of color. This conflict and the resulting racial myths can be illuminated by ideas in Ernst Cassirer's *The Myth of State*. In Cassirer's writings on "race worship," one can find ideas which help define the sort of racism which is exemplified in Millin's novel. Cassirer writes that

> those who think of themselves as the superior races can only know what they are and what they are worth by comparing themselves with these other races that are crouching their feet. Their self-

confidence cannot be complete without this element of contempt and disgust; the one implies and demands the other.[5]

One can see in Millin's ideas Cassirer's analysis of the dependency of racists on their concocted notions of the inferiority of their targets as a crutch to support their own "idealized image,"[6] to borrow Karen Horney's term. Millin's novel represents the massive amounts of psychological energy spent in 'proving' the inferiority of Blacks and 'Coloreds' in an effort to prove implicitly and explicitly whites' supremacy. This staunch defender of white supremacy and non-white inferiority, therefore, is essential in examining the connection between racial conflict and identity.

In order to more fully understand Millin's saga of miscegenation, it is important to begin with the character who sets it in motion, the Rev. Andrew Flood. Flood leaves England and travels to South Africa as a missionary. He soon marries one of the members of the African tribe he tries to convert. His marriage to the African woman, Silla, results in their having a daughter, Deborah; Deborah becomes pregnant by a white man and gives birth to Kleinhans; Kleinhans and a 'Colored' woman have a daughter, Elmira; Elmira marries a white man and gives birth to a son, Barry. As Andrew Flood is at the foundation of this genealogy of race mixing, he represents people for whom Millin has complete contempt. This contempt is evident in a number of ways.

From the outset, it is clear that Millin questions and wants the reader to question, Flood's intentions. First, she denigrates his personal qualities; second, she makes one question the validity of his desire to become accepted by Blacks as so much vanity. Albert Memmi's words in *The Colonizer and the Colonized* can explain this development, as he reflects Millin's feelings: "Humanitarian romanticism is looked upon in the colonies as a serious illness, the worst of all dangers. It is no more or less than going over to the side of the enemy."[7] This attitude in Millin's mind is immediately evident as she describes the influence on Flood to go to Africa as a missionary: "He had recently heard a tremendous sermon preached about the essential equality of all human beings, whatever their color, in the eyes of the Creator. It was, throughout Britain, the Creed of the moment."[8] In this passage, for the reader the validity of the "creed of the moment" — i.e., a fad — is immediately questionable by its temporarily fashionable status and by the fact that it is being propagated hypocritically by one of the world's foremost colonizers.

In addition, Millin's biographer, Martin Rubin, points out an important reason for her disdain for such missionaries as Flood:

> While still at school, she had read about missionaries in the early part of the nineteenth century who had married African women in order to win over their congregants. This had slipped her mind, but she was reminded of it when she received an appeal for money from a former schoolmate of hers, a German who had become a missionary among the Africans. From her recollection of this fervent young man and the impression of missionaries of the past century, whom her teacher had no doubt depicted as fanatics, came her conception of Andrew Flood, the dominating figure of *God's Stepchildren*.[9]

An interesting question is whether, in putting together the ingredients for failure, Millin plants intrinsic flaws into Flood's character. As Peter Abrahams briefly comments on Millin's writing of *God's Stepchildren*, Millin felt both "that it was high time to discover the tragedy of being half-breed! And only a weak and spineless caricature of a man such as Reverend Andrew Flood could possibly father a line of half-castes" (59). Thus, the answer is a clear yes, in both minor and great aspects of Flood's character. Also, as Rubin writes, "In making Andrew Flood a pathetic, stupid, and generally unattractive man, Sarah Gertrude is underlining her contempt for idealists who try to bring the black and white races together" (81). Flood is such an unsavory character that Mary, the white woman in whom he is interested before he leaves England, "could not bear to listen to him, and whenever she saw him approaching her she would look around in helpless desperation for some means of escape" (27). More important are Flood's stupidity and egotism. These are major qualities which are designated, it seems, to make the reader question the rectitude of his desires towards the Africans. The two qualities are shown in the following passage:

> He was not a clever man, and he knew people did not consider him clever; but he believed that was because they did not understand the essential mystery of his being. He often felt that if they could see the wonderful things that went on in his mind, while his speech so lamentably failed him, they would be touched and surprised and impressed. He was anxious to touch and surprise and impress people. (22)

This same egotism as a spur to his desires is evident later: "he only wanted to snatch these black souls from Hell, and thus to vindicate himself" (55). Both egotism and futility may be behind Millin's writing, after his marriage to the African Silla, that Flood realizes the "vanity . . . of his sacrifice. He had lost everything to give them nothing" (75). Millin's line of thought in this sentence is best illuminated by recalling Cassirer's interpretation of one of the roots of racists' fears of miscegenation: "With the passage of the purity of the race its strength goes and its organizing power. The higher races become victims of their own work, the slave of their slaves" (308).

Millin further undercuts Flood's character by making clear that Flood's egotism and romanticism are important aspects of his decision to marry one of the Africans in order to prove his devotion. These qualities are evident in several passages. In order to deliver himself from the "futility" (44) of his life, he decides to give himself up to the people, to realize his ambitions of performing such an act. Millin repeats these qualities in a few passages. For example, she writes: "[H]e would remember how all his young life he had aspired to sacrifice; how he had wanted to give the boots from his feet, to suffer misunderstanding in silence, to pray in isolation"(51). At this point, it would be significant to ask if Rubin is right as he says that Flood "is seen [by Millin] as a fanatic who is little more than insane . . . at no time is Flood given credit for trying to follow Christian doctrine and break down racial barriers" (79-80). Is Flood's impulse to "sacrifice" himself given no more validity that this? No. The subsequent complete failure of his endeavor to become closer to the people by 'sacrificing' himself in marriage makes clear the total incorrectness of the thoughts he tells Mr. Burtwell: "I know my actions will be misinterpreted. But . . . *I am prepared for the sacrifice*" (italics mine; 62). He continues, " 'Blessed are ye when men shall revile you and persecute you, and shall say all manner of evil against you falsely, for my sake' " (62). Thus, the idea of sacrificing his soul and suffering the condemnation of the world appeals greatly to Flood.

Millin's writing of this egomaniacal self-sacrificing drive lace her condemnation of Flood. Furthermore, the total failure of his 'sacrifice' makes evident his real desire for romanticism. As Memmi writes, "to adopt the colonized and [to] be adopted by them is another" matter (22). Millin makes clear that Flood's 'sacrifice" is such a colossal failure that he is even rejected by the Africans (of whom Millin's descriptions make clear she sees as barely human): after Flood and

Silla marry, her relatives go to church and "The people were all more friendly with him too. He told himself that at least he had won them. They despised him utterly, and his religion" (66). Moreover, " the Hottentots did not regard him as a brother; they regarded him as a fool" (69). Clearly, the Africans' rejection of Flood and their disapproval of race-mixing is, to be sure, Millin's.

Warren Breed's essay on "Suicide and Loss in Social Interaction" also sheds light on Flood's fate after the collapse of his marriage and 'sacrifice'. (It is important to say here that I would like to widen the notion of self-destruction beyond suicide, as Millin makes clear that Flood's actions are a form of social and cultural suicide; suicide 'from' being white and a part of white society.) One major aspect of self-destruction, according to Breed, concerns a great "disruption in interpersonal social relationships"[10] in the person's life which may result in loss of one's roles before oneself and others. "Loss of Position" is defined by Breed mainly in terms of what can happen at a job. "The loss here," writes Breed, " is of a position . . . that had conferred identity and prestige upon the man" (191-2). This loss for Flood — of the alleged superiority of being white — is clear as Millin writes of Flood's realization that "he had lost everything to give them [the people] nothing" (75).

Moreover, Flood seems to reach a point where he 'reverts' from whiteness after the collapse of his experiment. For example, Millin twice makes it clear that European clothes are a sign of "civilization" (25) in Burtwell's mission: also, Millin points out that Silla and Cachas are Christians and "among the most civilized of the tribe," as is marked by their European clothes (46). In contrast, Flood becomes ragged, dirty, with his toes coming out of his shoes. Moreover, Millin writes, "By the time the Reverend Andrew Flood had been at Canaan for fifteen years he was himself in many ways a savage. He was dirty and unkempt, wild looking, he seldom read, he wrote to no one; he knew nothing that was going on in the big world; and it embarrassed him to meet a civilized person" (77). Thus, Millin underlines both Flood's growth away from 'whiteness' and his exile from humanity as following his failure in his position. These ideas not only point out the centrality of loss of position as in Breed's analysis but raise another issue. Flood's exile from humanity and his shame at meeting other whites (civilization equals whiteness to Millin) bring to mind Breed's comments about the significance of "Loss of Mutuality" (195) to a self-destructive person. By "loss of mutuality" Breed refers to:

A weakening of mutual social relationships in general. As a type it is much like Durkheim's "egoistic" category in which the individual lacks bonds and ties to other persons and does not share a community of sentiments with others. Usually, the individual's "personality" has been characterized either by shyness, a lack of gregariousness", or he has evidenced traits which are found to be aggravating or insulting to other persons. (195)

This passage is especially important, as it pinpoints both the personal traits that made Flood an off-putting character to others and the larger issue of his exile from society as a result of his thoughts and actions. And certainly, Flood experiences "the loss of "expected" mutuality, or the kind of social life" (197) to which he had aspired in marrying an African. This loss, and his consequent exile from white society, clarify why he so disintegrates or, to use Breed's works, "drift[s] into . . . [a] mode of deviant behavior" (200) after his failure. Flood achieves mutuality with neither society (his own or his adopted one), is ashamed to interact with whites, and his decline seems the consequence. These factors bring to mind passages from Breed concerning both self-evaluation and loss of mutuality. Breed writes that

[O]ne attitude central to the human being is his attitude toward himself and that he must maintain, on balance, favorable self-conception. The source of this attitude is his estimate of the assessment other persons make of him. . . . [Furthermore] in presenting an interfactional theory of neurosis . . . adverse reactions to the individual, received from other persons, result in a series of flaws to self-conception which lead to anxiety sufficient to render the individual unable to perform roles. (199)

Consequently, when one reflects on the fact that Flood's desire to "touch, surprise, and impress people" results in his alienating and revolting both races, it is clear that there is a vast gap, curtailing mutuality of Flood's desires with either Black or white society. Moreover, at the foundation is the lack of mutuality between Flood's desires and his author's beliefs. As Rubin writes, "Indeed, the divisions between the races (and, at the genesis, between Flood and Blacks) are shown to be invincible and the author reveals her utter contempt for what she feels to be his futile and misguided assault on the colour bar" (80).

Though Millin was inspired partly to write about Flood by her memory of stories about white missionaries who married African women, another missionary, much revered by whites and significantly held in much less esteem by many Africans, not only illuminates what Millin may have considered proper behavior by a missionary but also illustrates the sort of self-congratulatory, condescending and racist liberalism reflected by those such as Millin who seem to believe that they know best how to act as guardians of Blacks' behavior, simultaneously making Blacks both targets of their superiority complex and of their beliefs on how to maintain the "correct" relations between white and Black. Though it is unclear whether Millin had read his work, Albert Schweitzer, in his 1922 memoir, *On the Edge of the Primeval Forest,* both mirrors and illuminates the bigotry which he shares to a significant degree with Millin. Thus, Schweitzer's book can also be read as an implicit critique of ideas represented by Millin's Andrew Flood and as an affirmation of the racial superiority reflected in Millin's (and Schweitzer's) racism.

In the following passage, Schweitzer sheds light on the belief that strict divisions of 'superior' (i.e., whites) and 'inferior' (i.e., Blacks) must be maintained between white missionaries and the African targets of their (alleged) *Christianity*:

> When, before coming to Africa, I heard missionaries and traders say again and again that one must be very careful out here to maintain this authoritative position of the white man, it seemed to me to be a hard and unnatural position to take up, as it does to every one in Europe who reads or hears the same. Now I have come to see that the deepest sympathy and kindness can be combined with this insistence on certain external forms, and indeed are only possible by means of them. One of our unmarried missionaries at N'Gomo — the story belongs to a period some years back — allowed his cook to be very free in his behavior towards him. One day the steamer put in with the Governor on board, and the missionary went to pay his respects to the high official. He was standing on deck in an elegant suit of white among a group of officials and military men, when a negro, with his cap on his head and pipe in his mouth, pushed himself into the group and said to him: "Well, what are we to have for supper tonight?" The cook wanted to show on what good terms he stood with his master![11]

Indeed, Schweitzer offers this as one of several examples of why he thought the "prevention of unsuitable freedom" (132) by Africans is central to whites as this freedom would upset the social order (i.e., resulting in Black equality at the expense of the inflated racist ego). His ideas indicate why maintaining white superiority and social distance were important issues to such whites as himself and, as her writings show, Millin.

Flood's failure to maintain a stance of white superiority to Blacks, therefore, is the central act both in setting in motion the plot of *God's Stepchildren* and in revealing Millin's ideology towards desires such as Flood's.

Again speaking about the supposedly correct relationship between missionaries (Europeans, in general) towards Africans, Schweitzer writes:

> The combination of friendliness with authority is therefore the great secret of successful intercourse. One of our missionaries, Mr. Robert, left the staff some years ago to live among the negroes as their brother absolutely. He built himself a small house near a village between Lambarene and N'Gomo, and wished to be recognized as a member of the village. From that day his life became misery. With his abandonment of the social interval between white and black he lost all his influence; his word was no longer taken as the "white man's word," but he had to argue every point with them as if he were merely their equal. (131)

Authoritarian distance, therefore — a sort of mental apartheid — is clearly the key to social order for both Schweitzer and Millin in the works under discussion.

In another passage which helps illuminate Millin's ideology in her novel, Schweitzer again emphasizes white superiority in recounting his observations and experiences as a missionary in Gabon:

> In this daily and hourly contest with the child of nature [i.e., Blacks] every white man is continually in danger of gradual moral ruin. My wife and I were once very much delighted with a newly-arrived trader, because in the conversations we had with him he was always insisting on kindness towards the natives, and would not allow the slightest ill-treatment of them by his foremen. The next spring, however, he had the following experience. Lying in a pond some sixty miles from here he had a large quantity of mahogany, but he was summoned to Lambarene to clear off some urgent correspondence just as the water began to rise. He ordered his foremen and laborers to be sure to use the two or three days of high water to get all the

timber, if possible, into the river. When the water had fallen he went back to the place and found that nothing whatever had been done! They had smoked, and drunk, and danced; the timber which had already lain too long in the pond was almost completely ruined, and he was responsible to his company for the loss. His men had been thoughtless and indifferent because they did not fear him enough. This experience changed him entirely, and now he laughs at those who think it is possible to do anything with the natives without employing relentless severity (133-34).

Furthermore, Millin's novel suggests that by not heeding such warnings as Schweitzer's, one could find oneself attacked on all fronts: as Memmi writes, "If he [the colonizer who attempts to become one with the indigenous people] persists [in trying to align himself with the colonized] he will learn that he is launching into an undeclared conflict with his own people which will always remain alive. . . . It is clear [to other members of the colonist group] that such a colonizer is nothing but a traitor. . . . What would logically result from the attitude of a colonizer who rejects colonization? Why shouldn't they vigorously defend themselves against an attitude which would end in their immolation, perhaps on the altar of justice, but nevertheless, in their sacrifice?" (21). By reflecting on these thoughts, one sees that Millin stacks the deck against Flood, making him an insane exile, at home nowhere.

Flood's disintegration, therefore, is an intrinsic part of Millin's argument against miscegenation. Here Schweitzer's book again can be utilized to illuminate Millin's view of Flood's — and any missionary's — unpardonable sin — clearly an unpardonable sin for any white person in Millin's eyes. Accordingly, Schweitzer sums up what he felt to be a key aspect of missionary life:

A word in conclusion about the relations between the whites and the blacks. What must be the general character of the intercourse between them? Am I to treat the black man as my equal or as my inferior? I must show him that I can respect the dignity of human personality in every one, and this attitude in me he must be able to see for himself; but the essential thing is that there shall be a real feeling of brotherliness. How far this is to find complete expression in the sayings and doings of daily life must be settled by circumstances. The negro is a child, and with children nothing can be done without the use of authority. We must, therefore, so arrange the circumstances of daily life that my natural authority can find expression. With regard to the negroes, then, I have coined the formula: "I am your brother, it is true, but your elder brother." (130-31)

Millin clearly intends her novel to represent the chaos which unfolds once a white person renounces the white supremacy best embodied in Schweitzer's comments.

Albert Memmi's thoughts on "The Colonizer Who Refuses" (20) in *The Colonizer and the Colonized* greatly enlighten one to the flaws in Flood beyond those Millin makes evident. (One might argue that South Africa was, until the late 20th century, a colonial situation with whites as the colonizers and Blacks as the colonized.) Memmi writes, "How can he go about freeing himself of this halo of prestige which crowns him and at which he would like to take offense?"(20). This passage from Memmi's book captures the dilemma of the Rev. Andrew Flood. Yet, Memmi's analysis of "The Colonizer Who Refuses" shows precisely why such efforts will be unsuccessful. Though Flood may at first want to prove his closeness to his African congregation, both their attitudes towards him — and, what is more, his attitude towards *them* — make his efforts futile. His attitude and experience are best summed up by Memmi when he writes:

> The colonizer [who refuses] refuses to participate in their [the oppressed's] suppression and decides to come to their assistance. At the same time . . . he has another civilization before him, customs differing from his own, men whose reactions often surprise him, with whom he does not feel deep affinity. The fact remains that he admits to a fundamental difference between the colonized and himself. (14-5)

Memmi pinpoints such attitudes as Flood's as he continues:

> The little strains of daily life will support him in [this] discovery. . . . Having first eaten *couscous* with curiosity he now tastes it from time to time out of politeness and finds that "it's filling, its degrading, and it's not nourishing". . . . Or if he does like *couscous* he cannot stand that "fairground music" which seizes and deafens him. . . . "Why so loud? How can they hear each other?" Many traits of the colonized shock or irritate him. He is unable to conceal the revulsion he feels and which manifests itself in remarks which strangely recall those of a colonialist. (25)

Memmi's metaphor is exceptionally appropriate if one applies it to the development of Flood's feelings for the Blacks he seeks not only to convert but to prove his closeness to. But as Memmi writes, such a relationship can only end in rejection of the people (26). In Millin's novel, as the author sets up the story to prove the damage of race-mixing, Flood acts out the author's pre-determined hypothesis that such an experiment will end in failure. Thus, about the author and her character, Flood, and the Africans, one is compelled to repeat a question from Memmi: "Who can completely rid himself of bigotry in a country where everyone is tainted by it, including its victims?"(23)

Millin's depictions of the 'Colored' characters is equally intriguing as her portrayal of Flood, and, perhaps, far more complex. In *The Souls of Black Folk,* W.E. B. DuBois writes of Black Americans that:

> The world . . . yields him no true self-consciousness, but only lets him see himself through the revelation of the other world. It is a peculiar sensation, this double-consciousness, this sense of always looking at oneself through the eyes of others, of measuring one's soul by the tape of a world that looks on in amused contempt and pity. One ever feels his twoness — an American, a Negro . . . two souls, two thoughts, two unreconciled strivings; two warring ideals in one dark body.[12]

In the passage, to reflect Millin's novel, one can substitute White and 'Colored' for American and Negro, respectively. Millin's 'Colored' characters have this double-consciousness by virtue of the fact that their actions and thoughts are shaped by the race theory of their racist white author. Her racism is evident in her representations of them in their internalization of racism against their Black heritage and in their self-alienation. Furthermore, their plight — their desire, unlike DuBois' analysis of American Blacks — to 'become white' and leave behind their black identity is illuminated by Barry D. Adam's *The Survival of Domination* in that Sarah Gertrude Millin's portrayal of her characters emphasizes that they want to flee from their Black ancestry and are hateful of it, as Millin's racist mythology contains a "composite portrait" of Blacks and 'Coloreds' which stresses their inferiority to whites.[13] Thus, self-hatred and denial of identification with those of Black ancestry are the results of 'Colored' characters' being depicted through the eyes of a white racist.

First, I will discuss aspects of Millin's "composite portrait" of 'Coloreds'; then I will examine her characters' self-alienation and attempts to flee from this black side of their racial heritage.

In "The Mythical Portrait of the Colonized," Memmi writes:

> From listening to him . . . one finds that the colonizer is not so displeased with that laziness [of which he accuses the colonized],

The "Nigger in Them": Sarah Gertrude Millin's Poetics... 13

whether supposed or real . . . [the colonizer in talking about the colonized's flaws] takes up all the usual expressions, perfects them, invents others. Nothing can describe well enough the extraordinary deficiency of the colonized. He becomes lyrical about it, in a negative way. The colonized doesn't let grass grow under his feet, but a tree, and what a tree! A eucalyptus, an American centenarian oak! A tree? No, a forest! (80)

In this passage, Memmi grasps such ideas about the oppressed as Millin's. For Millin, people of Black heritage are barely human and are unintelligent. In this regard, Millin shows a tendency of which I.A. Newby helps explain the intention in *Jim Crow's Defense,* a comparative study of race theories in Europe and America; i.e., Millin's physical descriptions of the Africans in Flood's mission. Newby summarizes racist myths:

[T]he negro's inferiority was not manifested by his low intelligence and deficient brain alone. The whole gamut of his physical features, from the top of his frizzled head to the bottom of his prehensile big toe attested his inferiority. His features, insisted racists, were generalized and primitive and much nearer to those of anthropoids than Caucasians. One of the oldest of racist beliefs, this idea has been reinforced by Darwinism and it persisted among extremists in the 20th century. "The anatomy of the negro exhibits a much closer approach to the anthropoid apes than does any other race," wrote one of the most immoderate racists, the physician R.W. Shufeldt. "Many vestigial or rudimentary organs and structures" which are constant in animals below man appear far more frequently in the negro race than in the white race. Even the scholarly and influential sociologist Franklin Henry Giddings . . . noticed "a large number of simian survivals" in the average negro's anatomy. [14]

In comparison, Millin, for example, dwells on the "monkey-like" (28, 54) appearance of the Africans; calls them "baboons" (36); refers to the dialectician's "brown paw" 949); says the Africans never wash themselves; writes that they spend a good deal of the day "dazed and stupid" (33) from dagga smoking; says that the old are left in the veld to be eaten by animals; states that " the Hottentot ideal of beauty" 947) is "grotesque " (47); that the "typical Hottentot figure" (67) is "stout to malformation" (67). Thus, Millin's physical descriptions of the people are loaded with judgments of them.

Millin's descriptions of the intellectual capability of the children of mixed marriages are also important. She makes clear that neither intellectually nor professionally can the 'Colored' rise to the status of whites. As Millin writes in her non-fiction book *The South Africans*:

> It is perhaps for the very reason that the colored man is so near the white man that the will to succeed is not in him. There is the constant comparison, the constant distinction, the instituted order of things. It has been held through the generations that he should stand below the white man. For him to aspire to compete against the white man, to have dreams of drawing, in any respect, level with him, would almost seem like a violation of nature. Although the colored voice vociferates sometimes that his heart is as white as the white man's, that he does not consider himself anyone's inferior, his attitude is a mere pathetic bluff. It is this very heart he speaks of, the spirit within him, that is not white. . . . [I]t is as if the darkness of his skin descends also upon his soul when it finds itself pitted against a white man. [15]

Consequently, once the races are intermingled in *God's Stepchildren*, Millin turns her guns for the most part away from the physical to the mental deficiency in the "soul" or "blood" (an oft use word in the text) that keeps 'Coloreds' from rising in the world of her novel. As Abrahams indicates, Millin stacks the fictional deck in illustrating these deficiencies in creating her novelistic race mythology, for "It was logical after the marriage of the staggeringly spineless Andrew Flood to the stupid and empty-headed Hottentot girl Silla [for Millin] to make the next claim: the Coloreds were the offspring of the worst vices of black and white alike" (Abrahams, 60). Thus, Millin tries to make 'logical' the human result of miscegenation: a race of beings inferior to any 'pure' race (especially, the white race).

Millin's descriptions of the intellectual capacity of Flood's descendants, his daughter Deborah and his great grand-daughter Elmira, point out that they will never advance beyond a certain minimal stage. For example, Burtwell thinks of Deborah:

> He had thought a child of a white father might be different. He knew that native children arrived at their full capacity very early. At the age of four or five they were far in advance of white children; but at fourteen or fifteen they would begin to falter, to lag behind, to remain stationary while their white competitors went ahead. . . . He had a vague theory that it had to do with the traditional hardness of their skulls. But he had certainly hoped that Deborah might be more white than black in intellect. (84)

According to Newby, similar to Burtwell's thoughts, in describing those features which made the Black person "a better animal" than the white man, racists began with the "exceeding thickness of his skull, a thickness so great that it made his head a battering ram", according to much racist literature (43). For Millin, it would be against the "instituted order of things" for Deborah to have a 'white' intelligence as she has a 'black heart' and, 'black mind' because of her 'black blood'. Comments in 1920 by S.M. Molema, later important in the African National Congress, provide an important critique of such lines of thought as Millin's ideas represent. In *The Bantu Past and Present: An Ethnological and Historical Study of the Native Races of South Africa*, Molema summarizes the ideas of racist myths concerning intelligence:

> It is confidently asserted [by racists] that at a certain age, shortly after puberty, the black child reaches its limit of intellectual acquirements. He can no longer take anything into his head, and the white child now invariably outdistances the black. To all intents and purposes the education of the latter is ended just at the age when education starts in earnest and takes a practical turn.[16]

He goes on to point out that *inferior* schools or irrelevant curriculum may account for difficulty in schools rather than anatomical and hereditary factors. Consequently, one can see the irrational nature of Millin's racial myths.

Millin's racial myths are further shown when Elmira, at whose white skin Deborah looks at with "proud amazement" (128) is no smarter than Deborah even for the 'white blood' in her: at school,

> she was not as clever at her schoolwork as she promised to be when a child. It was as if her brain, running a race against the brains of white children, was very quick at starting but soon tired and lagged behind, so that the time came when it fell altogether out of the running. At sixteen Elmira had ceased to make any mental advance. (152)

Furthermore, this racial myth brings to mind a comment in Newby's *Jim Crow's Defense*, by H. L. Mencken, who, according to Rubin, wrote to Millin that he admired her novel so that he ranked her alongside E.M. Forster as a novelist as the "only two first-rate English writers, not counting the old stages" (85). According to Mencken, Blacks are doomed to inferiority to whites because whites are "fifty generations ahead" of Blacks and will continue evolving even as Blacks do, so that

Blacks will never be equal to whites (Newby, 75). This echoes Millin's sentiments, which are stated explicitly in *The South Africans* and which are implicit as an integral characteristic of the 'Colored' characters in *God's Stepchildren.* It is understandable, then, why Mencken would find *God's Stepchildren* "an absolutely first rate contribution to the sum of human knowledge" (Rubin, 85). Thus, it seems that Millin strikingly made her point on the permanent inferiority of 'Coloreds' and 'pure' Blacks. While she credits some Blacks for going abroad to universities, she also states that "the young African . . . does not succeed gloriously either. . . . [H]e has not the persistence, the temperament, the tradition, the mental quality, the general capacity, to compete against his white colleagues" (213). Hence, Millin, instead of considering environment — and this is stunning since the environment of South Africa certainly would affect racial advancement — creates an innate flaw for her 'Colored' characters which will intrinsically prohibit them from advancing to the status of white people. Furthermore, Millin uses Cape Town, where 'Coloreds' would have had more opportunities to advance, to show that they cannot. For example, as Barry, the last generation of Flood's 'Colored' descendants, grows up and he

> began to look around him to see where the Cape people stood, he could find nowhere an obviously Colored man in a commercial enterprise, in a learned profession or an artistic endeavor. They were many of them astonishingly capable with their hands, they made good masons, or carpenters, or mechanics; but there they ended. They often remained to the end of their days gamins by dispositions, imitative and monkey-like, and that was the far back Hottentot blood in them. (249)

Again, therefore, black 'blood' makes one permanently inferior. This idea is raised again in Millin's aforementioned non-fiction book on South Africans. Millin emphasizes throughout the 'Coloreds'' inability to advance in comparison to whites. She states that the 'Colored' person

> does not seem to have in him the ability to rise. It is as if the offspring of the originally mixed union had, through generations, and through circumspection of life and interbreeding, achieved a definite, inferior and static race . . . a race made up of weak materials and without the capacity for a great spiritual or intellectual growth. (215)

It is clear in Millin's works that as Memmi writes, the traits superimposed on the oppressed by the oppressor are all to the oppressors' advantage. For example, Millin states in *The South Africans* that just as Blacks and 'Coloreds' cannot advance, even " the less civilized peasant of Europe is to this extent the colored man's superior: *the blood in him* is stronger for advancement" (italics mine; 215). Most importantly, the devaluation of the oppressed is clear in such characterizations as Millin's. As Memmi writes:

> The humanity of the colonized, rejected by the colonizer, becomes opaque.... What is left of the colonized at the end of this extraordinary effort to dehumanize him ... is hardly a human being [to the colonizer]. He tends rapidly toward becoming an object.... The extraordinary efficiency of this operation is obvious. (85-6)

These ideas are certainly true of Millin in *God's Stepchildren*.

Significantly, Memmi states, "Willfully created and spread by the colonizer, this mythical and degrading portrait [can] end up being accepted and lived with to a certain extent by the colonized" (87). This statement is certainly accurate about Millin's characters, for she projects onto them her own racist beliefs about 'Coloreds.' Thus, infused with self-directed and outwardly directed racism, her 'Colored' characters show signs of self-alienation, inferiorization, internalization, flight from identity, lack of identification with 'Coloreds' and a drastically split double-consciousness — of being Black and of being white — to which there seems no solution which is not deleterious to the characters themselves.

Kleinhans, his daughter Elmira, and her son Barry show these traits. Kleinhans exhibits the hatred that Millin states those of mixed blood may feel for their parents and he also is both alienated from himself and 'color-struck'. As Millin writes, "He was bitter with hate. He hated the people he lived among for the blood that was in them; he hated his mother for her fuzzy hair, her high cheek bones, her thick eyes, her yellow brown skin; he hated his own flesh" (104). Millin, in *The South Africans*, writes that such hatred against one's non-white parent may result on the part of the child of a mixed union. And Kleinhans portrays Millin's thought in *The South Africans* that "Of his white blood he [the 'Colored'] is terribly proud. It is the black man which calls up bitterness in his heart, the reflection of the shamed, betrayed, and desolate half within himself" (206). This statement is certainly accurate of Kleinhans, for "he did not hate the white man who had idly begotten him" (104) and, in fact, he has a longing to join whites — and especially to have a white wife. Kleinhans wants nothing more than to be able to flee from a group whom he sees as being inferior and unattractive to the point of being repulsive to him. He wants to flee identification with a group of whom he is not, as he is of his white ancestry, "proud" (104). Kleinhans is so eager to take flight from the 'Colored' race whose ancestry he shares that "He despised a man in proportion as he was brown. Just physical lightness or darkness alone was his only test" (104). Thus, Millin creates a character who is as emotionally inferiorized as his creator believes him inferior. And his double-consciousness is shown in his knowledge of having Black ancestry and his desire to be white; and in his hostility for his Black forebears and pride in his white forebears. This kind of split Millin only makes insoluble, as Kleinhans can never be accepted by whites (e.g., the Afrikaners he approaches rebuff him) nor can he accept being Black. For all his days, therefore, he is doomed to live in an emotional no man's land.

Kleinhans' family, including Elmira, his daughter, continues the dilemmas her father faces. Moreover, Elmira adds to her father's racism by directing it at her family, looking down on her brothers and sisters, because they seem 'Colored' to her, as she is passing for white (indirectly encouraged by Kleinhans and his wife, for they "idolize" her; 143). Elmira also looks down on other girls she meets as she 'passes' at school: "[S]he actually got to the stage of putting on airs and of looking down on other children for this or that" (141). She is arrogant towards girls because of their fathers' status and, significantly, feels hostile to other girls because they are Jewish (as was the author of the novel). Furthermore, both her mother, Lena, and grandmother, Deborah, show their internalization of racism as the white, old Lindsell approaches her for marriage. To Lena, the family will rise in some vague way (whiten up?) through marriage to a white man. And Deborah is happy, for her attitude is that "nothing . . . mattered except to be white" (196). Yet, the marriage and the 'whitening' process are unsuccessful, for as had Flood, to a degree, as Elmira grows in unhappiness and prepares to abandon her marriage, she 'goes Colored': "She had grown stout [like Silla after her marriage — an alleged 'Hottentot' trait], her skin had become darker and coarser, and even her hair had lost the suggestion of gold. She was no longer as white as the baby Deborah remembered her to have been" (217). Thus, flight from the group, bigotry, trying to 'become' white (as Elmira had earlier hoped in her relationship with a white man, Krell), and a split consciousness — simultaneously wanting to be white and being 'condemned' to blackness — are main features in the story of Kleinhans' family.

In the story of Barry, the son of Elmira and her white husband, Lindsell, Millin has also infused the character with a rejection of identification with 'Coloreds' and a double-consciousness, which, in this case, Millin tries to resolve in a way that, one supposes, she expected was the only possible affirmative outcome.

Like Elmira, Barry is proud before other children, especially those who are not white or are of a lower class. Yet, Barry, the whitest of Flood's descendants, is endowed with "a kind of pathetic intelligence" (229; "pathetic" is an interesting word choice, perhaps indicating that although he is the least 'Colored' of Flood's descendants, he still must ultimately opt to 'become' 'Colored'). Significantly, Barry passes for white and could live as a white man, unlike any of his ancestors, but to ensure his consciousness is split, his adult white half-sister, Lindsell's daughter, Edith, with whom he lives after the death of his father, tells him of "the shame and sorrow in [his] blood" (271), reminding one that a tenet of racism is that the races are unassimilable — even when they co-exist *within oneself*. Moreover, after Edith tells Barry that if he married it would be unfair to the woman, Barry shows the double-consciousness of which Edith seems the agent:

> What right had he, after all, to resent her [Edith's] warning about his blood? Was not what she said just? . . . Yet, on the other hand, how were the white-skinned people whom rumor credited with black blood different from other people? How different was he, except that he was afraid he was different? . . . Of course, it was an unspeakable thing for a white man to cut off his own children from the civilization that was their due, to throw life backwards to the inferiority that black blood meant. But what noticeable effect on future generations could his own drop of black blood have? (277-78)

This passage shows Barry's split consciousness, and his lack of resolution. And, the reader may feel Barry's final question is rhetorical, for it may seem sensible, in the logic of many readers. Yet, Flood had earlier answered his daughter Deborah when she told him she was pregnant with Kleinhans: "There can be no more white children" (98). Thus, Barry must resolve his dilemma, Millin seems to say, by accepting his blackness.

In the resolution to the novel, Barry, Millin seems to say, represents all 'Coloreds' and must ghettoize himself as 'Colored.' Barry can only, implies Millin, be his true self at that point. After Barry visits his mother, Millin wants us to believe that self-alienation, denial, double-consciousness and self-hatred are all resolved by Barry's acceptance of a mission to go live among 'Coloreds.' "I found myself" (325) is the signal of his resolution. Yet, Millin inadvertently undermines this resolution by making clear that living with 'Coloreds' not only is a penalty — "for my sin" (326) in begetting a child with a white wife, but by earlier saying that he "had deposited in him the same religious germ that had made his great-great-grandfather [Flood] want to give the boots from his feet to a beggar and walk barefoot" (262) and by using the same word — "sacrifice" (323) — that she uses to describe Flood's desire to become closer to his mission by starting the line of miscegenation she so detests. Hence, instead of the resolution that she may have wanted, one that says that at long last the saga of the results of Flood's miscegenation is resolved by an affirmative action by Barry to accept Black ancestry, it seems Millin merely succeeds in 'dumping' Barry into 'Coloredness' and thereby gives short shrift to the very complex issues raised in the novel as she depicts the emotions of Flood's descendants.

In the development of Barry's life, therefore, Millin inadvertently offers an example best explained by Franz Fanon in *Black Skin, White Masks*:

> While I was forgetting, forgiving, and wanting only to love, my message was flung back in my face like a slap. The white world . . . barred me from all participation. A man was expected to behave like a man. I was expected to behave like a black man — or at least like a nigger. I shouted a greeting to the world and the world slashed away my joy. I was told to stay within bounds, to go back where I belonged.[17]

Ironically, Millin seems to be aware, to a degree, that her hyper-vigilance concerning racial purity is an "intoxication", to use Cassirer's word (308). This awareness is embedded in the negative traits Millin gives to her alter-ego in the novel, Edith. Indeed, many of Edith's motives in preying on Barry's fears concerning his racial heritage, and her telling him he must never intermarry and produce more children with Black heritage, are traceable to Edith's own sexual repression, sexual fears and romantic deprivation. If one connects the main theme

The "Nigger in Them": Sarah Gertrude Millin's Poetics . . . 21

of several passages, one sees how Millin, unconsciously, it seems, undercuts the fictional embodiment of her own concern with racial purity. Perhaps, first it would be beneficial to examine passages which establish Edith's emotional deprivation — a deprivation which causes her to be reliant on Barry to fill the emotional void in her life. For instance, Edith decides to take Barry to live with her after the death of his father because "It was the first time any human had ever needed her" (244). Soon afterwards, one hears Millin's own critical view of the connection between Edith's emotional deprivation and her behavior towards Barry. First, Millin points out how society views Edith as an 'old maid' and couples this fact with Edith's relationship with Barry. Millin writes:

> It was, in a way, pathetic that here was this woman of thirty-six with the child of seven that she told people was her half-brother, and no one paid her the compliment of believing for a moment that Barry might not really be her brother. She had the look of the undesired. She bought herself a house in the Gardens suburb of Cape Town, and there for many years she remained with Barry. It was a quiet life. They were both unapproachable. Edith had a natural hostility towards the world. (295)

This passage establishes the loneliness, isolation and alienation towards others which both mark Edith's life and fuel her link to Barry. These qualities are the seeds of greater flaws which totally undercut Millin's use of Edith as the representative of Millin's own argument for racial separation.

More serious in damaging Edith as the carrier of the banner of racial purity is Millin's development of the aforementioned deprivation in the depiction of the connection between the dashing of Edith's own romantic desires with her campaign of mental torture on Barry concerning his own romantic and marital prospects, with Edith's telling Barry he must never marry or have children. Importantly, Edith's total devotion to prey on Barry's fears about his Black heritage begins after she despairs of winning the love of Rev. Raill, whose interest she had clumsily and pathetically tried to arouse. (In this part of the novel, Millin's exaggerated feeling of the tragedy of being an unmarried woman is clear, as Martin Rubin states in his biography of Millin; 360). The reason for the heightening in Edith's obsession with Barry's racial identity and her telling him that he must remain — like her — unmarried is a central issue in the novel and provides a key turning point. Before

Edith's hopes of love with Rev. Raill are dashed, she uses Barry to fill her emotional void. As Millin writes, "he really had a natural affection for her. . . . And she, shut off from all love, could not but respond. As time went on, too, she thought of his ancestry seldom and more easily . . . " (255) What then, triggers the change from this gradual acceptance of Barry's heritage to her hyper-sensitivity to it — a hyper-sensitivity she forces Barry to internalize?

First, as Millin writes this section of the novel, she unintentionally undercuts completely her own argument for segregation of the races and against inter-racial marriage by making it impossible for one not to tie these concerns in her alter-ego to Edith's own inability to have any sexual or romantic relationships. Indeed, after Rev. Raills's engagement, Millin's implicit and explicit emphasis on Edith's desire that neither should Barry experience such relationships makes Edith seem like a neurotic who wants to displace her own alienation, isolation and humiliation onto Barry rather than her seeming like someone who has clear views of any possible *actual* or logical validity to demands that Barry not 'taint' any future generations with his Black heritage. Millin herself terms Edith, in her aforementioned demands on Barry, "a crusader against love" (270). Another passage sums up the way Millin undercuts the validity of her spokeswoman for 'racial purity,' Edith:

> Edith's disappointment [with Raill's engagement] reacted curiously on Barry. He became a need to her so intense that it colored their association with bitterness. If she had not Barry, she would be cut off from the human world, she felt. She followed him about, hungrily. She not only loved him; most extraordinary, she hated him at the same time. And she hated him because she was afraid he might not love her as she loved him; might love someone else better. . . . She was dreadful of his friends, his occupations, even his religion. All day long she went round dreading the possible girl who might come into his life. She felt it was a kind of mania with her, and she tried to control herself; but by the time he was sixteen or seventeen she was always talking to him about girls — about how silly they were, how affected and selfish, how mercenary, how ruinous to a man's endeavor. . . . The news of an unhappy love affair or marriage released from her an excited flow of triumphant exposition. (269)

Millin's having Edith also feel that these ideas are "mad" (269) destroy any validity to her saying to Barry that "you ought not to allow yourself ever to care for a girl. Because it would be unjust to her — and to the race" (272). (Clearly, Edith's concerns are focused on Barry's potential feelings towards white women.) Indeed, though Barry has internalized white racism in his view of people of Black ancestry which gives Edith's racist words weight in his mind, Millin makes clear that Barry can still see through Edith's motives in demanding that he be without love and romance (273).

Moreover, that sex plays a role in Edith's desire to keep Barry from experiencing love and marriage is clear in at least two important ways. First, her concerns about Barry's relations with girls occur after he matures sexually, during his teenage years. Second, Edith's angry remarks to Barry about his interest in religion belie her innermost desire: "[S]he wanted him to live celibate like a priest" (278). Thus, Edith clearly wants mainly for Barry to live an asexual life more than she wants him to segregate himself from whites (as he chooses to do at the end of the book). Consequently, castrating or neutering Barry is Edith's central concern — not the racial purity that Millin consciously wanted to be the main developing argument of the novel; an argument Millin clearly meant to have its apex in the section of the novel concerning Barry and Edith.

That Millin emphasizes Edith's desire for Barry to become a celibate being (as she is) raises intriguing issues concerning what this topic reveals about the connection between racism, fear of the Black male sexuality and the racist desire to "contain" it.

The aforementioned psycho-sexual aspect of the novel is illuminated by considering other ideas by Fanon in *Black Skin, White Masks*. As I have stated, Fanon states that "The negro is a phobogenic object, a stimulus to anxiety [for whites]" (157). He further explains that a major focus of this phobia in whites centers on myths of Black male sexuality. Fanon makes evident that " 'negrophobia' has as its target the genital level" (157) of Blacks' existence (i.e., white myths about this aspect of Blacks lives). States Fanon:

> For the majority of white men the Negro represents the sexual instinct (in its raw state). The Negro is the incarnation of a genital potency beyond all moralities and prohibitions. The women among the whites, by a genuine process of induction, invariably view the negro as the keeper of the impalpable gate that opens into the realm of . . . delirious sexual sensation. . . . We have shown that reality destroys all these beliefs. But they all rest on the level of the imagined. . . . The white [person] who ascribes a malefic influence to the black is regressing on the intellectual level. (177)

Thus, Fanon's ideas clearly help to clarify the "intoxication" with matters of sex and race that are the foundation of central aspects of Millin's imagination — an intoxication most clearly manifested in Millin's somewhat confused and fascinating portrayal of Edith.

In addition to Fanon's insights, Thomas F. Pettigrew's essay, "Prejudice", provides one with a key to understanding the neurosis within such racism as Millin writes in Edith. First, concerning the affective factors of prejudice, Pettigrew writes that prejudiced

> [a]ttitudes can also reduce anxiety by serving an externalizing function. This occurs when an individual senses an analogy between the object of the attitude and some unresolved inner problem. One adopts an attitude that is a transformed way of dealing with an inner, affective problem. People project their emotional problems onto the external world through particular social attitudes. If you have sexual problems [e.g.,] you may regard Latins as dangerously hypersexed.[18]

And so, it is 'logical' (in the irrational logic of racism) that Edith's own thwarted sexuality makes her hypersensitive to Barry's sexual and romantic development.

Furthermore, Pettigrew's descriptions of externalization theories of prejudice help to illuminate the psychological meaning of such behavior as Edith's towards Barry. Pettigrew focuses on the theories of authoritarianism and the frustration-aggression hypothesis. Lack of self-awareness, and displacent of negative feelings onto a less important person than the one who actually aroused these feelings (as is the case when Edith takes out her disappointment not on Rev. Raill but on Barry, who as Edith's ward is thus at the losing end of power imbalance) are both essential to the authoritarian syndrome. As Pettigrew writes,

> Central to the [authoritarian] syndrome is anti-intraception, the refusal to look inside oneself and the lack of insight into one's own behavior and feelings. Authoritarians refuse to accept their emotions and try to deny them. (16)

Moreover, and especially relevant to the unintended emotional complexity of Millin's characterization of Edith, authoritarians

> are outwardly submissive towards those they see as authorities with power over them, and aggressive towards those they see as beneath them in status. This hierarchal view of authority links directly with ethnic attitudes. High-status ethnic groups are respected, and

authoritarians treat them with deference. But low-status ethnic groups are disparaged. Prejudice becomes for many authoritarians "a crutch upon which to limp through life." (17)

These ideas further help to explain the psychological depth of Millin's characterization of Edith. For instance, as stated earlier, Edith has 'authority' over Barry both as his guardian and as a white person in a racist society. And Barry certainly is "disparaged" — sadistically preyed upon — by Edith. Moreover, unleashing her racism on Barry gives Edith a "crutch" of many functions: her treatment of him bolsters her self-importance, for the message she clearly gives to him is that 'white is right'; she has a reason to obsess on something else (i.e., Barry, as the target of her racism) instead of her own loneliness and isolation; and she can attempt to be less tortured by being unloved if she sees to it that another may also be condemned to a loveless life. Consequently, the authoritarian theory certainly sheds light on Millin's novel.

Pettigrew's discussion of another externalization theory of prejudice also helps explain the pivotal section of Millin's novel, Edith's relationship with Barry. Pettigrew writes:

> The frustration-aggression hypothesis asserts that all aggression is preceded by frustration. . . . Though frustration is created by an inability to attain desired goals, aggressive behavior is frequently not directed at the agents that actually keep people from achieving their goals. Frustrating agents are usually older, stronger, more powerful, or protected by cultural traditions. So hostility often gets channeled onto approved, vulnerable objects, scapegoats that have little to do with the original frustration. (18)

Pettigrew goes onto stat that "Usually, however, scapegoats bear some symbolic relationship with the frustration" (19). It thus becomes clear why it is psychologically explainable that as a result of her frustrated love for Rev. Raill Edith bedevils not a respected man of the cloth but someone who is dependent on her — more centrally, a person of Black ancestry who is dependent on her. Thus, frustrated love provides the "symbolic" link between Edith and Barry that results in Edith's racism being mobilized to ensure that Barry will share such frustration.

In this section of the novel, Millin's focus on interracial romance and marriage between a man of Black ancestry and a white woman as the apex of her multi-generational saga also raises important issues. I. D. MacCrone's ideas in *Race Attitudes in South Africa* are relevant on this point. MacCrone writes of the European race attitude . . . which sooner or later finds expression in the question: 'Do you want your daughter or your sister to marry a black man?' — one of the implications being that white women would have no hesitation in so doing, and, in fact, would readily do so once there was genuine social equality between white and black. This obsession with race purity is, of course, so much rationalization, since its real aim is to keep sexuality in the form of a potentially superior sexual rival at bay. [19]

MacCrone's diagnosis mainly explains the possible white male point of view, i.e., that white men fear the existence of and having to compare with men who may be sexually "superior" to them according to racial myths. Still, the issue of sexuality seems to stand behind much of Millin's concentration on Barry and on the obsession of her fictional counterpart, Edith, with protecting 'the purity of white womanhood' from a man of Black heritage. Perhaps more relevant in helping to understand why interracial romance and marriage between a Black man and a white woman is so unacceptable to Millin that they are clearly the point that she felt was the apex of the degenerate nature of race mixing (thus making the issue the climax of her novel) is Walter Aidan Cotton's *The Race Problem in South Africa*. Published a couple of years after Millin's novel, Cotton's book illuminates why intermarriage between a Black man and white woman was, to many racists, the unpardonable sin. Consistent with Millin, who reaches the zenith of her racial hysteria in writing of Barry's marriage to a white woman, Cotton implies that it is somehow worse for a white woman to intermarry than it is for a white man:

> Not only would [a white woman], married to an African feel far more than [a white man] the cutting off from the society of her own kindred and all the protective contrivances of her home conditions; not only would she be companioned, in most cases, by one below herself in culture; but whatever the man's merits, and in spite of the status belonging to her race, she would be confronted with the very deeply rooted conviction of the essential inferiority of her sex. Indeed, as between the white man and the white woman who oversteps the racial bar, the lot of the latter must be, to any reflecting mind, incomparably the more full of danger.[20]

Thus, the evidence is there that white racists' imaginations often work feverishly overtime when contemplating objections to a union between a Black man and a white woman.

In helping to provide a critique of such racism as exhibited by Millin and like-minded racists, MacCrone writes: "The idea of a white woman in the arms of a black man, especially, if she is there of own free will, is enough to give rise to the most pronounced emotional reactions in the white man" (301-2).

Again, the sexist language (the reference to "the white man") is again strikingly inappropriate, as the idea, for our purposes, is markedly relevant to the writings of a white woman. And though MacCrone's statement may seem a statement of the obvious, that a psychologist whose idea is based on observation and research corroborates this mainstay of racism is certainly a relevant point. MacCrone's and Cotton's discussions clearly support, in different ways, Fanon's remark made decades later than that for racist whites who are intimidated by *their own myths* of Black sexuality, "The Negro is taken as a terrifying penis" (177). These anxieties and fears are at the foundation of Millin's focus on Barry as being the breaking point beyond which the author could no longer imagine her novelistic cycle of miscegenation, at which point she, by her characterization of Edith, makes a 'Negrophobic' and, therefore, neurotic rescue of white womanhood from a Black — 'Colored' in South African parlance — man. In the final, central section of the novel, therefore, it seems that Millin (and her fictional alter-ego Edith) suffers from the following aspect of the neurosis of racism of which Fanon writes: "over a series of long days and long nights the image of the biological-sexual-sensual-genital-nigger has imposed itself on you and you do not know how it get free of it" (202). This sentence sums up both the pseudo-scientific elements of Millin's racism as well as the "sensual" aspect which comes through in Millin's portrayal of the conflict between Edith and Barry. When one analyzes the complexity of this aspect of Millin's novel, it is clear that Millin achieved much more than she intended: she made her writing a case study in many aspects of the psychology of racism.

Reflecting R.F.A. Hoernle's earlier idea on the emotional symbolism of race, J.M. Coetzee's statement about *God's Stepchildren* is especially relevant: "Race theories . . . of the blood . . . [are] material for fantasy."[21] Nothing could capture more perfectly Millin's ideology in the novel. And, as Coetzee points out in "Blood, Flaw, Taint, Degeneration: The Case of Sarah Gertrude Millin," in Millin's tale of the misery encountered by four generations of the products of miscegenation, Millin was not aberrant in her approach to the topic, which makes clear her belief that Blacks and so-called 'Coloreds' are inferior to whites. Going beyond Coetzee's analysis, one again finds that Cassirer's ideas can be applied to Millin to illuminate not only her own racism but the racist 'race theories' which influenced her. Cassirer's critique of one of these race theories, Count Arthur de Gobineau's *The Inequality of the Human Races*, sums up a line of thought reflected both by Gobineau and by many other writers, some of which I will discuss, upholding white superiority and racial separatism; a line of thought clearly represented by Millin. Cassirer summarizes this type of bigoted thinking: "Cooperation between different races means cohabitation, cohabitation means blood mixture, and blood mixture means degeneration. It is always the beginning of the end" (308). Furthermore, Millin believed that 'Coloreds' are inferior to 'pure' Blacks as, states Coetzee, "The hybrid is . . . damned in that the two bloods in his veins are debased bloods to begin with"(54). As I.A. Newby explains in *Jim Crow's Defense*, a specific target of "racist scorn"(32) was the person of mixed blood. Mirroring Millin's idea in *The South Africans* to "[c]onsider his ancestry. In his veins run, on the one side, the blood of slaves; on the other side, the careless the stupid the vicious"(395), Newby writes,

> In the opinion of racists the mulatto was inferior for several important reasons. Not only was he the progeny of basically different racial stocks, but he descended [many racists believed] from the most depraved elements of those stocks as well, from coarse, impure, degenerate white men and grossly immoral and lascivious Negro women. Inferior and debilitated themselves, such parents could beget only inferior and debilitated offspring. (132)

Moreover, in explaining Millin's racial view, Coetzee points out, as does Newby, that such racist ideas were prominent worldwide before and during the time Millin was writing in the 1920s in such fields as eugenics, genetics, biology, geography, sociology, and anthropology, among others. Charles Darwin's cousin, Francis Galton, for example, in *Hereditary Genius* (1869) writes on "The Comparative Worth of Different Races." According to Galton:

> [T]he number among Negroes of those whom we should call half-witted men is very large. Every book alluding to Negro servants is full of such instances. I was myself very much impressed by this fact during my travels in Africa. The mistakes Negroes made in their own matters were so childish, stupid, and simpleton-like, as frequently to make me ashamed of my own species.[22]

In addition, the nineteenth century writings of Count Arthur de Gobineau, such as the aforementioned *The Inequality of the Human Races,* concluded that only Aryans could create strong civilizations and that, quotes Newby, "[A]ll civilizations derive from the white race, that none can exist without its help, and that a society is great and brilliant only in so far as it preserves the blood of the noble group that created it" (9). Newby also quotes Gobineau as stating that "strict despotism" (9) is "the only way of governing the Negro" (9).

Moreover, shedding light on Millin's ideology are many white South African writers who certainly wrote a significant amount of racial myths during race theory's 'Golden Age', the late 19th and early 20th centuries, when such pseudo-scientific observations were abundant. One relevant example is Alexander Davis' 1903 *The Native Problem,* which reflects the influence of other race theorists and which purports to give "a bird's-eye view of the [South African] native's present stage in evolutionary civilization."[23] In Davis' work, as in Millin's *God's Stepchildren* and *The South Africans,* we see racist assumptions hardened into 'facts'. Davis writes, for instance,

> The South African native is frequently compared with a child. This mental estimate inspires the mode of treatment almost universally recommended in dealing with him. Any person experienced in native management will enjoin the necessity of being strict but just, as any weakness of a master or employer is at once taken advantage of and real kindness or consideration is absolutely wasted. (19)

Davis' groundless pontifications on Blacks' intellectual capacities and potential for advancement include the following:

> Though intellectually underdeveloped, mentally [the native] is robust; that is to say, though intellectually in knowledge of matter and life he is a child, his mental powers are high and above the grade of cunning. . . . His low intellectual level is mostly due to a lack of imagination and a lack of necessity. . . . He would stake an engine for years without seeking to discover the sector of its working; be taught to take the whole machine to pieces without connecting the piston rod with the steam. Mechanically you could teach him anything, scientifically you would find him a hopeless case. You may teach him to read and write; but the writer has never met or heard of a case where anything higher has resulted than facile powers of expression and strong common-sense thought. (12)

Furthermore, though it would be interesting to know with which South African race theorists Millin was familiar, Coetzee states that Millin had read Galton and Darwin, among others, and was aware, therefore, of some of the prevailing race theory — which might better be termed race mythology — of her day. Writing *God's Stepchildren* in the 1920s, Millin was certainly in a world where, according to Newby and Coetzee, many of the dominant race mythologies were, in fact, racist and where, as I.D. MacCrone points out in *Race Attitudes in South Africa*, "pseudo-scientific" ideas were a strong factor in racist attitudes (262).

Significantly, Coetzee writes that Millin is "neglected nowadays because her treatment of race has come to seem dated and morally offensive. [But] Millin's ideas on race . . . are not a hotchpotch of colonial prejudices but the reflection of respectable scientific and historical thought" (42). Thus, it is no wonder that Millin would produce a novel in which her own theories are racist, especially about miscegenation, and which represents those who are a product of it as damned to eternal inferiority. Moreover, as Coetzee writes of Millin's view of miscegenation, "[I]t is the nature of the taint that no matter how thinly spread it [black blood] is in the blood-pool of the community, it remains black (it is thus not like a dye but like an oil)" (51). This "oil" of blood forever condemns Millin's 'Colored' characters, for in her ideology, it never truly mixes or diminishes in future generations, but always taints its bearer with the alleged inferiority of prior Black and 'Colored' ancestors. It is certainly true that in Millin's novel the drama of mixed blood is played out in such a way that it is clear that the non-white heritage of a mixed union forever relegates the 'victims' of it to having an almost sub-human mind and life. And this constitutes the "poetics of blood" of *God's Stepchildren* (Coetzee, 48). In addition, Hoernle's comments on some of the reasons why white supremacists were (and are) adamantly opposed to miscegenation explain to a degree Millin's hidden agenda in writing a novel whose most important aspect is racist myths about people of mixed race. Hoernle writes:

> Insistence on social distance, as we have seen, has the effect, and presumably, therefore, also the aim, of preserving group-integrity. It keeps aliens in race out of the dominant group. It is, clearly, in line with this aim if the entry of aliens in race by way of marriage is resisted. Similarly, the public condemnation of miscegenation, or race mixture, in the form of extra-marital unions, rests on fear of the

"bastardization" of the "White" blood in their make-up. After all, the cry for a "White South Africa," which, we have seen, is a cry for a South Africa dominated by the White group would become meaningless, if there were no White group to be dominated, owing to its absorption by wholesale race mixture into the numerically preponderant non-White group. The avoidance of race mixture, in order to preserve the integrity of the White group, is thus part of the technique of White domination. (39)[24]

In essence, the racist obsession with the threat to white domination by race mixture is the chief pillar of *God's Stepchildren*.

In order to more fully understand Millin's race theory in her novel, it aids greatly to examine more extensively Newby's aforementioned *Jim Crow's Defense*. As stated earlier, Newby emphasizes, for example, racist attitudes towards the mulatto in America that greatly mirror Millin's attitudes towards 'Coloreds' in both *God's Stepchildren* and *The South Africans*. Newby, for instance, summarizes racist arguments:

> [W]hatever his accomplishments, the mulatto was a product of discordant heritages. He had two souls, two temperaments, two sets of opinions and was unable to think or act strongly in any direction. Mentally and spiritually he was attuned to the traditions of neither race, and his soul was the scene of perpetual conflict of inharmonious tendencies. Restless and dissatisfied, he forever protested his station in life, but his protest, said racists . . . was the desperate rebellion of "a forceful Aryan in soul entanglement with an utterly strange being," a Caucasian spirit imprisoned in the forbidding circle of mongrel blood, inimical inheritance and pernicious environment. (134)

These thoughts are most certainly accurate reflections of Millin's portrayal of her characters who are the descendants of the missionary Andrew Flood. For example, Kleinhans' "White blood felt a longing for its kind" as he approaches an Afrikaner group (109). Also, Elmira hates her brothers and sisters because she, passing for white as a result of her light-skin, considers herself white and them 'Colored'.

Newby continues to recap race theories which Millin seems to share:

> And as if to intensify his sense of tragedy and protest the mulatto was often educated and given a glimpse of the possibilities of life in the white world. Drawn thus between conflicting inheritances and

wistfully longing for white man's society, he was brutally relegated to the status of the Negro. No wonder he was dissatisfied! Sensitive and self-conscious to an extraordinary degree and possessing a tragic sense of loneliness and isolation, he was perpetually discontented. He was a man without a race and . . . [this] explained his fanatical determination to smash the color line. (134-35)

This passage is especially applicable to Elmira, who is given a chance by 'passing,' to go to school, to socialize with whites and to think of herself as one of them. Furthermore, Millin's belief in the 'whiteness' of Elmira's desires is shown in the passage after her true race is exposed:

She had lost her white status and her white hopes; and she was old enough in these days to realize that, wherever she went, the past [of being exposed as being 'Colored'] stalked her, panting close, audible, audible at her heals, waiting its opportunity to leap at her, to lure her to the ground and tear her flesh. And it was not even, justly, her own past; it was the past of others. (163-64)

One can see in this passage that once Elmira has experienced life as a white, the vision results in emotional turmoil and estrangement from both races. Knowing that she is not white, Elmira nevertheless tries to disown her 'Colored' heritage. Thus, while she emotionally longs to live as a white, she knows she can never fully do that; and yet she remains totally alienated from her 'Colored' heritage. Consequently, while, as Newby indicates, she belongs emotionally to neither race, she still longs to destroy the barrier that prevents her from 'becoming white. Newby's analysis of racist myths about mulattoes in the United States, therefore, greatly enlightens one's understanding of *God's Stepchildren*.

In making one think further about such racism as Millin exhibits in her book, Jacques Barzun's *Race: A Study in Superstition* is also useful. Barzun lists objectives to show the logical fallacies in racist arguments, several of which are applicable to Millin. Take, for example, Millin's assertion that it would be against the "instituted order" of things if Blacks could advance to equality in deeds and mental capacity to whites. She takes it as a given that such a thing has never happened. Barzun would call such thinking a "circular argument"[25] He writes: "Race theories of whatever kind all lead to a point where the proponent . . . begs the question. He says in effect: the Nordic race is a group apart: it is the greatest race. Why? Just look at its triumphs,

The "Nigger in Them": Sarah Gertrude Millin's Poetics . . . 33

look at Columbus, Nelson, Shakespeare, Edison — all Nordics. But what made these men great? The racial something they had in common" (204). Such thinking clearly collapses under its own weight. Another charge which more greatly applies to Millin is her illogical view of heredity, as 'Colored' "blood" forever overpowering white "blood" and leading in almost all cases to the characters' decline. Barzun would refer to such attitudes as Millin's as belonging in the category of "Predestination and Obscurantism" (206). Barzun states:

> The upshot of race-thinking is that by offering us the mystery of heredity as an explanation it diverts our attention from the social and intellectual factors which make up personality. Race interpretations presuppose that from the moment of conception and by conception alone, the nature and mind of an individual are predestined. The thousand incidents and accidents that make a life are mere footnotes to a text that was written *ab ovo*. (206)

These characteristics are clear in Millin — heredity of 'Colored' 'blood' forever dooms those who possess it. This is the central theory of Millin's novel. This fact leads to the final charge I will quote from Barzun: "Absolutism" (206). Barzun states that for race theorists: "Race stands as an absolute, a first cause, an unmoved mover. In the familiar world of shifting appearances, race satisfied man's demand for certainty by providing a single, simple, and adequate cause for a great variety of large complex events" (207). One certainly sees these absolutist tendencies in Millin, for in *God's Stepchildren* all complexities of the human character seem to boil down to race and miscegenation.

Comparing Millin's ideology of race to the following passage Mark Twain's *Pudd'nhead Wilson* yields interesting results. After Tom, whose mother, the slave Roxy, switched him with a white baby, finds out that he is, in fact, Black,

> If [Tom] met a friend, he found that the habit of a lifetime had in some mysterious way vanished — his arm hung limp, instead of involuntarily extending the hand for a shake. It was the "nigger" in him asserting its humility. . . . And the "nigger" in him was surprised when the white friend put out his hand for a shake with him. He found the "nigger" in him involuntarily giving the road, on the sidewalk, to the white rowdy and loafer. When Rowena, the dearest thing his heart knew, the idol of his secret worship, invited him in, the "nigger" in him made an embarrassed excuse and was afraid to enter and sit with the dread white folks on equal terms. The "nigger"

in him went shrinking and skulking here and there and yonder, fancying it saw suspicion and maybe detection in all faces, tones, and gestures.[26]

Tom's thoughts in this passage from *Pudd'nhead Wilson*, are part of Mark Twain's attempt to explode the "myth of blood," in Coetzee's words (42), which so obsesses Millin. For Twain, Tom, who is "thirty-one parts white, and by a *fiction* of law and custom a negro" (italics mine; 29) doesn't think it is his *shock* at Roxy's revealing to him that she is his mother that makes him so paranoid about some Black 'essence' which seems to determine his actions but instead his own belief that there is such an essence. To Twain, such a belief is ridiculous. To Millin, such a belief is the crux of her race theory. For Millin, one drop of Black 'blood' is enough to confuse and to threaten to ruin a life; to expel one from happiness in any society; and to condemn one to a life of emotional upheaval. Millin believes, as Newby writes of racist theory, that "among individuals of every race there was a 'consciousness of kind', a 'call of race,' a 'call of the blood'" (47). For Twain in *Pudd'nhead Wilson*, such an idea would be ludicrous; for Millin, in *God's Stepchildren*, such an idea would seem fact. For when one asks what, according to Millin, is the tragedy in the lives of the generations of Flood's descendants, there is but one answer: "It's the nigger in them." Such is the result of the novelistic equivalent of what Cassirer states in critiquing such race theories as those which influenced Millin and are embodied in her novel. He describes them as "intoxication, an intoxication of race worship and self-worship" (308). In Millin's novel, one is left with a document which demonstrates the intricacies of this intoxication, allowing one to "denaturalize" and deconstruct the mythologies Millin perpetuates.

In summarizing this chapter, I would like to reinforce a few main points. But first, I would like to ask a question which may be on some readers' minds: Why discuss a South African novel from the 1920s at the turn of the century? In answering this question, I will state in no uncertain terms that anyone who thinks *God's Stepchildren* is a mere museum piece is foolish. Not only does the novel reflect the racism of its time, as Coetzee points out, but it is also a compendium of many symptoms of the neurosis of racism, many of which are with us to this very day. Some of these symptoms are the misrepresentation of non-white people (think of many reports on so-called Black on Black violence, as mentioned in the introduction); racist whites' desire to be 'guardians' — i.e., controllers — of blacks; and rationalizations to justify racist thoughts and actions.

One can readily see, therefore, that *God's Stepchildren* is not a work that has been made 'safe' by obsolescence for it is both a reflection of its time and of many enduring elements of the psychological and sociological problem of bigotry as is evident when one analyzes the novel in light of the ideas of the theoreticians employed in this chapter. Hence, any idea that feels *God's Stepchildren* is unrelated to our time overlooks key aspects of "the problem of the twentieth century."

Notes

1. Peter Abrahams, *Return to Goli* (London: Faber and Faber, 1963), 59.
2. R.F.A. Hoernle, *South African Native Policy and the Liberal Spirit* (1939; reprint, New York: Negro Universities Press, 1969), 131.
3. Bobby Seale, Lecture, Cornell University (Ithaca, New York: 4/18/89).
4. Franz Boas, *The Mind of Primitive Man*, Rev. ed.(New York: The Macmillan Company, 1938), 4-5.
5. Ernst Cassirer, *The Myth of the State* (Garden City, New York: Doubleday and Company, Inc. 1955), 308.
6. Karen Horney, *Our Inner Conflicts* (New York: W.W. Norton, 1945), 96,114.
7. Albert Memmi, *The Colonizer and the Colonized* (Boston: Beacon Press, 1965), 20.
8. Sarah Gertrude Millin, *God's Stepchildren* (Johannesburg, South Africa: AD. Donker, 1986), 109. All references are to this edition.
9. Martin Rubin, *Sarah Gertrude Millin* (Johannesburg: AD. Donker, 1977), 79.
10. Warren Breed, "Suicide and Loss in Social Interaction"; in *Essays in Self-Destruction*, ed. Edwin S.Shneidman (New York: Science House, Inc., 1967), 188.
11. Albert Schweitzer, *On the Edge of the Primeval Forest* (London: A. and C.Black, Ltd., 1922), 131-32.
12. W.E.B. DuBois, *The Souls of Black Folk* in *Three Negro Classics*, ed. John Hope Franklin (New York: Avon, 1965), 214-15.
13. Barry D. Adam, *The Survival of Domination: Inferiorization and Everyday Life* (New York: Elsevier North-Holland, Inc. 1978), 89-90.
14. I.A. Newby, *Jim Crow's Defense* (Baton Rouge: Louisiana State University Press, 1965),32.
15. Sarah Gertrude Millin, *The South Africans* (New York: Boni and Liveright, 1927), 395.
16. S.M. Molema, *The Bantu Past and Present: An Ethnographical and Historical Study of the Native Races of South Africa*, (1920; Cape Town: C. Stuick, 1963), 328.
17. Franz Fanon, *Black Skin, White Masks*, trans. Charles Lam Markham (New York: Grove Press, 1967), 114-15.
18. Thomas F. Pettigrew, *"Prejudice"* in Thomas Pettigrew, et al., ed. *Prejudice* (Cambridge: Harvard University Press, 1982), 16.
19. I.D. MacCrone, *Race Attitudes in South Africa* (New York: Oxford University Press, 1937), 262.
20. Walter Aidan Cotton, *The Race Problem in South Africa* (1926; reprint, New York: Negro Universities Press, 1969), 109.
21. J.M. Coetzee, "Blood, Flaw, Taint, Degeneration: The Case of Sarah Gertrude Millin," *English Studies in Africa*, 23 January 1980: 48.

22. Francis Galton, *Hereditary Genius* (Cleveland: The World Publishing Company, 1962), 19.
23. Alexander Davis, *The Native Problem* (1903; reprint, New York: Negro University Press, 1969), 19.
24. Hoernle does argue against intermarriage in *South African Native Policy and the Liberal Spirit* because he feels it would subject such couples and their offspring to "social ostracism" (98).
25. Jacques Barzun, *Race: A Study in Superstition* (New York: Harper and Row, 1965), 204.
26. Mark Twain, *Pudd'nhead Wilson* (New York: New American Library, 1980), 75.

Chapter 2

"The Ways of Whitefolks" II: White Sterility in Gordimer's *A World of Strangers* (1958) and La Guma's *Time of the Butcherbird* (1979)

Nothing could be more diametrically opposed to Millin's mythology of white superiority to Blacks than the counter-mythology offered by the images of whites in Nadine Gordimer's *A World of Strangers* and Alex La Guma's *Time of the Butcherbird*. The identities of whites who either unthinkingly uphold the status quo regarding race relations with their very passivity as well as those who actively support it are either sterile or downright racist in their attitudes and actions. Before delving into this subject, however, it is important to consider Gordimer's and La Guma's ways of conveying the racial representations of such whites in their novels. For insight into Alex La Guma's and Nadine Gordimer's characters under discussion, consider a passage from Gordimer's *Occasion for Loving*. In this novel, Gordimer writes of the reaction of Jessie, the main character, on reading Thomas Mann's *The Magic Mountain*:

> Now she was making the discovery that the massive style was not a Victorian catalogue of "character" and furniture but a terrifying

descent through the safety of middle-class trappings to the individual anarchy and ideological collapse lying at their center. Even a comfortable description of a man's walk with a dog . . . fell away suddenly underfoot like a rotten mahogany floorboard — "you indulge in the illusion that your life is habitually steady, simple, concentrated, and contemplative, that you belong entirely to yourself . . . whereas the truth is that a human being is condemned to improvisation and morally lives from hand to mouth, all the time."[1]

This passage illuminates both Gordimer's technique of characterization and Alex La Guma's in *Time of the Butcherbird*. Both authors rely on an *accumulation of detail* to portray essential underlying aspects of their characters. Moreover, perhaps the most striking thematic similarity between Gordimer and La Guma is that they both emphasize the sterility of their unthinking or pro-apartheid characters. Often, this sterility is tied to what Gordimer calls "the extraordinary sense of whiteness, of having always been different, always favored, always shielded from the vulnerabilities of poverty and powerlessness."[2]

In this chapter, the ways in which the authors convey a mythology of the sterility of certain white characters will be shown by analyses of La Guma's *Time of the Butcherbird* and Gordimer's *A World of Strangers*. Connected to this issue is Gordimer's statement in "A Letter from Johannesburg" that a key element of apartheid was that for most South African whites there was "a physical and mental cordoning off of areas of unrest. The police and army take care of the first, and that extraordinary sense of whiteness . . . takes care of the second" (39). Perhaps this is why Nadine Gordimer states that many white South Africans need a *"change of consciousness,"* a change in their sense of self as the country changes for the better (40). Interestingly, in her descriptions of many of the white characters in her books, most prevalently in *A World of Strangers*, who display an indifference to or ignorance of the *reality* of the South African situation, Gordimer writes of their hollowness. It is clear, then, that facing reality and turning away from a world of mere form and appearances are so important to her. Perhaps these are the reasons why she implicitly attacks, in her detailed descriptions, those whites who are least conscious of their role in maintaining white privelege and Black deprivation in South Africa.

Those whites who want to pretend that they are sitting on a fence above Blacks and beyond apartheid and those whites who support racism are special targets of Gordimer's. In addition, Gordimer writes that "concurrently with engagement in the political struggle for the end of apartheid, there exists an awareness of the need for a new conception of culture, particularly among whites" (39). Those whites who cling to the old culture, either by directly supporting white privelege, or indirectly supporting it by turning their backs on reality, are the targets of Gordimer's cerebral venom. Thus, as with Alex La Guma in *Time of the Butcherbird*, it is important to look at the *details* of characterization and/or description in Gordimer's *A World of Strangers*.

Here it is central to note the risk that the authors take in focusing on a detailed delineation of white sterility in order to deconstruct notions of white supremacy. First, this approach is both standard and innovative in protest literature. A staple of protest literature, certainly as far back as the 19th century American slave narrative, is the author's intention to argue that an oppressive system which is advantageous materially to whites is also disadvantageous morally and psychologically to those whites who support such a system. More innovative than this topic in Gordimer's and La Guma's representations of whites who are indifferent to or racist towards Blacks is that by detailing intricately the moral and emotional bankruptcy of such whites, the authors risk alienating the reader who may not at first understand the relevance of why these writers focus on characters who are, frankly, alienating. Moreover, the critic who analyzes this aspect of the authors' representations of whiteness risks making the readers find these alienating whites so annoying that their patience is tried by the full examination of the authors' critiques of such bankrupt characters. But the centrality of a detailed examination of precisely how the authors convey a critique of racist identity is clear — precisely when it is this identity that has occupied the position of power in South Africa, and that has created flattering and narcissistic myths about this identity for the past few centuries. How Gordimer and La Guma destroy this mythology presents an important landmark in the literary argument against white supremacy and requires a very detailed examination of the subtleties of the texts.

In *A World of Strangers*, Gordimer writes of many minor characters who especially display a "sense of whiteness" that emphasizes their hollowness and sterility. That this sterility is linked to the incapacity to deal with reality is shown in the reaction of the white protagonist, Toby, who leaves England for South Africa, as he is on the ship to Africa. Especially striking is Toby's reaction to those on the ship, especially a minor character named Stella, in the book's prologue:

> I felt a sickening at them all. A spoilt woman who got ill from the idea that she had put her foot back in Africa again. So that was the

reason for the romantic, genteel life in Italy; inability to face the husband, the marriage, the reality, inability to face even the fact of this inability, so that husband, marriage, reality took the discreet disguise of Africa. . . . [Stella] could not bear to alight in the one place where she was, conventionally, bound to live. . . . Were these the sort of people Africa gets? Christ, poor continent![3]

Though Gordimer is certainly not saying that these types of whites are all that populate Africa, her novels make clear that these sterile types form much of the white population which surrounds her main characters. These people who shun reality and Africa are the kind that form the human landscape for *A World of Strangers*. These people are the ones condemned in Toby's observation: "I encountered what I was soon to recognize as a familiar desire among South Africans; an unexpressed desire to dissociate themselves from their milieu" (68). This dangerous choice of unconsciousness of the reality of the racist system which influenced every aspect of life in South Africa is what Gordimer intricately exposes, analyzes, and, ultimately, condemns in her representation of such irresponsible whites who populate *A World of Strangers*.

The theme of sterility is introduced almost immediately on Toby's arrival in South Africa. The minor white characters are marked by their hollowness. As Toby is introduced to Miss McCann, the typist at his workplace, for instance, he types her as "one of those common little girls to whom anemia gives a quenched look which can be mistaken for refinement, and who, appropriately, smelled of sickroom cologne. I should have to find some means of getting rid of her" (41). Indeed, she does leave his employment, and her reasons for doing so make clear Gordimer's reasons for making her so unappealing when she first enters the book. For instance, she looks suspiciously at the mail the Black delivery man brings, thinking something must be amiss with it simply because a Black man has brought it (41). Moreover, Miss McCann finally reaches the point of no longer being able to tolerate the visits to the office of Toby's Black friend, Steven; thus, she quits. Gordimer may be indicating here the equivalency of racism and sterility — a point she implies elsewhere.

Sterility is most evident as Toby visits The High House of Marian and Hamish Alexander, which is frequented by upper class whites. Importantly, Hamish Alexander is a hugh gold mining mogul — meaning he has 'dirty hands' in the exploitation of Black labor. Indeed, Toby chooses to frequent The High House in great part as a result of his

"The Ways of Whitefolks" II 43

desire to avoid the political and intellectual types suggested by his mother and uncle as

> 'worth-while people'. . . . A newspaper editor. A university professor. An ex-chairman of the Institute of Race Relations. A priest who was something to do with the Penal Reform League. A women doctor who was superintendent of a hospital. Reverend This, Doctor That. An Indian who was secretary to some congress or other. An African leader. An M.P. (47)

It is important that Gordimer points out that Toby decides to contact the Alexanders of the High House only after recalling that his mother had "hesitated over" giving Toby their name as people to look up after his arrival in South Africa, indication that they are not politically progressive, as are his parents. (47)

The sterility evident in these whites of the leisure class at first is noted in Gordimer's elaborate descriptions of their physical unattractiveness. The growth in Gordimer's development of the hollowness of the Alexanders is complex and gradual. This is the case because the novel's narrator, Toby, starts out very naive about how apartheid affects both white and Black individuals and because the growth of his consciousness in this regard is the main theme of the novel. As Gordimer's physical description of racist and indifferent whites needs to be contextualized mainly by writing of Toby's enlightened evaluations of the whites he knows at the Alexanders', it is important to analyze mainly Toby's later realizations of the passive and at times racist attitudes of these people.

The social and political indifference to the South African racial and political situation by those who frequent The High House is noted by Toby after he has come to feel the Alexanders' home to be the main source of his social life with other whites:

> The few times I heard politics talked at The High House, it hardly seemed to be concerned with the same country or spoken by the same people in the same situation as the talk I heard in [the Black township] Sophiatown or in houses where black and white people met. The people at Alexanders' were almost entirely preoccupied with the struggle between the Afrikaner and the Englishman; that is the Nationalists and themselves. To the other people I knew [Blacks and the dissident Anna Louw] the squabbling of the two white people was simply picayune; dwarfed by the towering bout between black and white. (209)

The political indifference of Toby's white acquaintances is further underscored: "They discussed a possible refurbishing of their United Party as they might have considered doing up a perfectly livable room they hadn't used much lately, or reconditioning a plant that hadn't been in production for a while" (209). Moreover, indeed, when the women at The High House join in the men's rare political discussions the scene is described with brief and striking condemnation: "[T]he women there never contributed except for the rare passing interruption of some piercing and paralysing generality" (208).

The negativity of the social and political indifference of those at The High House is emphasized by Toby's rich, meaningful relationships with some Blacks, especially Steven Sitole, which make him negatively evaluate those whites with whom he has become involved, e.g., Cecil Rowe (that her name is a play on Cecil Rhodes is clear). Reflecting on his double life, i.e., his time with Blacks, on the one hand, and with whites, on the other, Toby reflects:

> I had another life, outside the parenthesis of the time I spent with [Cecil]. . . . I heard her say to some people with whom we were having coffee after a cinema, "Toby does a lot of work among the natives." Later, when we were alone, I asked her, "What made you tell the Howards I do a lot of 'work' among natives?" "Well, don't you?" she said yawning. "I never have", I said. She let it drop; she assumed that anyone who had anything to do with Africans was concerned with charity or uplift, and that was that . . . I knew that if I told Cecil that my closest friends in Johannesburg were black men, and that I ate with them and slept in their houses, I would lose her. (163-64)

This yawning, the view of patronizing as white's only possible interaction with Blacks, and the vision of total unacceptability of whites' being friends with Blacks mark the characteristics of one who is psychologically bankrupt vis-a-vis race relations. Such is the sort of person Toby meets among his white acquaintances.

This vacuousness, which masks — or is an intricate part of — racism, is a quality Gordimer seems to say is totally repugnant to a conscious white person. Gordimer uses Toby and his breakup with Cecil to make this point. Toward the end of the book, as Gordimer has Toby realize most fully his alienation from whites of The High House, the theme of those whites as representative of people who keep racism and prejudice in place both on the social and political level is made evident. In a striking dialogue, Toby tells Cecil of his friendship with Blacks, during which Cecil makes him feel "as if I were trying to make comprehensible a liking for the company of snakes, or chimpanzees" (263). Indeed, Gordimer makes Cecil representative of those whites who while ignorant of Blacks, accept the racist myth that Blacks cannot, after all, be quite human. Cecil says such things as,

> You mean you can actually sit down to dinner with them and it doesn't make any difference to you? . . . And they seen like other people to you? . . . You know I can't imagine it — I mean a black man next to me at a table, talking to me like anyone else. The idea of touching their hands. . . . (263)

This passage certainly explains Cecil's earlier comment, meant by Gordimer here as a statement both of the acceptance of racial myths and the desire for racial separation: "How can you live with savages around you?" (202). Thus, one must consider the entirety of the novel to explain what ostensibly may seem to be merely Gordimer's concentration on white characters whose sterility might first seem to some readers to be an apolitical aspect of the novel.

Having discussed the vapid and, at times, racist attitudes of the characters Toby meets at The High House, I have set the stage for the reader to be able to see the deep meaning in Gordimer's initial negativity in describing these characters. For instance, Gordimer details Toby's reactions to the whites to whom he is introduced by Hamish Alexander:

> 'Archie Baxter' — a thin, youngish man with the good looks of the distinguished drinker in the whiskey advertisements. 'Kit Baxter', an equally good-looking young woman, also with a commercial finish about her; they were the kind of couple whose clothes — in this instance, riding clothes, might have been donated by some firm in return for having them worn to advantage, and in the right company. 'And this is Margaret Gerling and her big sister, Cecil Rowe.' At this they laughed and looked alike, the two pretty girls who were also in riding clothes. (49-50)

Gordimer notes all of this with a cerebral distance which connotes her own alienation from hollow opulence of the characters. Moreover, some descriptions show the awful sterility underneath the glistening facade of The High House. After describing more of the cosmetic beauty of those at The High House, Gordimer makes it clear that her recording of the features of the guests is more than mere description but is like the description she recalls in *Occasion for Loving* of a man walking a dog — a detail which makes a descent into the man's inner horror. Gordimer writes:

> There were middle-aged couples, the wives looking far younger than they could have been, in cotton dresses which displayed a lot of well-preserved flesh. But they were good looking women who smelled luxurious. The men wore the clothes of whatever sport they had just left off playing, or, pasty and wattled, sat, stranded in a well-pressed get-up of flannels, silk shirts, and scarves that covered the ruin of the hardened arteries, the damaged liver, or the enlarged heart that lay heavily in the breast. One of these last sat next to me, eventually; and I felt myself moved to a kind of disgusted pity, as I always am by the sight of these old bulls of finance, still sniffing the sawdust, with the broken shafts of money-tussles, overwork, overeating, over-drinking stuck fast in their thick necks. (50-51)

Indeed, this description of the upper class descends into the miserable state that is hidden by the beautiful facade. And, indeed, the description of the sterility of those at The High House continues. For example, the description of Marion Alexander points out her horribly painted face which "no doubt . . . was how she imagined she had looked and so it was what she had chosen to fake" (52). Another point about Marian that she took to the leftist causes of the 1930s "just as she had taken to cloche hats" (54) provides a negative commentary on her which, perhaps, in part, explains the critical description of her. Indeed, Kenneth Parker states that "for Ms. Gordimer, the world of The High House is not just a world where money rules, but a world where money and privilege evoke insincere responses."[4] Moreover, a description of two other male guests states that they were "youthfully apoplectic, blond, somewhat small, flat, lobeless ears, short noses, and bloodshot blue eyes. Every feature of their faces looked interchangeable" (53). Kit Baxter is another target of Gordimer's:

> Uproot her again tomorrow and she will begin again at once to attempt to make the next shell of habitation conform to this master setting. In this primitive cause, those waxy, inutile, decorated hands would work as tirelessly and instinctively as any animal's claws making ready the nest and in the nest would be — she herself. It was a perversion of the nesting instinct that you see often in sophisticated women; the drive remaining crazily fixed, while the purpose for which it was rooted in human nature has been lost, truly forgotten. (59)

Gordimer points out an illusory self-protective drive in such nesting as Kit's, making clear the negativity of her perception by implying that Kit, like some of the others, wants a "nest" away from reality — something, Gordimer makes clear in her essay, "Letter from Johannesburg," that was both easy for white South Africans to have and decadent for them to keep. John Hamilton also exposes the hollowness in Kit and Archie's relationship: "You know those ventriloquists who have marvelous dolls, and the ventriloquist's the stooge, and the clever things come out of the mouth of the doll? — Well, that's Kit and Archie. Whatever he seems to think or do, it's Kit pulling the strings and thinking for him" (66). Thus, the hollowness and sterility beneath Kit and Archie's facade is also exposed.

In a world where form is so important, it is intriguing that many at the High House possess the form of gentility, with not only no substance but also with a horrible internal emptiness. Even Cecil Rowe, with whom Toby becomes involved, is described disparagingly as Toby is at the High House. Moreover, it becomes clear as the novel progresses that she is all facade, with nothing underneath. Her make-up is a symbol of her outer gleam and inner hollowness. Her entire being possesses a "cosmetic sheen" (108). In addition, her hair is "gilded" (109). Indeed, to Toby, "[S]he belonged to the unreality through which I had fallen" (110). And, indeed, unreality pervades her whole being: "[S]he clutched a young English woman's bright social manner about her as if it were a disgusting old coat that she'd love to throw away. Now and then . . . she would lapse, quite unconsciously into perfect mimicry of the part she was dressed for — the languid object, that is the languid object that is the mannequin, showing herself off like a diamond whose facets must be turned in the light" (111). Indeed, the key to Cecil's character is her unreality, which is shown in her reaction to Toby's having gone to the townships. She asks "Where? What townships?" (140) as if Black South Africa must be on another planet. To be sure, Blacks play no role at The High House except as shadowy servants, and they play no role in Cecil's life except as her own servant. This aspect of Cecil — her distance from reality — is shown in one of the first descriptions of her, at the High House. In addition to her and her sister's exaggerated English manner, Gordimer writes:

> With her face in repose, I noticed that, although she was too young to have lines, I could see the pull, beneath the skin, of the muscle that always exerted the same tension when she smiled; her mouth,

too, though pretty enough in its fresh paint in contrast to the worn make-up on her cheeks and chin had about it when she talked the practiced mobility of having expressed much, and not all of it pleasant. (63)

This passage foreshadows the sterility and triviality of character that Cecil is shown to possess after becoming more involved with Toby.

While reading Gordimer's description of the human landscape which populates white South Africa, it is essential to remember Gordimer's remarks in "Letter from Johannesburg" about how the fragmentation between Black and white made the South African situation under apartheid seem like 'business as usual' for many whites. To be sure, the people in The High House seem to have little or no awareness of the overall situation in their country, no curiosity and no care to find out. The High House is a mere fantasy world for high society. Perhaps for this reason, Gordimer turns it into a fantasy world with a dark underside, for its false appearances and ugliness are constantly underscored by her. As Gordimer has stated:

> People who don't live in South Africa find it difficult to hold in their minds at once an image of the life lived by the banished, banned, harried and spied upon active opponents of apartheid, and the juxtaposed image of life in the sun lived by a prosperous white population that does not care what happens so long as it goes on living pleasantly. . . . To [the indifferent] the desert seems absolutely foolproof, reassuringly unpassable. . . . Kindly and decent, within the strict limits of their 'own kind' . . . the indifferent do not want to extend that limit by so much as one human pulse reaching out beyond it. Where the pretty suburban garden ends, the desert begins.[5]

Indifference is what characterizes the inhabitants of The High House. Erecting the impenetrable barrier of their 'high society' facade, the inhabitants of The High House seem grotesque in their unreality. Indeed, they represent the "indifference"[6] of which Christopher Heywood speaks and, clearly, Gordimer is implying a change of consciousness among such escapist whites is needed if South Africa is ever going to resolve its fragmentation and stop turning from the true problems of reality.

The decadence and sterility that characterize many of the white characters in Alex La Guma's *Time of The Butcherbird* and Nadine Gordimer's *A World of Strangers* offer depictions of white South Africa which no doubt fly in the face of the self-conception of many of those in the group. Instead of a group worthy by 'election' or being chosen by God, Alex La Guma's Afrikaners in *Time of the Butcherbird* are mainly small-minded bigots who are all facade, hiding brutality. And Gordimer's characters who live in The High House in *A World of Strangers*, who cling to European and English facades, show no alleged English liberalism but merely thrive on the status quo. When one thinks of the age-old charges by racist South Africans and whites elsewhere that whites are the bringers of civilization to Africa, it is clear that to both La Guma and Gordimer these ideas are not mere implausible myths but lies. Indeed, the idea that South Africa is populated by whites who are "the best of Europe" is proved false.[7] If this is the best, according to the depictions in *Time of the Butcherbird* and *A World of Strangers*, then it is a 'best' that is tawdry, corrupt, and decadent.

Similar to Gordimer, Alex La Guma, in *Time of the Butcherbird*, points out the sterility of whites who are indifferent to or supportive of white privelege in South Africa. Certainly, as *Time of the Butcherbird* is organized along juxtapositional lines (i.e., scenes and characters are juxtaposed), by contrasting the rebellious Mma Tau, who leads Blacks to resist being removed from their land, with the white women in the book, La Guma reveals the sterility and triviality of the latter; and the strength and courage of the former.

Mma Tau is first juxtaposed with her brother, the "dwindling" old chief, Hlangeni.[8] La Guma, who stated that each character was to represent some aspect of South African society, clearly chose Mma Tau to be the voice of Black resistance in the book. It is important to remember that *tau* means lion and the equally rebellious Shilling Murile thinks of her as being as "ferocious" (46) as a "she-lion" (46). In addition, some of her thoughts about the whites mirror Aime Cesaire's ideas on colonial powers in *Discourse on Colonialism*. Cesaire states that colonizers become especially strong-handed and vicious about holding onto their possessions not, in fact, because they are secure in their strength but instead their actions reveal the last gasps of a dangerous, dying beast. As Mma Tau says,

> Listen, it is said that the whiteman's laws and his weapons and his money make his heart bad, that . . . with these things he can destroy manhood. But it is his own manhood . . . which he has killed. So be it, but he has not killed ours. We are still a people. With laws and guns and money he knows nothing of people, does not sense the dignity of people. This inability mystifies him, baffles him for he cannot understand it, and he is defeated because in him there is no

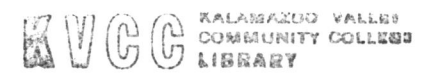

heart, no dignity. He does not understand, he is afraid of it, so he laughs very loud at the dignity of the people; but it is a defeated laughter, a mask over the defeat in his heart. The evil one laughs to conceal his defeat even while he waves his gun and his authority over the people . . . and so against the evils of the bad one there is a defense and a remedy, the people's will and dignity and it is possible for the heart to remain whole, the times to be good, the years to be fat. (46)

The issues, thoughts, and activities faced by Mma Tau — the Blacks' removal from the land — are also to be juxtaposed with the activities and thoughts and issues of the white women in the novel. By making this comparison, one sees the strength of Mma Tau compared to the hollow and silly lives of La Guma's white female characters.

The second most important female character in the novel is Maisie Stopes, the wife of the English-descended salesman, Edgar. Critics are sometimes baffled by or silent on her presence. Yet, as Cecil Abrahams states in *Alex La Guma*:

> The Afrikaner community receives most of La Guma's attention because it dominates most aspects of South Africa's political and social existence. Since the writer, however, is attempting an evaluation of the attitude of the entire white community toward the blacks, English speaking whites must be considered as well. The story of Edgar Stopes and Maisie Barends is therefore more than that of a marriage that has failed or simply a dramatic device to link Stopes's death with Hannes Muellen's by Shilling Murile.[9]

Abrahams continues:

> Through the story of the failed marriage of Edgar and Maisie Stopes, the writer provides a good portrait of the shabby, boring, aimless life-style of the urban, middle-class English settlers. La Guma indicates that it is only because of their skin color that these settlers enjoy rights and privileges that are superior to those of the blacks. (132)

Relevant to Maisie's contrast to Mma Tau and to her own character are Richard Wright's thoughts in *American Hunger,* which are triggered by the white girls with whom he worked in a Chicago restaurant in his youth. Wright states:

> I learned about their tawdry dreams, their fear of feeling anything deeply, their sex problems, their husbands. They were an eager,

restless, talkative, ignorant bunch . . . I often wondered what they were trying to get out of life. . . . They lived on the surface of their days, their smiles were surface smiles, and their tears were surface tears . . . their constant outward-looking, their mania for radios, cars, and a thousand other trinkets made them fix their eyes upon the trash of life, made it impossible for them to learn a language which could have taught them to speak of what was in their or others' hearts. The words of their souls were the syllables of popular songs.[10]

Certainly, as in Wright's analysis of certain white American women, cheap romance, money and the illusion of upward mobility are all that matter to Maisie. Indeed, in Maisie's distance from Mma Tau, Wright's words are also relevant:

It was in the psychological distance that the deepest problem of the Negro lay for me. For these poor, ignorant white girls to have understood my life would have meant nothing short of a vast revolution in theirs. And I was convinced that what they needed to make them complete and grown-up in their living was the inclusion in their personalities of a knowledge of lives such as I lived and suffered containedly. (13)

Clearly, Maisie lacks a knowledge of anything beyond the "trash of life" (Wright, 14) which she pursues and dreams of — even to the point of fantasizing about her husband's death.

Yet, ironically, Maisie (even more than her husband, Edgar) is a political character. Cecil Abrahams brings out the political nature of both characters when he writes that if the Afrikaners are parasites on the backs of the Blacks, the English are parasites twice over. Abrahams explains this parasitic quality by saying that the English are leeching off of the backs of the Blacks indirectly, because they leech off of the Afrikaners' system of running the country in a way to benefit and protect whites. Though Maisie may at first simply seem to be a caricature, the political nature of La Guma's depiction of her soon comes out.

In fact, the caricaturish descriptions of Maisie when she is first introduced are an indication of the shallowness and triviality of her reactions to political events. La Guma, in a way which is relevant to Wright's descriptions of whites in *American Hunger*, emphasizes Maisie's trashiness on her date with Edgar, among other places: "The orange mouth smiled boldly, but somehow it didn't match the bleached but carefully dressed hair, yet the frock she wore emphasized the young hips and that horrible mother of hers had even allowed a bit of upper tit to show" (37). Furthermore, the make up, the facade that covers the hollowness, is a technique also found in Gordimer's novel. Moreover, Maisie's "lust for trash" is shown as she imagines the men she meets resembling film stars. In fact, her entire inner life is a trivial fantasy: "[S]he went to the bioscope, the one for Europeans only. She knew the histories of most of the film stars, especially the males; and she had her hair done in the styles the female ones introduced. One week she was Alice Faye or June Allyson, another she was Greer Garson or Alexis Smith, Lana Turner" (32-33). Harmless fantasies one might ask? But, as in Gordimer's work, the damning details accumulate. For instance, she failed to complete high school because it was "a bore" (32) and thus she ceased to pay attention to her studies. Furthermore, Maisie's sterility is reinforced when she meets Edgar, her future husband, and significantly, in light of their later dismal marriage, she fantasizes that he resembles Van Johnson or Brian Donlevy (two men completely unalike in appearance). Her entire measuring stick of reality is films, which are juxtaposed with the bleak reality of her life. For instance, when she first goes home with Edgar, "She had thoughts of a tall apartment block, a modern bachelor flat, but he wasn't Cary Grant after all, only a salesman, with a future maybe. Yet the alternative was that great meal-bag of a woman [Maisie's mother] with the clashing teeth of a movie dinosaur. [Yet Edgar's] place was a flat down a flagstone pathway across a rough, narrow lawn behind a bungalow. The flat . . . perhaps . . . had once been servants' quarters" (39). Maisie marries Edgar in order to escape the barren (Barends') home life. Importantly, Maisie is *not* awakened by the reality which surrounds her — she sinks even more deeply into a fantasy world in which political dissidence is a mere spy movie and Black unrest seems to be a wild party at which she is an observer.

How can such a stupid and trashy character be endowed with characteristics that make her of political significance? For example, La Guma once again reveals Maisie's incredible "lust for trash" which reaches its greatest proportions in her thoughts of murdering Edgar in order to collect his insurance money, even as he is being killed, unbeknownst to her (in a masterly stroke of juxtaposition), by Shilling Murile. Nevertheless, if Maisie represents a certain type of white character, her feelings towards Blacks, politics, and political unrest are significant. Maisie's attitude towards Blacks, which is one of total distance and disdain, may be a product of her childhood. As a child,

Maisie was kept upstairs, in order not to be exposed to the many Blacks in the neighborhoods. (This is before the Group Areas Act.) Of course, the tram cars she used in order to go to school, La Guma points out, were segregated, as was her school. Yet, she is exposed to Blacks for part of her life as her family owns a store which serves many Blacks — a fact of which Maisie is supremely conscious. At one point, Maisie thinks, "God, how could she bring any fellow home? Right on the edge of coolieland?" (34) She also thinks of the customers as "niggers" (38) and "coons" (40). Thus, even though she has a somewhat supportive attitude towards the Blacks' bus boycott, pointing out Blacks' poverty and the fact that the bus fares had been increased (support which she fails to reiterate after Edgar dismisses her points with his race theory of Black inferiority), she still feels that Blacks are "coons" whom she wishes to escape. Moreover, Maisie has deeper feelings about Blacks. During her marriage, for example, she has a Black maid who she "order[s] about" (49). She also joins a gun club and buys a pistol because "one never knows when some terrible Kaffir will run amok" (50). Yet, not even this thought brings her closer to reality. The gun makes her feel like "James Bond" (50). The fact that Maisie is still distant from reality the closer she gets to political unrest is also shown in a few incidents. In one key scene as she waits at a restaurant, she sees a policeman prod with a stick a Black woman with a baby. Totally failing to register the Black woman's mistreatment, Maisie's sole reaction involves her fantasy world of films: "Maisie noticed a policeman, white helmet, breeches and boots, gun and sun goggles. . . . stop to tower over the black woman. Like something out of those space movies, Maisie thought absently. *Invader from Mars*" (52). Furthermore, when Maisie's former schoolmate is arrested for being involved in political activities with Blacks, her reaction is typically sterile and trivial. "'Messing with Blacks? But he's white, like us.' The memory of a black woman with a baby just seen flashed through her mind. 'Them?'" (52) Her reason why she failed to read about it in the papers underscores her attraction to the trash of life: "Oh, I don't read things like that. The magazine part, maybe the comics on Sundays, 'Blondie and Dagwood.' To think that nice Donny Harris could of gone and done a thing like that" (52). Thus, Maisie intentionally keeps herself ignorant of the volatile political situation in her country — even as she has a gun.

Interestingly, Gordimer writes of a real conversation of a similar nature with people who had seemed to like a friend who was later imprisoned without trial for helping Blacks. Noting their amazement and distance from this man on hearing the news, Gordimer writes: "How could the indifference keep at a safe distance this man whom they had accepted and who was at once the same man who sat in prison, nothing whatever to do with them? The subject was dropped into the dark cupboard of questions that are not dealt with" ("Great Problems in the Street," 54).

A final central incident in revealing Maisie's attitude comes as she watches a peaceful protest of singing Black people, who are attacked by the police. From the balcony of a cafeteria, a group of whites can see the "armed men in helmets, some carrying long riot staves" (114). And some of the crowd wants to see the "fun" (114). This attitude is reminiscent of Gordimer's remarks in " A Letter from Johannesburg" on life in South Africa seeming like a movie where some whites are on a balcony safe, while unrest boils over in the townships. As Gordimer writes, " I remember a film I saw once where the camera moved from destruction and its hateful cacophony in the streets to a villa where people were lunching on a terrace, and there were birds and flowers" (42). The difference in La Guma's novel is there is not as wide a gap between both sides; instead, he reveals the distant stance of denying reality that some whites indulge in as tear gas is thrown at the Blacks and "the muzak and the sound of battle stir" (115). Maisie watches the riot and is reminded of an English holiday:

> She saw through a triangle made by a sunburnt and peeling elbow that the crowd of blacks had broken, some running back and others defiantly closing with the place in the gas that hung foggily in the street. A window broke with the sound of falling bells. Police sirens bayed in the distance. In the gutter and on the sidewalk lay bundles of clothes that sprouted feet, hands, and faces like red-painted masks. Maisie was momentarily reminded of Guy Fawkes night when she was a child. A woman went up the street holding her bleeding face, and Maisie, extricating herself, thought illogically, Poor old Edgar. I reckon I'm stuck with him. Pity stirred in her, an alien worm, and she resigned herself, with a last glimpse of a huddled mound, I reckon I'm stuck with him. (115)

This scene is the highpoint of Maisie's sterility and triviality. Confronted with the reality of Black protest and police brutality, she shrinks further within herself, reifying the mistreated Blacks — seeing them only as mounds of clothes sprouting feet, hands, and heads — and thinking "illogically," as La Guma points out, of her marriage to (the now dead, unbeknownst to Maisie) Edgar. Therefore, the trash that has filled Maisie's head stays with her to the end of the novel. Still, though Maisie does possess "the sense of whiteness" — of invulnerability (as do the other watchers on the balcony) — La Guma makes clear that whites — Maisie as a representative of a certain type — will not go getting off "scot free" to borrow Gordimer's phrase ("Letter from Johannesburg," 42) for Maisie's husband, to whom she has just resigned herself, is killed even as she finally accepts him. Thus, although Maisie may try to deny and escape reality, La Guma makes clear that in her case, too, it is the "time of the butcherbird."

Concerning Maisie, and the others who watch from the balcony, Peter Lambley's comments in *The Psychology of Apartheid* are applicable. Lambley writes:

> Normal signs of human emotions of sympathy, concern and fairness were foreign. . . . In this place you were expected to deny your hurt, anger, dismay or whatever by many of the institutionalized rituals available — 'drink yourself mindless, drive recklessly, bunk school or work, fuck indiscriminately, beat someone up' . . . anything but show the proper emotions, the proper shock, or recognize the ungodly mess that you live in the first place. I had entered, it was clear, into a brutalized society living on its wits and on its nerves.[11]

Maisie, interestingly, shows the callousness which Lambley says can result from life under apartheid in her attitude towards her acquaintance Donny Harris' jailing for helping Blacks with trade unions, the Black woman harassed by the police, and the Blacks she views from the balcony. And, if one examines her similarity to those with her in these scenes, "Moreover, there was an inverted sense of unity and charity. There was always an underdog, someone else lower down on the social scale who could be the victim, who was worse off . . . [there was] no sense of upward-directed anger" (Lambley 128) — for example, at the police or the government for harassing, attacking or jailing people.

Maisie's mother, Mrs. Barends, is another sterile character. As with Maisie, La Guma's description of her puts the reader on guard for her negative qualities. He writes, "She wore big dentures that seemed to clatter when she talked. . . . a formidable woman with red hair and a face like a limestone crag (31). Later, La Guma describes her dentures as being "like miniature tombstones" (36). More importantly, Maisie seems to have inherited, to a degree, her mother's ignorance of Blacks, her ambition, and her prejudice. Running the store, for instance, Mrs. Barends reduces her husband to "ghost" (31). In addition, she states, "I'm not interested in politics. . . . that's alright for the government and the kaffirs" (32). Her ambition for her daughter Maisie is shown in thoughts close to some of Maisie's later ones that Edgar would make a good husband because he has "go-ahead" (36) and he has already taken out life insurance — a detail which much later makes Maisie contemplate his murder. Interestingly, Mrs. Barends doesn't mention love and affection as reason for marriage, but mere ambition. Thus, La Guma paints Maisie's mother as another spiritually empty character.

Mrs. Kroner, the hotel proprietor, is another hollow white character, possessing nearly nightmarish qualities. These are brought out especially in La Guma's descriptions of her. He talks of her "shrill and nerve-pinching laughter" (6-7) and describes her as a "small birdlike woman, the frail body hidden in dark cloth like widows' weeds . . . her thin, red, clawlike hands fluttering, while she screamed like a jaybird" (7). La Guma uses such words as "shrilled," (7) "screamed," (7) "screeched," (7) "screaming," (7) to describe Mrs. Kroner. And similar to the death imagery in equating Mrs. Barends dentures to small tombstones, decay is also prevalent in Mrs. Kroner; her dark dress and also her illness make her seem a small, unsavory woman clinging to life. In addition, she rules over a decaying hotel. Indeed, in the hotel, she lords over her Black servant. La Guma briefly but importantly shows this quality. In berating the Black servant who forgot to bring Stopes his beer, she "shamed" (22) him by "shrill[ing]" (22) at him, "Stupid . . . you can't tell these things [Blacks] anything. All day I must talk to him. Can't you remember what the *baas* tells you?" (22) She continues "shrilling at the servant to get on with his work and stop being so stupid" (22). Thus, the nightmarish qualities Mrs. Kroner possesses are linked to the bigoted and power-mongering ways she deals with the servant. La Guma uses his unsavory descriptions of her, therefore, to both foreshadow and underscore her racist attitude towards and treatment of her Black servant.

The direct contrast to Maisie, Mrs. Barends and Mrs. Kroner is Rina Steen, the fiancee of the Afrikaner politician Hannes Muelen. Rina might seem to incorporate the antiquated ideal of the Afrikaner woman, the epitome of 'civilized' refinement. She is educated, but passive; beautiful and virginal. La Guma's description of her certainly contrasts greatly with his description of Maisie and her mother. As Hannes silently admires her, for example, La Guma describes: "Firm young breasts, not an ounce of fat on her body and the past boyishness of her limbs had softened into the beautiful lines of a well-made woman. Her curly blond hair gleamed in the lamplight. . . . [and] there was a certain demureness about her mouth, an innocence which one expected to find in a well brought up Boer woman" (59). Yet, she is the daughter of a man who refers to "those black things" (61) and who unquestionably supports Blacks' removal from their land. Indeed, in her reaction to the removals, one sees Rina's moral blindness and emptiness of thought. Concerning the removal, Rina's *sole* reaction is that the plants and flowers must be "rescue[d]" (62) and that she needs Hannes to see she has trucks for the task. She requests trucks to rescue the plants because, as she compassionately states, "[T]here are hundreds and hundreds of wild flowers out in the veld and they'll die from thirst if they are not moved to places where they can be preserved. There are aloes, cycads, even orchids, which must be transplanted. The idea is to mount an expedition to go out into the veld, find the plants and flowers and move them to certain public gardens and parks for preservation" (62). One might think this concern is admirable, and La Guma makes no direct comments criticizing Rina. Yet, he achieves showing the negative aspects of her character through detail and juxtaposition. She is silent as the men— her father and finance — speak of the removal of "the kaffirs" (61) and only registers concern for plant — not human — life. Moreover, Hannes makes clear the order of concern — his own and Rina's — as he states that the trucks will take "sheep where there is more water, and . . . two lorries . . . to transport the kaffirs tomorrow" (63). She doesn't even comment negatively on his use of the word "kaffir" as her father had. Furthermore, the priorities of Rina and Hannes are clear — first, sheep; second, plants; third, "kaffirs". Consequently, Rina can listen silently to the discussion of removals for she really is indifferent to the Black plight; thus she adds

> nothing else, knowing that these things were really the affairs of men. She was wearing Hannes' engagement ring and that meant that she would stand by him in everything he wished to do. That was her duty. Her college education would be an asset to him too. She would be his good wife and the mother of his children, live under his protecting arm, and she would watch him grow to something in this community, and her heart fluttered with pride (65).

In other words, Rina is the ideal unquestioning fool, idealizing a racist man, limiting herself to such things as plants as the 'affairs of women,' and showing no concern, with her 'demure' and 'sensitive' nature, for the removals of Blacks from their own land. She merely wants to live and prosper through her husband (as Maisie fantasized about doing — which could be La Guma's sly way of commenting on Rina's character). When all the details are put together, then, though La Guma may seem silent on criticizing Rina, he is not — she is, finally, a morally bankrupt character who indeed exudes "the sense of whiteness" — of privilege and invulnerability.

Yet another central character in the discussion of white sterility is Edgar Stopes. Gerald Moore, in "Through Suffering to Resistance" in *Twelve African Writers* makes remarks that connote his own confusion about the presence of the Stopeses:

> The tawdriness of this whole subplot is perhaps La Guma's way of situating the English-speaking petty-bourgeoisie . . . Stopes and his Maisie are Identikit characters who could be reconstructed in Pittsburgh or Peterborough without any change being necessary in their horizons or their vocabulary. La Guma may be implying that their involvement in the South African tragedy, which is in essence the struggle between Boer and Bantu for mastery of the land, is as random as Stopes' involvement in the death of Muelen.[12]

Moore undercuts his own reading of the Stopeses place in the novel, for he is most certainly onto something when he says that La Guma is making a point about the English presence in the South African conflict. Yet, the Stopeses are not unspecific to South Africa as Moore later conjectures, for it is important to realize that the players in the South African situation are not merely Afrikaners and Blacks, but also include those who maintain white power, and this group includes the Stopeses. Maisie and Edgar are not, therefore, "Identikit characters" who might appear in Pittsburgh or elsewhere. They are characters who are integral parts of the South African situation.

Significantly, according to Cecil Abrahams,

> In discussing this group of [English-speaking] whites La Guma portrays an inferior people who are benefiting from a system that has dispossessed the majority. Furthermore . . . the English settlers . . . simply wrap themselves in a cocoon and ignore the problems of the country. The English settlers are bloodsuckers or "ticks" twice over: first, they live off the backs of an Afrikaner-devised system of apartheid that ensures rights and privileges to all whites and second, like the Afrikaners, they live off the back of

stolen black land and cheap black labor. . . . In bringing about he death of Stopes in the manner in which it occurs in the novel, La Guma contends that Stopes' death is as inevitable as Muelen's if South Africa is to be cleansed of negative forces. (133)

Moreover, as mentioned earlier, La Guma himself pointed out, each of his main characters is representative of some aspect of the South African situation. Thus, one must look closely at the character of Edgar Stopes in order to realize his significance in La Guma's novel.

Edgar Stopes is a character of decay and sterility. As La Guma lets the details of the novel reveal the characters, it is essential to note what details are intrinsic to characterizing Stopes, who will soon be killed by Shilling Murile. The "dusty landscape" (2) and "dusty blue sky" (2) which envelope Stopes as he is introduced to us are indicative of decay both without and within Stopes. Immediately after describing the drought-stricken landscape, for instance, La Guma cuts to Edgar and his thoughts about himself and his car, mentioning the aging of the engine and springs and, most significantly, Edgar's analogy of himself to the car. Edgar thinks, "We're getting on in years. . . . we're crocked up" (2). Indeed, La Guma's description of Edgar underscores this decay. La Guma writes of Edgar's "pale blond hair falling back from the scalp, the pink face starting to go pudgy, the near-blond mustache" (3). Nothing in the description seems 'complete'; indeed, Edgar seems like the "shadows" (3) that La Guma reiterates surround him on the landscape.

A major point in Edgar's sterility is that he is a mere facade, a hypocritical form without substance. A salesman, even when he is angry he feels that "one had to maintain goodwill all the time" (3). Rather than this being an admirable sentiment, it makes evident Edgar's arrogance and anger. For instance, in the midst of an Afrikaner town, he attempts to dissociate himself mentally from the Afrikaners:

> Here in the countryside he was like a foreigner and he had learnt that he would make no headway with these people unless he submitted to their narrow arrogance. He considered himself a broad minded man: live and let live, but why couldn't a man talk his own language instead of having to struggle with their mumbo-jumbo? . . . Yet in order to maintain good will, to obtain the orders of plastic combs, drag chains, electric light bulbs, he had to surrender his identity, become a bad imitation of one of these bloody dutchman. (4)

Yet, although he feels estranged from the Afrikaners, and moreover, from Hannes Muelen when they meet, he also seems to envy their 'insiderness.' Indeed, he claims to be apolitical (28) — or politically blind — considering this attitude in South Africa. Clearly, he resents being make to feel like "a bloody nigger" (24) by his status as an outsider in Afrikanerdom. Inside, he really wonders what Hannes, who is running for Parliament, has that he doesn't. Thus, he doesn't want to change the system so much as be a part of it. As La Guma writes of Stopes's thoughts towards Hannes, "[B]last them all, the long and the short and the tall . . . bloody Member of Parliament my bloody eye. What's he got that blokes like me haven't?" (109) Consequently, Stopes's envy of and anger at Afrikaners make clear that he is a mere shell of "goodwill," a hollow facade.

Stopes's decay is also emphasized. As La Guma writes of Stopes:

> Failure and hopelessness hung to him like hairspray — new style aerosol cans of failure at thirty-five cents each at wholesale. . . . Hopelessness hung on the stained walls of hotel rooms. . . . Hopelessness and failure were double images peering at one from cracked mirrors over dusty dressing tables; tickled at sweaty skin in the beds made up with sheets frayed by bitterness and darned with despair (108).

It is not surprising, therefore, that Edgar is killed along with Hannes, for not only is he a member of the racist society he scorns (his "nigger doll" (2) in his windshield is a significant detail) but he also seems to be, according to LaGuma, a junior, inferior Hannes, the salesman being a junior politician. The decadence and death of both types are part of La Guma's agenda — a revolutionary agenda of the time of the butcherbird ridding the country of both "major" (Hannes) and "minor" (Edgar) objectionable sorts.

In addition to Edgar, the politician Hannes Muelen is a central character who must be examined in light of La Guma's criticisms. It is important to analyze the details concerning Hannes Muelen in order to uncover the sterility of his character. On entering the novel, he is described as "handsome" (27) and seems to possess the goodwill towards his fellow whites that Edgar puts such a premium on in his own line of work. Stopes recognizes their similarity immediately: "Another one after good will, eager for friendly public relations" (27). As with Gordimer, as La Guma makes his points by the accumulation of details, rather than blatantly writing out massages, it is important to notice that these details are a central part of the author's method of characterization. It is significant for example, that as this "handsome," crafty politician (28) talks to Edgar Stopes, "Behind them the finger pulling match was going amidst cries of excitement" (28). This juxtaposition serves to undermine "the man of the handsome face and white teeth" (which are later likened to fake pearls) who is a young politician on the rise.

Moreover, like Stopes, Hannes is also a facade hiding corruption: "[A] good man to represent this region. He has our people at heart. Some years ago there was trouble with a kaffir and he got a suspended sentence, but it was really a small matter and nobody around here thinks about it" (29). These lines tell of the most important actions of Hannes' character. As the finger pulling match continues, La Guma points out, Kroner tells of this "small incident" — the killing of Shilling's brother Timi. The fact that Hannes is silent on the issue makes clear that it is a small, forgotten matter to him. Not only that, but he remains the staunch racist he was on the night of Timi's death, berating Timi and Shilling as "Kaffirs" (74) who are "getting too smart" (74). As he ordered Opperman to "tie up those baboons" (74) and fasten them to the post, the ugliness behind the attractive facade is revealed in a flashback.

Relevant to the portrayals of the Afrikaner characters are details La Guma gives about the (racist) Afrikaner self-conception.

Aspects of the Afrikaner identity as defined by La Guma and borne out in T. Dunbar Moodie's *The Rise of Afrikanerdom* are made clear in Dominee Visser's sermon, which Hannes and Rina attend (along with the other Afrikaners of the town). Echoing Sarah Gertrude Millin, Visser states that

> Blood pollution and the lowering of the racial level which goes with it are the only cause why old civilizations disappear. The causes are not lost wars, but the lost power of resistance which ensures the purity of blood. In the purity of blood also lies the guarantee of our honorable mission. It is the duty of all of us to unshakably keep our aim, spiritually and earthly, which is to secure for our children their God-given land and soil on this earth. (106)

This idea of white election is made clear in Moodie's book and in David Harrison's *The White Tribe of Africa*. Another idea which is made clear is the notion of life as a fight against Blacks in order for whites to maintain supremacy of power over them. As La Guma writes in Visser's sermon: "The heathen beats his spears against our door . . .

they are breaking into our civilization, into the minds of civilized people, civilization is threatened. . . . Take up again the sword of your forefathers so that the land may be protected from the heathen and made safe for God and our nation" (107). The ideas of white supremacy and of life as a fight to maintain it in the face of a threat by inferiors are central in this passage. The ideas of election and supremacy are central to La Guma's depiction of Hannes Muelen, who is the embodiment of the Afrikaner who innately accepts such ideas as in Visser's sermon. In his depiction of Muelen, La Guma debunks the ideas of supremacy and election, revealing the sterility of the 'model' Afrikaner. And, indeed, Hannes learns about South Africa from a father who "loved the land" (57):

> to him country was not only a geographical entity, an anthem, celebrations of Dingane's Day, the day of Blood River. For him country was a matter of who owned the flat, dreary red and yellow plains and the low, undulating hills, the grass and the water. This was a heritage which had been gained through the sacred blood of their ancestors and the prophetic work of God. It had come to their fathers through the musket and the Bible; they had come into this land like the followers of Joshua. Any other conception was anathema. (57-58)

This passage makes clear the proprietary nature of such men as Hannes. It also explains why such a man would support massive removals of Blacks ("country was a matter of who owned" the land) and why, having been taught that *not* believing in Afrikaners' chosen status of ownership is anathema, Hannes would feel free to punish Shilling and Timi severely and never show any conscience about Timi's resulting death. In fact, to Hannes, Blacks are mere "Kaffirs" (61) to be moved at the will of whites. Furthermore, his dinner conversation with his future father-in-law, Steen, reveals that Hannes is in accord with the reigning white supremacist ideology. As Hannes says,

> Our course is set. What might appear to be divergences, faltering, like Rina's schoolmates [some of whom believed that a minority could not keep power from the Black majority], are entirely superficial, I'm sure. After all, the foundation and cement of our people, which is as everlasting as the monument we set up in the capital in honour of our forefather, that cement and foundation is the ethic of our racial, cultural and religious purity. (64)

Interestingly, Hannes' fixed view of history and of whites' place in it are seriously undermined, La Guma makes sure, by Hannes' death at the hands of Murile. He who dismissed the idea that whites couldn't control Blacks is exterminated by a Black man; and if his fixed ignorance and past crime weren't enough, La Guma makes sure the reader notes Hannes' responsibility for his own fate by having Hannes killed with his own gun. (Even as he hubristically wonders "why the black man had it [a shotgun] because that wasn't allowed"; 110). Thus, La Guma totally undermines Hannes' "sense of whiteness," of privilege and of safety. And, moreover, La Guma smashes the handsome facade which he himself had created: ". . . the next thing there was slither and a heavy thump together with a wet slap across his [Stopes's] cheek which was made by one of Hannes Muelen's ears as his head was blown off, and the white-wash of the passage-wall was suddenly decorated with a blossom petalled with blood and brains and pieces of bone and fragments of teeth like pomegranate pips" (110). To juxtapose this passage with "the handsome face and white teeth" (29) mentioned earlier and the rosy future Hannes imagined with Rina, with himself a Member of Parliament, is to see just what the mechanism behind La Guma's technique is in depicting Hannes. To be sure, the facade of civilization can be very weak. This idea fits Hannes in a few important ways. His veneer as a 'civilized' man is thin when one is told of his responsibility in Timi's death. It is also thin as his carefully indoctrinated ideology makes him believe that Blacks are mere "kaffirs" to be moved at will. Moreover, as many white South Africans prided themselves — and men such as Hannes — as being the preservers of civilization, in this depiction La Guma makes sure that the reader realizes the handsome facade hides something sterile and corrupt underneath.

La Guma's depiction of Hannes' grandfather shows to the utmost the decay and sterility of the whites in the book. As La Guma writes, "[T]he old man's ancient, decaying body shifted, fragile bones seeking further warmth as life seeped unseen from it" (90). The house is "crumbling" (93) and "[t]he rats wriggled in the rotting, overhanging eaves, the ruins of the grand armchair disintegrated on the step — the old man was far too feeble now to sit out there" (93). As Shilling approaches, nearing his mission of death to his brother's killers, La Guma points out the decay in the Muelen family by focusing on the old man. In fact, this scene maybe viewed as transitional — introducing the actual and more blatant decay which has been so prevalent in the novel in relation to the white characters by the reiteration of dust, ghosts, and shadows and leading up to the actual deaths of the decadent whites whom Shilling Murile kills.

> It was in the psychological distance that separated the races that the deepest meaning of the Negro lay for me. . . . [S]haring the culture that binds him, and seeing that a lust for trash is what blinds the nation to his claims, is what sets storms to rolling his soul. (13-14)

Richard Wright's words in *American Hunger* echo the plot of *Time of the Butcherbird*: Hannes' bigoted lust for power; Stopes's petty desires to build artificial 'friendships' and 'goodwill' with other whites to increase his customers; and Maisie's drive for realizing a cheap movie fantasy life are some of the "lusts for trash" which create an unbridgeable gap between Black and white in La Guma's novel. Moreover, the decay associated with many of the characters underscores their corruption — or their closeness to becoming themselves "the trash of life." Hence, the decadence of racist and/or passive whites is one of the major themes of *Time of the Butcherbird*.

To those who are committed, perhaps there is no group more reprehensible than the uncommitted. Surely, though the target of their protests are lowest on the scale of morality, the dedicated ones have endured a sacrifice — alienation from their compatriots, jailing, banning, or worse — that those who play it safe would never think of risking. Perhaps this is why Nadine Gordimer and Alex La Guma write so damningly of those characters who represent those uncommitted to racial equality. Gordimer, a member of a self-acknowledged "minority-within-a-white-minority" ("Letter," 33) as a result of her stance regarding apartheid and her writings; and La Guma, spending time under arrest, having been an exile from South Africa and a long-time member of the African National Congress— these are people who have paid a certain price for their dedication (though certainly La Guma to a greater degree). It is not surprising then that both the uncommitted and the opposition should incur literary venom from those to whom they represent the upholders of bigotry.

"So much sterility, and to what end! This topic is rather annoying!" I agree — and try living under the heel of people who are so vacuous and you will *really* be annoyed. That power can be in the hands of morally bankrupt people who are in denial of their bigotry is precisely one of the most maddening aspects of racism. And one service performed by the novels under discussion by Gordimer and La Guma is to smash the narcissistic mirror held by those who benefitted from racism and to show their true inner ruin. This is one of the reasons why *A World of Strangers* and *Time of the Butcherbird* are important not only as responses to apartheid but also as social criticism which will be relevant as long as bigotry exists.

Notes

1. Nadine Gordimer, *Occasion of Loving* (London: Virago Press, 1983), 206.
2. Gordimer, "A Letter from Johannesburg" in *Apartheid in Crisis*, ed. Mark Uhlig (New York: Vintage Books, 1986), 33.
3. Gordimer, *A World of Strangers* (New York: Penguin, 1958), 26-27. All subsequent references to this edition.
4. Kenneth Parker, "Nadine Gordimer and the Pitfalls of Liberalism" in *The South African Novel in English,* ed. Parker (London: Macmillan Press Ltd., 1978), 120.
5. Gordimer, "Great Problems in the Street" in *The Essential Gesture*, ed. Stephen Clingman (New York: Alfred A. Knopf, 1988), 52-3.
6. Christopher Heywood, *Nadine Gordimer* (Windsor, Berkshire, England: Profile Books Ltd., 1983), 17.
7. P.W. Botha's daughter, *Children of Apartheid*, CBS documentary, 12/5/87.
8. Alex La Guma, *Time of the Butcherbird* (London: Heinemann Educational Books, 1979), 43. All subsequent references to this edition.
9. Cecil Abrahams, *Alex La Guma* (Boston: Twayne, 1985), 131.
10. Richard Wright, *American Hunger* (New York: Harper and Row, 1977), 12,14.
11. Peter Lambley, *The Psychology of Apartheid* (Athens: University of Georgia Press, 1980), 128.
12. Gerald Moore "Through Suffering to Resistance," in *Twelve African Writers* (London: Hutchinson and Co., 1980), 119.

Chapter 3

In the Grasp of White Primitives: The Fight for Humanity in Andre Brink's *A Dry White Season* (1984)

> In the tradition we are dealing with it [is] frowned upon to have a will and mind of one's own.
>
> Alice Miller, *For Your Own Good*

Andre Brink's *A Dry White Season* provides an important landmark in the portrayal of white identity among the books under discussion and in creating a counter-mythology to racist myths. It is certainly one of the most powerful condemnations of apartheid. The Afrikaner protagonist, Ben Du Toit, because of his trying to help Black acquaintances, is placed in a position where others—the upholders of apartheid—force him to question and redefine his identity as an Afrikaner as well as his relationship to Afrikanerdom. Moreover, in portraying these topics, Brink raises such issues as whether during apartheid South Africa was an oppressively dysfunctional society which treated its citizens as children who must unquestioningly uphold the order of things as they are—or risk being crushed. Before discussing these topics, however, it is important to consider some aspects of Brink's ideology as a writer.

In *Writing in A State of Siege,* Brink states that he believes in

> the view of the writer as the rebel who fights in the name of the essentially human values—against everything which threatens the human, against everything which is essentially *inhuman*. . . . this is not a "human" country. The entire system which determines every aspect of private and communal life in the country is a contradiction of all the basic attributes we have termed "human": movement; growth; change; communication; the right to think, to read, to speak, to write; the right to choose a sexual partner and relate one's experience to that of others; the right not to be killed; the small, precious, personal right to be — to be in awareness, in compassion, in humility, in defiance, in anger, in pain, and—if it must be so—in violence. However, if I am pleading a literary cause, it is the cause of a literature wholly committed to humanity . . . and to the imperative need to speak the truth fearlessly.[1]

The passage is clearly relevant to *A Dry White Season*, for the questions of the quality of humanity and of human rights are essential to the novel. Moreover, Brink clearly informs Ben, the main character, with his thoughts as Ben reflects on a variation of the author's ideas:

> 'Humanity': Normally one uses it as a synonym for compassion; charity; decency; integrity. . . . Must one now go on in search of an entirely different set of synonyms; cruelty; exploitation; unscrupulousness; or whatever? . . . The problem is: once you've caught a glimpse of it [reality], once you've merely started suspecting it, it is useless to pretend it's different . . . the only question that matters is . . . What now?[2]

What indeed, as Brink depicts Ben's facing the fact that his efforts will be endlessly frustrated in his desire to find out the truth of how the Black gardener at his school, Gordon, died in detention and also to discover the true details of the earlier death of Gordon's son, Jonathan. With most of his family, the authorities, and society against his search for truth and justice, Ben faces many charges of disloyalty to family and Afrikanerdom. Furthermore, he finds himself in the existential situation where he realizes some of the previous 'truths' of his life— for example, belief in the justice of the police and legal system—are mere oppressive myths. Ben, therefore, finds himself on a quest not only for justice but for his own true identity in the face of an alienated and *alienating* family and society. These themes are central for one to explore in order to more fully comprehend *A Dry White Season*.

In Brink's novel, Ben's revelations about himself, family, and the society Ben encounters as a result of his quest for justice and truth in Jonathan's and Gordon's deaths bring to mind passages from Lambley's *The Psychology of Apartheid*. Ben, as an Afrikaner who questions, and then dissents from the system is, to borrow Lambley's analysis of such alienated Afrikaners, "analogous to [a] large animal once free, who [has] now to spend the rest of [his life] in captivity—both die a long, slow, agonizing death out of loneliness and isolation."[3] Ben is "psychologically savaged" (220) because he and people like him, to continue Lambley's analysis of such Afrikaners, may be "cut off from the process of being Afrikaans and as such, they show the true weakness of the Afrikaans system" (220). To Lambley, this weakness is that without being in the system, Afrikaners who make the break may be prone not merely to emotional upset but also to emotional illness. This dangerous assertion may be interpreted to mean that it is `healthier' for Afrikaners not to threaten shaking up their own world by breaking with racism. Yet, though this particular conclusion is highly questionable, Lambley's previous assertions raise vastly interesting issues and other possible conclusions when examined in light of Brink's novel.

The process and results of Ben's questioning the system, a process first begun with full faith in the system, result not in the mundane conclusion that he might have been 'better off' had he not devoted himself to a quest which separates him more and more from Afrikanerdom. It is significant that Brink not only affirms Ben's struggle but also explores the defense mechanisms with which Ben's family confronts him and which eventually bring about his greatest betrayal— his daughter Suzette's cooperation with the Special Branch in working against her father. It is Ben's family whose mental health should be questioned, for along with the authorities, they squeeze him out of existence. The personal (family) and authoritative (Special Branch) cancellation of Ben represents a microcosm of the most dangerous effects of the Afrikanerdom-devised system on its own — dissident — kin.

This danger which Brink emphasizes is that Ben's existence is no longer allowable once he moves from unquestioning Afrikanerdom to questioning the system to the extent that even his family, except for his son, no longer care about him. His family is a main agent in his fate, as are most members of the society of the novel who aid in Ben's isolation. Ben's family's actions are central in understanding Brink's view of pro-apartheid Afrikaners' defense of the system in the face of what it feels is a challenge—especially, if it be by 'one of its own.' Ben's family is an example of the type of Afrikaners who view conflict with their own, to quote Lambley, "as a kind of seeable threat which encourages them to keep turning inwards" (199) and to withdraw from the person who 'rocks the boat.' Not only that — "Frightened people tend to act rashly and to strike out at any point that threatens them: it is a kind of survival-at-all-costs mentality — 'us or them' fashion" (Lambley 216). And when, Brink seems to be saying, the target of such destructive behavior is a member of one's own family and society, this tendency is especially censoring. It is important, therefore, in examining the characters in the novel and their attitudes towards Ben to remember Brink's words in *Writing in a State of Siege:*

> Apartheid, as I see it, denies what is best in the Afrikaner himself. It reveals only that side of him which is characterized by fear, by suspicion, by uncertainty, hence by arrogance, meanness, narrow-mindedness, pigheadedness. What it denies is the Afrikaner's reverence for life, his romanticism . . . his generosity, his compassion. (19)

The former qualities are revealed by Ben's family, society, and the authorities; the latter by Ben himself. It is a split of unhealable proportions. As Ben states,

> I have the feeling that deep inside every man there's something he is 'meant' to do. Something no one but he can achieve. And then it's a matter of discovering what your own personal something is. Some find it early in life. Others drive themselves to distraction trying to find it. And still others learn to be patient and prepare themselves for the day when, suddenly, they'll recognize it. Like an actor waiting for his cue . . . [t]he main thing is to be ready when your moment comes. (29)

Said in the prologue to the narrator, and some seventeen years before the main action of the novel, Ben's abstract thoughts predict his future split from Afrikanerdom. It is a future — a "something" — which will cause his family, acquaintances, and authorities and then, fittingly, all of these together, to attempt to cut him off from his quest to find out the truth about Jonathan's and Gordon's deaths; from his burgeoning openness to South Africa's Black majority; and as these things are the "something" Ben is "meant to do," from his very existence. Consequently, one sees earlier, in the prologue, the seeds of Ben's later actions for which others isolate and destroy him. The prologue reveals another incident which foretells that Ben's character is one which may lead him on the road he takes in examining Jonathan's and Gordon's fates. The seed that will cause the pro-Nationalist Afrikaner society to destroy him is in his character from early in his life. Thus, taking up the "something" he is "meant to do" is an intrinsic part of his character. That this "something" challenges the foundations of Afrikanerdom is what causes Ben to be first hindered, then betrayed and, in essence, killed by his family and by the authorities. The key incident in Ben's youth which foreshadows his future occurs when the narrator and Ben are in school together. Ben emerges from "his attitude of placid withdrawal" (17) and from his "habitual lethargy" (17) to protest a substitute lecturer's singling out of the narrator for throwing a paper missile because the rest of the class shared his guilt in such acts. Ben goes on to threaten a student boycott unless an apology is offered, and when it isn't, he leads the boycott, causing a "sensation" (17). The incident does not end there, for when the Head of the Department asks Ben to apologize, Ben instead repeats his initial demand of an apology from the lecturer. The upshot is that Ben is suspended for the rest of the semester. In this incident, Ben shows the "doggedness" (16) the limited narrator notices initially only in his chess playing. What the reader realizes, however, is that it is this doggedness which Ben will show later in questioning Jonathan's and Gordon's fates. Most importantly, it is this doggedness which will be important in fulfilling Ben's desire "to be ready when your moment comes" (29) and the "something" he is "meant to do" arrives. Brink intends the prologue to reveal, therefore, the qualities which will cause Ben to be criticized, cut off, isolated and betrayed by others.

Other important issues are revealed in the prologue. As Mel Watkins writes in the *New York Times Book Review,* "Ben's descent into isolated pariah" is a central aspect of the novel.[4] Ben's family plays a great role in treating him like a pariah, and an essential aspect of the prologue in setting up an analysis of Ben's family is what Brink reveals about Ben's wife Susan during the narrator's visit some seventeen years earlier. Susan's attitude of control over Ben is striking. Susan states, "I've brought him to where he is today" (26); and she later says, "It's up to me to keep the family going" (26-7). She confesses, furthermore, that her earlier feelings for Ben were prompted by "imagin[ing] him the way I wanted him to be" (24). Unhappy with her own life, she states additionally that she feels "It's not easy for a woman to admit that she's married to a loser" (24). Thus, to Susan, Ben is merely a lost cause whose life, at best, must be controlled by her. This drive for control, both in Susan and daughter Suzette, as I will discuss later, is a primary element in Ben's later estrangement and in his ultimate destruction.

Another minor point foreshadows the familial discord that revolves around Ben's quest for justice for Jonathan and Gordon. At one point Susan says, "Do you think I should resign myself to the thought that one day my daughters may do something on my behalf?" (25) Contrast this with Ben's desire for a son: "I'd love to have a son. . . . I feel I cannot come to grips with all my former selves unless I relive it through a son" (29). Indeed, the sentiments of the parents foretell the later battle lines: Suzette, and ultimately, Linda, on Susan's side; Johan on Ben's side. Thus, the ultimate battle for control of Ben's actions is drawn upon sex lines in the Du Toit family. And, it is a battle which shows the family, except for Johan, to possess unhealthy qualities which help to alienate and isolate Ben. Consequently, the reference to Tolstoy by Susan is certainly not fortuitous — "every unhappy family is unhappy in its own way" (23) — for the family is a central part of Ben's opposition.

It is significant to remember the familial distance from Ben, considering that one might view the Special Branch as Ben's main and only foe. Moreover, it is important in light of the familial hostility Ben encounters, that, in the prologue, during the action that takes place near the end of his life, Ben doesn't identify the all-encompassing "them" (12) from whom he is hiding his papers, leading one to suspect that those who plague him may include his family. (Especially in light of the fact that Suzette discovers his hiding place for his papers and betrays him to the authorities.) Ben states:

> They've taken everything from me. Nearly everything. Not much left. But they won't get that [his papers]. . . . If they get them there was no sense in it at all . . . that's what they're aiming for. They want to wipe out every sign of me, as if I'd never been here, And I won't let them. . . . I can't go on for very much longer and I think they know it too. (13)

Here, Brink shows Ben to the hunted animal of Lambley's description of a dissident Afrikaner. And certainly, in this passage, "they" refers in great part to the authorities. But if one reads more deeply, and considers his abandonment by his family and his betrayal by Suzette, it seems that his family is elevated alongside the authorities as the unspecified "them" who plague Ben. This part of the book is especially relevant if considered alongside MacCrone's analysis in *Race Attitudes in South Africa* of the attitudes of racist whites towards the targets of their disdain. In considering his analysis, it is important to understand that in Brink's portrayal of Ben's treatment by the authorities and by his family, the point seems clear that by empathizing with mistreated Blacks, a dissident can be perceived as a member of that 'outgroup' against which the dominant group acts, with the following results:

> [T]he existence of the out-group as an object of hostility itself leads to an increased intensity of identification between members of the in-group, since a common object of hate is, in some respects, a stronger bond between individuals than a common of object of love.[5]

Especially revealing of the family's and the authorities' common stance against Ben is MacCrone's statement that "A common object of hostility may indeed make strange bedfellows even in the personal relationships of everyday life, so that two individuals scarcely on speaking terms with one another may become positively cordial as a result of their dislike of a third party" (253). Consequently, Brink's portrait of the 'unity in hostility' that can meet a dissident represents some important psychological theories. Moreover, in a section called "The Functional Analysis of a Group Attitude towards the Native," MacCrone states that bigotry towards Blacks

> preserves group unity and identity [among whites]. It is a commonplace in group psychology that the unity of a group depends on the ways of believing, feeling and acting which are shared in common by its individual members. The attitude towards the native is one such way; hence any tendency to deviate on the part of an individual member has very little chance of developing so long as he wishes to regard himself, or to be regarded, as a member of a group. In other words, the [white] attitude towards the native becomes the criterion of group membership. (256)

This passage illuminates the psychological validity in Brink's portrayal of how various parts of society unite to react against someone who dissents from the prevailing bigotry. Furthermore, and especially ominously, MacCrone continues to state that criticism of the in-group (i.e., whites) can have the effect of strengthening it, since the negative response to a dissenter can be based on "the preservation of group identity as against outside interferences" (256). This unity is precisely what Brink wants to expose as a hindrance to change in South Africa — but a hindrance he wants to demythologize, to demystify and thereby destroy the authority of it.

Perhaps the most essential aspect the novel is that Brink's portrayal of Ben's family makes evident the connection between the dysfunctional family and dysfunctional society. First, I would like to establish the precise the familial and societal dysfunctions illustrated in Brink's novel. Former psychoanalyst Alice Miller, in *For Your Own Good*, focuses on the cruelty of oppressive and rigid parenting as a key ingredient of dysfunctional families. This parenting is transmitted through the "poisonous pedagogy" of one or both parents.[6] And while Miller makes connections between the dysfunctional family (as she defines it) and the characteristics of the relationship between the government and the citizens of Nazi Germany, my research yields that a parallel can also be drawn to South Africa under apartheid , particularly as represented in Brink's novel, if one substitutes Miller's references to parents with the South African Nationalist governmental system and those institutions and individuals who upheld it.

As Alice Miller defines the "poisonous pedagogy" of authoritarian figures, the intention is to prevent people from having a consciousness both of what is done to them and of the true nature of reality, as these qualities would give rise to questioning authority and to its construction of reality and of society. As Miller writes: "[A]s long as you are not allowed to see something you have no choice but to overlook it, to misunderstand it, to protect yourself against it in one way or another" (9-10). In addition, "The pedagogue must also put a very early stop to the desire to know" (30). As Miller states in *For Your Own Good*, totalitarian demands for obedience to authority demand that people "(1) willingly do as they are told, (2) willingly refrain from doing what is forbidden, and, (3) accept the rules made [supposedly] for their sake" (13). Furthermore, "poisonous pedagogy" of a parent is defined in Miller's list:

1. Adults are the masters . . . of the dependent child.
2. They determine in godlike fashion what is right and what is wrong.

3. The child is held responsible for their anger.
4. The parents must always be shielded.
5. The child's life-affirming feelings pose a threat to the autocratic adult.
6. The child's will must be "broken" as soon as possible (59).

In addition, as Miller states earlier, "Causing a child to feel shame can also be a strategy in the struggle against willfulness" (47).

It is also important to note that the threat that the dysfunctional familial and societal system feels because of dissidents and critical individuals underlines the fragility that both masks and makes overt the ironhandedness which often marks tyrannical systems. Thus, one can clearly apply the following ingredients of "poisonous pedagogy" to the racist system and its upholders in Brink's *A Dry White Season*: the desire to "create the belief that [authorities] would not survive being offended"; that "strong feelings are harmful"; and that "authorities are always right" (60) is shown both in the scorn that Ben meets with as a result of the appearance of a newspaper photograph of his hugging a Black woman, Emily, at the funeral for her husband, Gordon, and by the fact that one of the final humiliations of Ben comes when an anonymous source (certainly South African police) sends members of Ben's family a photograph secretly taken of Ben having sex with his lover Melanie. Thus, affection and sexuality are portrayed by poisonous pedagogues and their followers as shameful and dirty acts, which, therefore, are tools to control or shame dissidents.

More importantly, in South African society which Brink portrays, the apartheid system as it is embodied both in the institutions — e.g., the educational and criminal justice systems, and the media — as well as in individuals was the equivalent of the dysfunctional parents and authorities of which Miller writes. Brink certainly portrays the apartheid system as one which, as exemplified by the aforementioned institutions, demanded unquestioning loyalty and obedience to mores that were defined externally and that individuals were expected to internalize. Furthermore, Brink portrays that the system was like the tyrannical parent of Miller's work who feels threatened by his children's questioning and independence. The retaliation — punishment, humiliation, isolation — is illustrated by Brink in the jailing and murders of dissidents, culminating in the destruction of the novel's protagonist, Ben. If one considers Brink's novel in light of Miller's theories, therefore, it seems that only people who function as children whose consciousness has been determined by authorities and who have no individual, questioning will concerning South Africa's racial policies and the resultant limitations they put on one's relationships can live contentedly in the face of injustice. Indeed, the 'perfect' citizens in such an oppressive society are people who conform to authority to the extent that, as Miller states, they surrender to oppression "without even being aware of their enslavement" (66). Miller seems to suggest that a conscious person who objects to the system must have two alternatives: to shield herself or himself by hiding behind "a false self" (269) which conforms externally to authority; or to express his or her dissidence and risk the intolerance and attempts to break his or her will by those who uphold the system and the status quo. Furthermore, Miller indicates, even if one does follow one's consciousness, this effort, even if morally righteous, may be derided even on moral and ethical grounds by those who support the white privelege. As Miller writes:

> It is clear . . . that a relativity of traditional moral values is an intrinsic part of this [oppressive] system: in the last analysis, our status and degree of power determine whether our actions are judged to be good or bad. This same principle prevails throughout the whole world. The strong person dictates the verdict, and the victor in a war will sooner or later be applauded, regardless of the crimes that have been committed on the road to victory. (64)

Consequently, Miller sums up the relativity of values based upon one's position of power, showing the complications facing those who dissent from an abusive status-quo.

Additionally, in light of the united force of a dysfunctional society against Ben, one might consider not only his desperation as the action moves towards its end but also the narrator's remarks about Ben's death. Though the narrator tries to dismiss the thought, he wonders: "Perhaps I would still have found it possible that he deliberately walked into the passing car that night to lend suicide the more respectable appearance of an accident. But there was something amiss" (perhaps implying murder) (33). In my analysis, it is not entirely relevant that he is on a path which leads both to his enlightenment and to his destruction. For the relevance of his family's abandonment of him comes via one's looking at Ben as trapped in a dysfunctional family system as described by Joseph Richman in "Family Determinants of

Suicide Potential," which bears a striking similarity to Miller's work on dysfunctional families. Though Ben may or may not have committed suicide, many of the destructive family patterns Richman describes are starkly present in his family. Moreover, as the foundation of Richman's ideas are relevant to Alice Miller's ideas on the dysfunctional family, his thoughts are especially relevant to Brink's novel. My interest here is not in arguing that Ben is a suicide; but solely in examining the undeniable fact that his family has some of the central qualities described by Richman, and it is these qualities which cause Ben to be isolated from and alienated by those who should be closest to him. Moreover, many of these traits are conducive to the destruction of a family member, and here it is important to remember Ben's desolation at the accumulated hostility of his family, which is highlighted by Suzette's betrayal of him. Some key aspects of Richman's list of characteristics which can aid in the destruction of a family member are essential in understanding the relationship of the family to Ben and how it affects him. Finally, and most importantly, in Brink's novel the dysfunctional family is a microcosm of a dysfunctional society.

In each system, "The house is on fire, but like the story of the emperor with no clothes, we are not supposed to look. We are to share a collective denial and cultural no-talk rule . . . [O]ne of the rules comprising the sacred rules is that we can't question any of the rules. This would dishonor authority."[7] This passage summarizes key psychological concepts that incorporate and transcend individual families; concepts which can come to permeate an entire society. Nazi Germany would certainly be one example of societal internalization of submission to autocratic authority. In addition, in fictional terms, George Orwell's *1984*, a key influence on Brink, is a classic representation of such phenomena which take place under totalitarian regimes. That the state is encompassed in Big Brother connotes a pseudo-familial bond which supersedes the actual familial bond. Orwell makes evident this usurpation in his portrayal of people — especially children — who will inform to the authorities on family members who are disloyal to Big Brother. Thus, the devaluation of the family and the displacement of the familial bond onto the state is one of the main features of Orwell's representation of the dysfunctional nature of a totalitarian society. Andre Brink's *A Dry White Season* is clearly influenced by Orwell in many ways. In fact, Brink himself has made the connection between Orwell's novel and South African fiction in "Writing against Big Brother: Notes on Apocalyptic Fiction in South

Africa." Importantly, Brink emphasizes the essential need for literature to smash the dysfunctional familial and societal "no-talk-rule" and obedience to authority which can greatly pervert relationships and corrupt morality in a state such as South Africa. Moreover, in my analysis, Brink, in *A Dry White Season*, portrays the fact that obedience to an immoral authority can be a sign of individual, familial, and societal dysfunction. For, as much of the novel focuses on the Afrikaner Du Toit family's abandonment of Ben, whose dissidence against the system grows slowly, Brink made it clear that the family is indeed a microcosm for much greater dysfunctional entities: the state and its legal and extra-legal machinery; and the 'ordinary citizens' who make up the society which actively or tacitly keeps a system of racism and white supremacy in place.

Now we will closely analyze the Du Toits as a microcosm of a dysfunctional system. A central characteristic of Ben's family found in Richman's discussion is the "closed family system."[8] As Richman writes,

> a 'closed family system' refers to a family that cannot tolerate any outside contacts that would threaten to change its established structure. A friendship by any member, for example, with someone whose standards or habits are different . . . [is an] example of such a threat . . . [and] the family closes itself off.(42)

These characteristics are clear when Gordon's wife, Emily, and a friend, Stanley, arrive during dinner at Ben's house (which I will discuss more later) and by Ben's abandonment by most of his immediate family as he refuses to let go of his quest to get justice for Blacks. The urge to cut out 'troublesome others' — i.e., Blacks — from the family as if they are invaders is shown in at least the two incidents mentioned above. Thus, members of the Black majority, to Ben's family, are to be ignored. Moreover, it is important to look at the nature of those who help to put Ben in such a desolate frame of mind and who aid and abet in his destruction. In this light, Ben's family acts as a force which not only represents pro-apartheid society (however passively, they still support the status-quo and thus are backers of the system) but also reveals in microcosm the people who force Ben's ostracism from and damnation by the vast majority of the white society of the novel. These facts are essential in explaining Ben's feelings of abandonment by the microcosm (his family) and the macrocosm (the authorities and the society of the novel).

Since Ben's family represents a major force in his desolation and isolation, it is important to examine them further. In fact, to do so provides a helpful explanation of Ben's feelings. In any case, Ben's family is certainly a "closed family system" regarding his activities with Blacks.

Another characteristic of destructive family systems which Richman discusses is "a symbiosis without empathy" (34). Richman defines symbiosis as entailing "exploitation and satisfaction of neurotic needs rather than . . . love and cooperation" (37). This element is most certainly found in Susan and Suzette, neither of whom love Ben but use him for their own purposes—mainly his increasing their security and respectability. Furthermore,

> In a symbiotic relationship one person cannot be seen and cannot see himself as an individual, but only as part of a larger whole, such as the family, or as an attachment to some other person. . . . If he does attempt to become an individual dire consequences follow. (37)

Moreover, the actions of the other person will only be recognized "dim[ly]," if at all (37). Centrally, for our purposes, "his motives, for example, will always be interpreted in terms of their effect on" other family members (37). Richman continues:

> Such a failure in empathy implies a deficiency in the ability to identify or take the role of the symbiotic other, to put oneself in his place and see things as he sees them, combined with the inability to separate. The symbiotic other, therefore, is seen only in terms of oneself . . . [The family shows] anxiety . . . usually associated with the other becoming a separate individual. It is particular when this type of unempathetic symbiosis is the threatened that [the person] receives the message [from family] not to be. (37)

This passage details much of the history of Ben's family: Susan's feeling that she 'made' him; the family's hostility towards Ben as Susan desires that he and she remain together and not let go of what they have built; her and her daughters' anxiety at Ben's involvement with his cause; and, finally, Suzette's betrayal of her father as he is at his most isolated. Her betrayal and Susan's finally leaving him leave alone (as his lover Melanie has been forced out of the country) set him on the road to becoming his most desolate and fearful of whom to trust. Thus, the ultimate message Ben receives from his family is, in essence, "not to be." Moreover, the quality of empathy which is largely missing in his family is precisely a main factor in Ben's involvement with Jonathan and Gordon. Thus, Brink illustrates that empathy is one of the keys to challenging a rigid, oppressive society. As Miller writes in *For Your Own Good*, authoritarian structures "lack of empathy" (62) is also a dysfunctional value in totalitarian states (as it allows powerful rulers and their underlings never to identify with those who are harmed by the ruling order). Yet, Miller states that those who are able to be empathic "are more likely to be open to the suffering of others, or at least will not deny its existence. This is a necessary precondition if old wounds are to heal instead of merely being covered up with the help of the next generation" (634). Nevertheless, Brink shows that those who try to heal the wounds may themselves be mortally wounded by those who maintain a closed, unempathetic society.

Another clear part of Ben's dysfunctional family is "a fixation upon earlier social roles," to use Richman's terminology (34). This directly pertains to Ben's membership in the Afrikaner community. A role, quotes Richman, refers to "the function played by an individual in a group," while status is "the position accorded, formally or informally, to a person in his own group. . . . It is always dependent on the others in the group or community and is partly a matter of how others directly perceive the individual" (39-40). With his involvement in Jonathan's and Gordon's cases, Ben's status as an Afrikaner is questioned and criticized by most of his fellow Afrikaners. Furthermore, regarding his social role, some of Richman's central remarks certainly apply to Ben. Ben certainly faces from family and acquaintants "undue stress upon social role due to the detriment of true individuality" (Richman 41). Moreover, as is clear with Ben, the person who violates the social role may become subject to public and private "scapegoating" (Richman 41).

In fact, "scapegoating" is a key part of Ben's family's attitude towards him. As Richman describes it, "[T]he scapegoat is the family member who is held responsible for the difficulties of the family. He is to blame" (44). Some forms of scapegoating include holding up the person to ridicule; isolation of the "scapegoat"; and criticism, before others and in private. Ben clearly is "blamed" by Susan for being a "loser" who is going to tear down all the security that she and he have built up over the years by continuing his activities on Jonathan's and Gordon's behalf. Moreover, society scapegoats Ben — acquaintances criticize him at dinner when Emily and Stanley show up to talk to him; as does Susan for Ben's being photographed being embraced by Emily;

and for his 'un-Afrikaner' search for justice for Black friends. The Special Branch is also relevant here, holding up Ben to great humiliation by circulating a photograph of him and Melanie about to make love. Thus, Ben's family mirrors the condemnation of Ben by the society of which they are a part, greatly magnifying his plight.

To continue the discussion of Ben's family in more detail, Susan's attitude, which shows both lack of empathy and a closed family system, is clear during the dinner party Emily and Stanley 'invade.' Though Emily is nearly hysterical from finding blood and broken teeth in the trousers of her detained husband, Gordon, Susan's feelings are entirely self-centered, unsympathetic, and closed. With amazing triviality, she tells Ben to "try to get rid of them soon. I can't wait with the main dish" (68). Thus, though she has answered the door and seen Emily's emotional state, she is only concerned about her dinner and guests. Her "deadly restraint" (70) on Ben's return, and her "disapproving stare" (70) as Ben begins to tell the story of Jonathan and Gordon also show her critical attitude and self-centeredness. Her "smiling" (70) mocking of Ben as "Don Quixote" (70) indicates the hostility with which she will openly ridicule Ben for disturbing her with outsiders. Her protectiveness of her home from Black 'intruders' and her perception of Ben as rocking the stability of their home life are shown as she says to Ben, "With a more urgent tone in her voice than he was used to . . . : 'Ben, everything we've built up together over the years — for God's sake, make sure you don't spoil it'" (74). This self-interest, rather than the danger and death Ben's Black acquaintances have faced, is her main concern. Moreover, Ben's telling about Gordon's blood and teeth in the trousers is only so much bad taste and bad manners to Susan though it is crucial to Ben's trying to make others understand his involvement in Gordon's case. ("'We're still at table,' said Susan, disapproving" (71)). Her great concern, knowing the danger that Gordon could be in and his wife's great upset, is that Ben "very nearly succeeded in wrecking the whole evening" (73) by dealing with Emily and Stanley and later being involved in the dinner discussion about it. Consequently, it seems that keeping her private world safe from upset is one of her main considerations, regardless of her knowledge that Blacks are suffering. Though she may be more savvy than Ben about the potential trouble he could be in for, she fears this trouble mainly for herself and her home, it seems, remaining conscienceless and uncaring about the clear violence Gordon has faced and about her husband's obvious concern for him.

Indicating the marriage is a "symbiosis without empathy" for her, Susan later says, "You've never been able to make me happy, Ben (141). Hence, what she is most interested in concerning keeping her marriage and family together is, to use Richman's analysis, not love, not mutual understanding — but selfishly preserving her own little world; even as Blacks and her own husband suffer. The lack of empathy between husband and wife is very clearly revealed as Susan states to Ben ideas similar to those in the prologue about her disappointment and about her only knowing the Ben of her imagination. She tells him: "Just be careful. Please. We've been married for thirty years now and sometimes it seems to me I don't really know you. There's something in you I feel I'm unprepared for" (74). Certainly, no empathy exists even after thirty years. Thus, there can be no healthy connection. Plus, Susan needs to keep "everything we've built up over the years" (though she also, ironically, feels that their life is less than it would have been if Ben had been more ambitious, indicating her permanent disappointment with him). "Everything" — home, moderate status, an unloved and unknown husband — these are the things to which Susan is tied and, partly because of her desire never to risk them, she can never empathize with Ben's main concern in the novel — justice for Blacks. Consequently, the entirety of Ben's family life is founded on estrangement and alienation from most other members of his family, most consistently his wife.

Not even after the farcically unjust inquest into Gordon's death does Susan empathize with Ben. When, for example, the photograph appears in the paper of Emily's embracing Ben, Susan (once again), instead of empathizing with Emily's state or Ben's concern, is merely concerned with appearances, refusing even to go to church, worrying about being stared at and about what people will think of Ben. Furthermore, her desire for enclosure and her lack of empathy are clear as she tells Ben, "If you'd kept out of it from the beginning you wouldn't have brought this shame over us now" (138). Also, Susan is far more concerned about the impact of the photograph on her father's political career than with Emily's grief or Ben's feelings (even his feelings about the photograph). More than any other scene, the family's reaction to the photograph shows the almost uniform lack of empathy for Ben: to Suzette, he has done the unthinkable — "Embracing black women in public" (139) — disregarding the fact that Emily's embracing Ben was done in grief and that the papers invaded that private moment. Her tone is "sharp" (139) and she is wholly unsympathetic, which is especially shown when Ben tells her to have a "sense of perspective"

(139) and she angrily dismisses him, "scathingly" (139), and only worries about the consequences to herself and to other members of the family — not about hearing Ben's side. Even his sister Helena shows "a touch of venom" (139) and thinks "it's priceless" (139) that Ben is in the papers being embraced by a Black woman. Only teenager Johan — reflecting Ben's sentiments in the prologue — defends him. Still, with that one exception, Ben is surrounded in his family by people who are unable to see things from his perspective and who are totally unfeeling for his quest for justice. Here, it is central to note that, as Miller states of dysfunctional families, a central method of preventing 'misbehavior' is "the method of withdrawing love, which can take many forms" (Miller 41). The connection between the dysfunctional family as a mainstay of a dysfunctional society is clear in Brink's portrayal of Ben's family's response to him, for his family's withdrawal of love is intended to make him regress from 'threatening' the political, social and legal systems.

In line with Susan, Ben's politician father-in-law also withdraws emotionally from him and completely lacks empathy for his quest. Again, self-interest is evident here, for his father-in-law is a Member of Parliament who clearly backs away from Ben when he mentions that the Special Branch has become interested in his (Ben's) activities. Even before Ben lets this information out, his father-in-law speaks of the potential "embarrassment" (210) Ben could cause him, clearly revealing his self-interest. Moreover, the two men are on completely different planes concerning their view of Blacks. Ben's father-in-law states regarding his own helping Blacks, "I appreciate your concern for them. I've been doing the same thing all my life, sacrificing myself for [my] neighbor, be they black or white. But no member of our family has been seen in public with a kaffir woman before, Ben" (210). His using the equivalent of the word 'nigger' to describe Emily shows his true feelings towards Blacks. Thus, completely cutting off Ben, as he makes clear a bit later, is inevitable. Ben has come to realize the injustice of the system; Brink writes that his father-in-law counters "contemptuously" (212), "You amaze me. . . . Don't you realize what the government is doing for the blacks? One of these days, the whole bloody lot of them [Blacks] will be free and independent in their own countries [i.e., homelands]. And then you have the nerve to talk about injustice!" (212). Once again, therefore, by dealing with a family member, Ben finds himself more isolated, a target of more hostility and once again a target of more familial lack of empathy.

Moreover, in Ben's father-in-law in this section of the book, Brink reveals an important function of myth as a maladaptive defense mechanism. Again, an analysis of Brink's novel reveals that this dysfunction exists on a familial and societal level. John Bradshaw, who has popularized Miller's theories, speaking the role of myth-making in the dysfunctional family, clearly illuminates not only Brink's portrayal of Ben's father-in-law's rejection of him but also sheds light on Brink's indictment of South Africa on both an individual and collective level. According to Bradshaw, "Mythologies are meanings given to events or actions in order to distract from what is actually happening" (74). In applying this statement to the novel, one can see that Ben's father-in-law clearly uses the implausible myth of the homelands being set up by the white-controlled government in Blacks' best interest in order to both displace the focus of the discussion from the brutal injustices done to Blacks to the self-righteous, self-justifying, oppressive myth that racial separation has been for the good of all. By deflating the argument in such a manner, Ben's father-in-law also reveals another purpose of myth-making in a dysfunctional family. According to Bradshaw: [T]he system remains closed and rigid. Anyone rocking the boat would upset the status quo" (74). Consequently, Ben's increased knowledge of the mistreatment of Blacks is a representation of the factual way in which many Nationalist politicians (which the father-in-law is) dismissed reality with self-serving myth; and attempted to silence dissidents by implicitly reinforcing the "no talk rule"; after all, why discuss facts when oppressive myths served to preserve the state and both whites' 'place' and previously held world view as well? Again, in essence, the family is a small scale replica of a warped society.

Brink's depiction of Ben's isolation further illustrates that Ben is the victim of a dysfunctional society. Ben is at his most isolated after the photograph of him and Melanie is sent to various people, including his wife and the head master at his school, Cloete. Furthermore, 'his' daughter, Linda, becomes ostensibly more distant than Suzette, who is closer in manner and thought to Susan. Yet, significantly, it is Suzette who acts as the Judas to Ben, after seeming to comfort him by making him feel understood and wanted. "I wanted you to know that I understand!" (295), says Suzette in a mockery of empathy. Indeed, all that Ben suffers as a result of his dedication to truth and justice bears out Alice Miller's ideas on the lengths to which totalitarians and the people who support them go to try to regulate — to the point of destroying — a person who will not accept injustice. As Miller writes:

> The methods that can be used [to repress dissidence and to fulfill the aforementioned aims of poisonous pedagogy] are: laying traps, lying, duplicity, subterfuge, manipulation, "scare" tactics, withdrawal of love, isolation, distrust, humiliating and disgracing, scorn, ridicule, and coercion even to the point of torture. (59)

Also, the relevance of Brink's portrayal of Susan's behavior is strengthened when one recalls Miller's statement that "Deception seems to be a universal method of control . . . ultimate victory is presented as "the successful resolution" of the conflict" (36).

Brink depicts the betrayal and withdrawal Ben encounters as his family's and society's way of 'resolving the conflict' a dissident brings forth. Suzette's betrayal is clearly the apex of this attempted undoing of Ben. Giving away Ben's hiding place to the authorities for material collected on Gordon is clearly her doing. Yet, tragic as this is for Ben, a bit earlier he certainly had come to grips with the ultimate outcome of his quest — a quest unsupported by his family and his society:

> If I act, I cannot but lose. But if I do not act, it is a different kind of defeat, equally decisive and maybe worse. Because then I will not even have a conscience left. The end seems ineluctable: failure, defeat, loss. The only choice I have left is whether I am prepared to salvage a little honor, a little decency, a little humanity — or nothing. It seems as if a sacrifice is impossible to avoid, whatever way one looks at it. But at least one has the choice between a wholly futile sacrifice and one that might, in the long run, open up a possibility, however negligible or dubious, of something better, less sordid and more noble, for our children. My own and Gordon's and Stanley's. They live on. We, the fathers, have lost. (304-5)

Consequently, although Ben is betrayed and abandoned by his family, he still longs to make a better world for them and others. Part of him, therefore, is inviolate from his destructive family (and society). In evaluating Brink's portrayal of Ben's experiences, it is central to recall what Miller has written in *For Your Own Good* about people who stand up to authoritarianism:

> Rejection, ostracism, loss of love, and name calling will not fail to affect them, but once they have found their authentic self they will not want to lose it. And when they sense that something is being demanded of them to which their whole being says no, they cannot do it. They simply cannot. (85)

She goes on to say that such people sometimes "risk the loss of love in order to regain their lost self. They will not be willing to relinquish it again for any price in the world" (85). Miller's ideas, therefore, shed light on Brink's main message in writing of Ben's persistence.

Still, obviously, Brink emphasizes that lack of empathy surrounds Ben. He is criticized, ridiculed, and shunned as a result of his quest for justice. More importantly, the family's relationship with Ben — symbiosis without empathy — grows to the point where it seems the family feels that, instead of trying to be empathic to Ben, or stopping the unhealthy symbiotic relationship, they should opt to obliterate their relationship with Ben and reduce him to, first, an antagonist; second, an enemy. In this regard, they are clearly microcosms of Afrikanerdom, with whom Ben may have a strained connection but which excludes any empathy whatsoever. Another classic work helps illuminate Brink's attempt to create a liberatory mythology in *A Dry White Season* by exposing the oppressive and dysfunctional nature of upholders of South African racism. As in criticizing Sarah Gertrude Millin's racial mythology, Franz Boas' thoughts in *The Mind of Primitive Man* can be applied to Brink's representation of the pro-apartheid whites who make one who questions the status quo into an outcast, providing an incisive critique of racial 'herds' whose main features are unity and feelings of superiority to those who are not a member of their herd. Before proceeding, I must emphasize that one of the results of Boas' ideas on "primitive" behavior is to destroy the traditional, prejudiced notions of the concept of "primitive" — e.g., its traditional application to societies who don't share in predominant Western modes of technology, religion customs, etc., and to make one ask, "Who, in fact, is primitive?" According to Boas' ideas below, one could clearly designate racist whites as the true primitives. Boas writes:

> There are a number of primitive hordes to whom every stranger not a member of the horde is an enemy, and where it is right to damage the enemy to the best of one's power and ability, and if possible to kill him. Such behavior is founded largely on the solidarity of the horde, on the feeling that it is the duty of every member of the horde to destroy all possible enemies. Therefore every person not a member of the horde must be considered as belonging to a class entirely distinct from the members of the horde and is treated accordingly. We can trace the gradual broadening of the feeling of fellowship during the advance of civilization. The feeling of fellowship in a horde expands to the feeling of unity of the tribe, to a recognition of

bonds established by a neighborhood of habitat, and further on to the feeling of fellowship among nations. This seems to be the limit of the ethical concept of fellowship of man which we have reached at the present time and which has superseded the local interest of lesser units; we recognize that it consists largely in the idea of the preeminence of that community whose member we happen to be — in the preeminent value of its bodily build, its language, of its customs and religious traditions, and in the belief that all external influences that threaten these traits are hostile and must be combatted not only for the justifiable purpose of preserving its peculiarities but even with the wish to impose them upon the rest of the world.[9]

Boas continues:

The feeling of nationality as here expressed, and the feeling of solidarity of the horde, are of the same order, although modified by the gradual expansion of the ideal of fellowship; but the ethical point of view which makes it justifiable at the present time to increase the well-being of one nation at the cost of another, the tendency to value our form of civilization as higher — not as dearer to our hearts — than that of the whole rest of mankind, are the same as those which prompt the actions of primitive man who considers every stranger as an enemy, and who is not satisfied until the enemy is killed. It is somewhat difficult for us to recognize that the value which we attribute to our own civilization is due to the fact that we participate in this civilization, and that it has been controlling all our actions since the time of our birth; but it is certainly conceivable that there may be other civilizations, based perhaps on different traditions and on a different equilibrium of emotions and reason which are of no less value than ours. . . . The general theory of valuation of human activities, as developed by anthropological research, teaches us a higher tolerance than the one we now profess. (224-25)

Certainly, one can see that Ben's family can be said to represent the intolerant primitive horde who is alienated from and unsympathetic to Blacks and all who question their bigotry. Yet, their feelings and actions are understandable if one examines the feeling of other members of society in the novel and on this point it is clear that Brink's critique of Ben's family broadens to a larger critique of South African society. To them, it is Ben, Brink makes clear, who is the aberration — an Afrikaner who cares for the Blacks whom he knows and who believes in justice — and not the injustice of racism. It is significant that most of the white secondary characters, with the exception of Melanie, her father, Johan, and Ben's colleague, Viviers, disagree fundamentally with Ben's being involved with Jonathan's and Ben's cases although Ben makes clear that, at first, he does not see himself as fighting the system. (That the system has taken *him* on is one of his main sources of knowledge as he grows from innocence to awareness in the novel.) Yet, the society that surrounds him makes clear that he is taking on the powerful horde. For example, at the dinner party at which Emily and Stanley arrive, only a young teacher Viviers, "an intense young man, fresh from university" (70) questions the Afrikaner system. (And, at this point in the novel, he is far beyond Ben's relatively 'innocent' position.) Dominee Bester, Cloete, and Susan's friends are all in a disapproving frame of mind. And Cloete's reminding Ben of the Immorality Act when his picture appears in the paper with Emily after Gordon's death makes clear that he is a spokesman for the horde who uphold the status quo. Added to this are Cloete's condemnation of Ben when a story based on Ben's information appears in the paper: "How much did they pay you, I wonder . . . thirty pieces of silver, Mr. Du Toit. . . . To think an Afrikaner should sell his soul like this!" (235). Another spokesman for apartheid is Dominee Bester, as is pointed out in a crucial scene when Ben comes to him for guidance. He tells Ben, "It is better to obey than to sacrifice" (144). (This statement is ironic since Ben later thinks that a "sacrifice" — of himself — is unavoidable.) Consistent with his thoughts in the prologue, Ben later counters, "What I think, Dominee, is that once in one's life, just once, one should have enough faith in something to risk everything for it" (144). Between two such men, there can be no meeting of the minds. While the Dominee's strongest advice for change is actually for Ben to pray for the government, Ben has grown to realize the injustice of the police and legal systems, leaving passivity no longer an option. For this reason, his society is at odds with him — and is a macrocosm of his family in their condemnation of Ben, making Boas' remarks even more relevant.

Others are representatives of a racist society. For example, Ben's secretary (somewhat similar to Toby's secretary in Gordimer's *A World of Strangers* who is put off when she has to deal with his Black friend, Steven) is "flustered and mildly disapproving" (52) when Emily visits Ben at school. Moreover, Dr. Herzog is a greater example of the racists in Afrikaner society. Dr. Herzog's racism, which is his attitude of shutting out Blacks from the human race, is extremely blatant. For instance, Ben tries to investigate the veracity of Dr. Herzog's testimony at the inquest, during which Ben feels the doctor lied about Gordon's true condition and about the nature of his visits. Herzog reveals his true attitude toward Blacks. Herzog asks Ben, "Why go to all this trouble for the sake of a bloody coon. . . . You know, if you'd been working with those people the way I've got to, day after day, you'd soon sing a different tune altogether" (149). Another comment he makes mirrors that ridiculing remark Susan made about Ben's being a Don Quixote. Brink writes, "His gold fillings gleamed. . . . 'It's good to know that there are still people like you, and I wish you the best of luck.' Now he was as glib as any after-dinner speaker. 'Only' — he smiled, but his eyes remained unchanged — 'it's such a hell of a waste of time'" (151). Ben, therefore, finds in society the same qualities of criticism, hostility, and damnation he experiences with his family, which makes his family clearly representatives of the larger horde.

In fact, in light of Brink's comment quoted earlier about Afrikaner identity, it is important that Ben, who is condemned by most Afrikaners, asserts his Afrikanerness, as others call him a traitor. Significantly, in *Writing in a State of Siege*, Brink also says that he is not only arguing "against what is evil in the Afrikaner but for . . . his potential good" (20). Ben is clearly an example of Afrikaner potential. This fact is relevant because the reality of people's lives is not some vague fade-out into 'transcendent' colorlessness, as Peter Abrahams might seem to argue at points in *The Path of Thunder*, but being what one is, white or Black, Afrikaner or English, with all the complexities that one must grapple with. And it is important and valuable, Brink is saying, to face hostility of one's own group in a society with clearly defined roles and ideologies regarding race and ethnicity.

The role of Ben's Afrikaner identity is clear at several points. To Ben's father-in-law, for instance, even Smuts was not an Afrikaner ("You call Smuts an Afrikaner?!" (212)). This man is so proprietary of Afrikaner identity that he, typical of racist Afrikanerdom, appropriates history to tell of the hardships of Afrikaners and to angrily brush aside Ben's charges of injustices to Blacks:

> Injustice! If you want to talk about injustice, then look at what our people had to suffer. How many of us were thrown in jail in the Forties just because this land was more important to us than to be drawn into England's war — the same English who used to oppress us? (212).

This conversation reveals Ben's father-in-law's deep concern for the 'traditional' Afrikaner identity as opposed to Ben's assertion of a different or progressive Afrikaner identity that is concerned with injustices against Blacks, though he is no crusader and his quest for justice is limited to Jonathan and Gordon and also those who seek him out (by referring the latter to the lawyer, Levinson). Ben's father-in-law asserts that there is a uniform "your people" (211) and "our people" (212), telling Ben that he ought to be "ashamed" (212) to criticize what Ben perceives as injustices. He also says, "Now that we have at long last come to power in our land" (212), making clear that the historical Nationalist identity is being thrust at Ben in order to shame him out of his feelings and concerns. Ben, in his analysis of his father-in-law, realizes that the man is an example of an Afrikaner who feels he is, in Lambley's words, "superior, godly, a descendant of brave men and women who fought for their beliefs and values, that the English tried to take his birthright away and that the African is simply waiting his chance to do the same. He is encouraged to be watchful, lest he be overwhelmed" (198). Furthermore, regarding his father-in-law, Ben rightfully concludes: "Now I know it is hopeless to expect any help from him. Not because he is malicious or obtuse; not even because he is afraid.... His benevolence, his dour Christianity, his firm belief in the rectitude of his people: these are a much greater obstacle to me than any enemy who squarely opposes me" (212-13). Thus, Afrikanerdom is also Ben's nemesis.

Therefore, it is of the utmost importance that Ben assert that he, too, (especially with his expertise as a teacher of history and geography) is an Afrikaner — which can open up notions of what an Afrikaner can be. (Here it is relevant that Ben's life — in his papers — is influencing the narrator — and the reader — of the novel. It is significant to think of Ben as a writer, for as Brink shows in the portrayal of Ben's life, as he states in *Writing in a State of Siege*, "It is the duty of the writer to probe below the surface to ask dangerous questions, to discover essential human truths" and to try to awaken others to these "truths" (38)). Moreover, on the subject of exposing truths, Miller's ideas in *For Your Own Good* are certainly relevant to Brink's novel:

> We admire people who oppose a regime in a totalitarian country and think they have remained "true to their principles" or the like. We may also smile at their naivete, thinking, "Don't they realize that their words are of no use at all against this oppressive power? That they will have to pay dearly for their protest?" Yet it is possible that

both those who admire and those who scorn these protestors are missing the real point: individuals who refuse to adapt to a totalitarian regime are not doing so out of a sense of duty or because of naivete but because they cannot help but be true to themselves. (84)

Thus, both Brink and Miller connect the individual's dedication to truth with personal authenticity and self-actualization.

Indeed, it is most significant that Ben is a history and geography teacher, for his alienation from traditional Afrikaner readings of history is an important stage in his search for truth and in his move away from Afrikanerdom. Rethinking parts of the history he teaches that implicitly justify apartheid, lines run through his mind:

> our entire history, children, can be interpreted as a persistent search for freedom. . . . Freedom expressed in terms of the new land, this continent. We Afrikaners were the way to others. And now that we have finally come to power in our own land, we wish to grant the same right of self-determination to all the other nations [Blacks divided by tribes and assigned to homelands by the government] around us. They must have their own separate territories [homelands]. Peaceful co-existence. Plural development. . . . It is an expression of our own sense of honor and dignity and altruism. After all, we have nowhere to go. This is our fate. At thy will to live or perish, O South Africa, our land. No, I'm afraid it's not good enough. (160)

Ben's alienation from prevailing historical mythology makes him realize he has not been teaching history but inaccurate myths about history; myths which obscure reality as they uphold white dominance:

> And in a few minutes we'll all be back in the classroom resuming our work as if nothing had happened. . . . I'll teach you where you come from: the three small ships that brought the first white men, and the first bartering with Harry's Hottentots, and the first wine, and the first free Burghers settling on the banks of the Liesbeek in 1657. The arrival of the Huguenots. The dynasty of the Van der Stel governors, and the options open to them: Simon aiming at a concentration of whites at the Cape, allowing natural class differences to develop; his son William Adrian opting for expansion encouraging the stock farmers to explore the interior and settle among the natives; racial friction, disputes, frontier wars. 1836: Boer emigrants, a mass exodus in search of liberty and independence elsewhere. Massacres, annexations of the newly conquered land; temporary victory for the Boer Republics. Followed by the discovery of

diamonds at Kimberly and gold at the Witswatersrand; the influx of foreigners and the triumph of British imperialist interest. Anglo-Boer War, concentration camps, Lord Milner, anglicization in the schools. 1910: Unification and a new beginning. "South Africa first." Boers rebelling against the decision of their own government to support Britain in 1914. Impoverished farmers flocking to the cities. . . . The indestructible dream of a Republic. At last a Nationalist Government in power. So you can see for yourselves, boys and girls, we've come a long way. (159-60)

This narcissistic view of South African history should be familiar to those who have done research into white South African views of history to support white centrality in the country, e.g., T. Dunbar Moodie's *The Rise of Afrikanerdom* and David Harrison's *The White Tribe of Africa*. The self-worship of race-worship is evident in those analyses of South African views of history and crystallized by Brink's passage. The passage makes clear the racist view that South African history begins with the arrival of whites (which implies that Blacks did not occupy the land before whites' arrival); that Afrikaner history struggles to predominate to near exclusion all else, especially Blacks; that Blacks — the overwhelming majority of the country — are merely (and briefly) presented as obstacles Afrikaners encountered in their search for freedom; that Black freedom and removal from *their* own lands in the Afrikaner "expansion" is a historically negligible item to race-centered whites (i.e., the majority of South African whites). And perhaps most important is the fact that as Leonard Thompson states in *The Political Mythology of Apartheid* and as Ernst Cassirer points out in *The Myth of the State*, such reconstructions of history are myths and create further myths that are meant to justify the status of the dominant group. Brink's passage also crystallizes what Cassirer points out in discussing the role of language in the creation of myth, for "magic words"[10] permeate the view of history — and reality in general — of those who support racism, who maintain white dominance as they declaim it, with words that clothed white privilege and white power in such phrases as 'separate development,' 'plural development,' 'homelands,' among other words (including the Nationalist government's repudiation of the word apartheid, as if a new *reality* could have been implemented foremost by changing terminology). Brink, therefore, illustrates a major aspect of the creation of perceptions of reality by the manipulation of language during the era of apartheid. Cassirer's analysis of the tie between "magic words" and social and political mythologies which are supported by them sheds light on Brink's critique of this subject, as Brink represents in Ben's awareness the inadequacy of both the magic words and the myths they express. Furthermore, Brink uses Ben's father-in-law and other upholders of apartheid to portray the meanings, feelings and passions embodied in these words. Equally importantly, Brink uses Ben's unfolding drama to expose the lies behind racist and enslaving mythologies and the upholding of them.

Consequently, Brink's point that on Ben's realizing all the alienating euphemisms and that for him the traditional reading of history is "not good enough" (160) is central to the novel. Thus, his knowledge of history and land, one can surmise though Brink is not explicit about it, prevents him from viewing the world as narrowly and blindly as those who persecute him.

Moreover, unlike most other whites in the book, Ben realizes the limitations of a closed Afrikaner upbringing. According to Alice Miller, "It is also a part of "poisonous pedagogy" to impart to the child from the beginning false information and beliefs that have been passed on from generation to generation and dutifully accepted by the young even though they are not only unproved but are demonstrably false" (59). Yet, through Ben, Brink illustrates that one reaches an irrevocable turning point in one's consciousness by realizing the closed and artificial nature of the system in which one has been ensconced. Similar to Lambley's analysis of this point, Brink writes of Ben's thoughts:

> From a very early age, one accepts or believes, or is told that certain things exist in a certain manner. For example: that society is based on order, on reason, on justice. And that, whenever anything goes wrong one can appeal to an innate decency, or common sense or a notion of legality in people to rectify the error and offer redress. Then, without warning, there occurs what Melanie said and what I refused to believe: you discover that what you accepted as premises and basic conditions — what you had no choice but to accept if you wanted to survive at all — simply does not exist. Where you expected something solid there turns out to be just nothing. . . . Nothing.(160-61)

And in reaction to this nothingness, Ben must redefine his view of life, of his identity; and thus finds others redefining him as the enemy, outsider, traitor to his family and to Afrikanerdom (making extremely relevant the line "if you wanted to survive at all"). And, consequently,

Brink writes of the existential realization: "Everything one used to take for granted, with so much certainty that one never even bothered to inquire about it, now turns out to be an illusion. Your certainties are proven lies" (161). Thus, Brink's point is that dissident Afrikaners must, as Ben does, quest to create a new, real justice, a more valid identity, 'solid' values and meanings in life.

Moreover, as a result of his struggle to get justice for Jonathan and Gordon, Ben experiences the modern condition as described by William Barrett in *Irrational Man*."[11] As Barrett describes, "homelessness" and "alienation" (35) are a part of the modern condition. And, as *A Dry White Season* progresses, Ben is both literally and figuratively homeless, abandoned by most of his family and alienated from his 'own' society and heritage. Furthermore, as Barrett writes, modern man is "trebly alienated" (36) from religion (after Ben becomes involved in the pursuit of justice, which Dominee Bester is against, he resigns his position as deacon); from much of society, feeling himself an "outsider" (35; which is certainly the case with Ben, both regarding his family, most of white society, and the authorities); and most importantly, from the world he inhabits, surrounded mostly by those who scapegoat him as a traitor. Thus, Ben's modern and existential condition as a result of his involvement in Jonathan's and Gordon's cases is crucial to the novel. Furthermore, Brink's theory on writing as stated in *Writing in a State of Siege* is relevant here on this aspect of the novel:

> The writer has two important responsibilities. The first is, quite simply, to keep the people informed. In a country dominated by official lies and distortions, and alarmingly, an increasing silence among those well-meaning people who have lost their curiosity and who have allowed themselves to be coaxed or bludgeoned into accepting without question whatever happens a number of whites simply do not know — and do not want to know — what is happening. The writer's second responsibility (much more important than the first) . . . is to explore and expose the roots of the human condition as it is lived in South Africa . . . [and to keep] alive . . . the search for meaning in a demented world. (151-52)

Consequently, the reasons for Brink's portrayal of Ben's modern and existential situation are clear.

Existential realizations are a major reaction of Ben to the abandonment, injustice and harassment he faces. The disintegration of the wholeness of the things he believed in — family, justice for Blacks, the justice of the security system, religion and his own identity — is central. Brink's admiration of Camus is evident here. In fact, Ben's existential feelings are best reflected by Camus' *Myth of Sisyphus*:

> [S]trangeness creeps in. . . . at the heart of all beauty lies something inhuman, and these hills, the softness of the sky, the outline of these trees at this very minute lose the illusory meaning with which we had clothed them, henceforth more remote than a lost paradise. The primitive hostility of the world rises up to face us across millennia. For a second we cease to understand it because for centuries we have understood in it solely the images and designs that we had attributed to it beforehand, because henceforth we lack the power to make us of that artifice. The world evades us because it becomes itself again. That stage scenery masked by habit becomes again what it is. [12]

Ben's main feeling of existential instability regards his identity. The initial seeds of Ben's existential 'nausea' are shown after first learning of Gordon's death. On returning home, "all at once *this* was what seemed foreign to him . . . His garden . . . His house . . . His life. As if he'd never seen it before in his life" (99). More important — central, in fact — is his existential estrangement from the traditional Afrikaner heritage. Melanie tells Ben of such a process as this during an early meeting with him:

> One morning you open up your eyes an discover something prickly and restless inside and you don't know what's the matter. You take a bath and go back to your room and suddenly, as you pass the wardrobe, you see yourself. And you stop. You look at yourself. You look at yourself naked. A face, a body you've seen in the mirror every day of your life. Except you've never *really* looked. And now, all of a sudden, it comes as a shock, because you're looking at a total stranger. . . . And then you realize that all your life you've been hanging around waiting for something to happen, something special, something really worthwhile. (129)

Ben replies that he knows the feeling, and, certainly, he expressed it earlier in his life, when he discussed his feeling that people are "meant" to do "something" which reveals their true identity to them.

Furthermore, when this something comes along, it both reveals to Ben and separates him from what he had been his whole life — a drifting Afrikaner. Melanie's speech is significant in this regard. Furthermore, it is important to notice that Ben is twice 'accused' of being a liberal. In the first instance, his response is "I'm not a liberal. . . . I'm a very ordinary man who's had it up to here" (150). In the second, "an unreasonable, atavistic anger sprang to life inside Ben, as it had during his visit to the District Surgeon [Herzog]. 'I'm not a bloody liberal,' he said fiercely. 'I'm an Afrikaner'" (181). It is essential to note that at this point Ben's life is being disrupted by the defenders of Afrikanerdom — the Security Police — who soon before started open harassment by searching his house. It is implicit in the novel with the familial estrangement and police harassment that perhaps Ben's anger results from his knowing that the certainty about his life and identity is disintegrating. Certainly, while Ben attempts to affirm his Afrikaner identity (ironically, before a Black man who distrusts him in the second instance) he has already had the experience Melanie describes in his dealings with Blacks:

> Something changes irrevocably. I stood on my knees beside the coffin of a friend. I spoke to a [Black] woman in mourning in a kitchen the way my own mother might have mourned. I saw a father in search of a son the way I might have tried to find my own. And that mourning and that search had been caused by "my people." Who are "my people" today? To whom do I owe my loyalty? There must be someone, something. Or is one totally alone on that bare veld beside the name of a non-existent station? (163)

Yet, though this existential moment makes Ben feel the nothingness which is a possibility for him, for Brink there must be a search for meaning.

Perhaps one might think that Ben's asserting his Afrikaner identity is an attempt both to assert meaning to his life and to forestall the feeling of disintegration. As Brink writes Ben's thoughts,

> Yesterday's visit by the Special Branch . . . a frontier crossed. So definite that now I'll be able to divide my life in before and after. The way one talks about the flood. Or the apple, the fruit of the fall, that perilous knowledge. . . . Everything wholly strange. Children who say "good morning" and whose faces you see without recognizing them or knowing why they are addressing you. . . . When you open your mouth it is without any foreknowledge of what

will follow. . . . Your own words seem unfamiliar to you, your voice comes from far away. Every building, every room, the tables and benches, the blackboards, pieces of chalk, everything is strange. Nothing wholly dependable. You have to assume that, previously . . . in some mysterious way you "belonged," but it is inexplicable now. (158)

Facing the existential moment here as described by Camus, Ben must create who he is, knowing that by moving against the system — and against his family and society — that the only meaning will come from being able to face and carry out the something he feels he is meant to do, even if it means he must become a new — and rare — Afrikaner, and go through the painful process of shedding his old identity and the underpinnings of his old world and proclaiming his new identity to hostile others and finding that his world remains unstable and uncertain.

In finally judging Ben's efforts, two works come into play: Camus' *Myth of Sisyphus* and Brink's interpretation of *1984*. To Camus, Sisyphus, who was eternally fated to roll a rock up a hill, one which it would roll down again, is

> the absurd hero. He *is*, as much through his passions as through his real torture. His scorn of the gods, his hatred of death, and his passion for life won him that unspeakable penalty in which the whole of his being is exerted towards accomplishing nothing. (89)

All of this could be applied to Ben: his scorn of the authorities and of the racist system; his hatred of the injustices committed against Jonathan and Gordon; his unstoppable passion to find the truth. In short, his whole existence is dedicated to something his family, the dominant society, and the authorities — i.e., the horde — reject and which he comes to feel, even as he is unstoppable, will bring about his undoing. Yet Camus' words on the affirmative aspect of Sisyphus' attitude towards his fate apply to Ben. Camus writes of Sisyphus' descent to retrieve the rock:

> I see that man going back down with a heavy yet measured step toward the torment of which he will never know the end. That hour is like a breathing space . . . that is the hour of his consciousness. At each of those moments . . . he is superior to his fate. He is stronger than his rock.(89)

Camus continues:

> If this myth is tragic, that is because its hero is conscious. . . . But it is tragic only at moments when it becomes conscious. Sisyphus . . . powerless and rebellious, knows the whole extent of his wretched condition: it is what he thinks of during his descent. The lucidity that was to constitute his torture at the same time crowns his victory. (89-90)

This passage also mirrors Ben's experiences. Brink's writing of Ben's thoughts reveals Ben's lucidity, his knowledge that he won't 'win' against the authorities, that he is "powerless and rebellious" and that his lucidity of his condition is one of the most compelling aspects of the novel. Yet, Ben will not stop, for, as Camus writes, "the struggle itself toward the heights is enough to fill a man's heart" (91). This idea is true in Brink's novel, for both Ben and the narrator are affected profoundly by Ben's struggle.

This point brings us to why Ben's writing and the impact on the narrator — and the reader — are another especially important aspect of the novel. One of the clues to the affirmative aspect of Ben's struggle is elucidated by some of Brink's thoughts on *1984*. The act of writing and leaving one's ideas behind is particularly important to both novels, for as Brink writes, they are political actions:

> [N]othing precipitates the confrontation with Big Brother so fatally as Smith's insistence on thinking for himself — and on committing his thoughts to his diary. In itself, the private revolt may appear absurd, guaranteeing nothing but the extermination of the dissident himself; yet there is a blind form of hope in the Sisyphean act: "I don't imagine that we can alter anything in our lifetime. But one can imagine little knots of resistance springing up here and there — small groups of people banding themselves together, and gradually growing, and even leaving a few records behind, so that the next generation can carry on where we leave off."[13]

Brink points out that *1984* "is generally seen as demonstrating the futility of this hope" (189). And indeed, Brink often has Ben reflect on the possible futility of his quest. Thus, it can be overemphasized by some readers that Ben already realizes that "the fathers have lost." Still, like Orwell, Brink has his protagonist realize that the following generations will perhaps lead a greater and more effective battle for justice.

In the Grasp of White Primitives 101

Moreover, the impact of Ben's writings on the narrator implies Brink's desire to show the growing pockets of future resistance in his own book — in addition to ideas which reflect Brink's beliefs in the role of the writer — that some readers will be enlightened by Ben's plight and at least intellectually become a part of the resistance. By affirming Ben's struggle, therefore, Brink affirms his own position as a writer who wants to appeal to the conscience and humanity of the reader.

Furthermore, it is especially important that Ben does have enlightenment into his identity and into his cause:

> I am Ben Du Toit. There's no one else but myself right here, today. So there must be something no one but me can do: not because it is "important" or "effective," but because only I can do it. I have to do it because I happen to be Ben Du Toit; because no one else in the world is Ben Du Toit. (161-62)

Ben continues: "And so it is beside the point to ask: what will become of me? Or: how can I act against my own people?" (163). These passages affirm the need to act, for whatever the cost, there are gains in self-knowledge and as Brink implies, for the future generations.

Another value of Ben's quest is found in examining what Lambley writes of a process which children often undergo and which he feels he has been missing in much of white South Africa. To be sure, this is a process which Ben undergoes, for in the beginning of the book he is an 'innocent' — like a child who faithfully believes what he has been taught to believe in: the justice of a racially corrupt system of white privelege and power. Thus, for the good of Ben's maturity, this innocence is disrupted. Jonathan's and Gordon's deaths are the disrupters and introduce Ben to a knowledge of the corruption of his own family and of the system in general. Brink's thoughts are relevant here on the impact the *knowledge* of oppression can have on those who are *not* members of the oppressed class: "[S]uffering is not reserved for the already deprived: it exists in a peculiarly agonizing form in the minds of those who are *aware* of it: our torture . . . is the existence of others as unequal" (*Writing in a State of Siege*, 47-8). Moreover, to borrow Lambley's description of this disruption for a child, through exposure to conflicting views values, and experiences,

> the continuity between his various cognitive attitudes is gradually broken: the child becomes aware of other views which conflict with

those of his family. These contacts with reality are the essential forces which shape not only a person's perceptions of the world and reality but also his personality and character. By creating conflict and anxiety, they create resistance, dilemmas and problems for the child; how he solves them determines the sort of person he will become. Intelligence and creativeness, for example, [can] arise out of problem-solving and coping with anxiety. . . . In adolescence, how the child solves or copes with these dilemmas [can help] the child develop mature concepts of reality of himself and his role in life and society. (200)

Lambley's ideas are certainly true of the process Ben undergoes, one of conflict which brings him to greater — and valuable — awareness of the true nature of reality, rather than the facade he had believed in. Still, one main dilemma for Ben is that his family and acquaintances — and certainly the authorities who hound him — have not undergone this process, and thus, accept the pseudo-validity of the racist structure of society. And, furthermore, the vast majority of the characters in his family, school, and the authorities who surround Ben are clear examples of the Afrikaner who has been, according to Lambley's theories, "saved from discovering that his ideology and conceptual system is at fault or inhuman or in conflict with reality by the fact that his system is supported" (201), one can say, by the (white) minority of South African society and by the Nationalist power. Consequently, Ben is fated to live in a society where lack of empathy with his dissident views, being isolated (especially after the departure of Melanie), and ultimately being destroyed are veritable givens in his life. Hence, although Ben may feel he has no victory, in contrast to the Afrikaner community of the novel, if Lambley's theories were applied, he does. For the Afrikaner society of the novel is representative of a "community that protects and insulates itself from reality, [and]the levels of intellectual and emotional development of the majority of its members are stuck . . . at a vastly myopic level" (Lambley 200). In contrast, resistance offers a deeper and growing pool of knowledge, including a knowledge of the nature of society's opposition.

Significantly, a passage which may at first seem like a defeat for Ben develops into an affirmation of his struggle. After being attacked by a Black crowd, Ben's thoughts are central:

I am white. This is the small, terrifying, broken truth of my world. I am white. And because I'm white I am born into a state of privilege. Even if I fight the system which has reduced us to this, I remain white, and favored by the very circumstances I abhor. Even if I'm

In the Grasp of White Primitives 103

hated, and ostracized, and persecuted, nothing can make me black. . . . On the other hand: what can I do but what I have done? . . . By not acting as I did I would be denying the very possibility of that guilt to be bridged. . . . Alone. Alone to the very end. I. Stanley. Melanie. Every one of us. But to have been granted the grace of meeting and touching so fleetingly; is that not the most awesome and wonderful thing one can hope for in this world? (304-5).

This passage is one of the most important in the book. For here, Ben realizes that suffering can build a bridge to the future. He also realizes that in such painful experiences, the future is being decided. Consequently, although to many South Africans Ben may seem quixotic, to himself he has proved adequate to the "something" to which he referred in the prologue.

Ben, therefore, may be hunted like a wounded animal and physically crushed by the end. Yet, it is his victory to which narrator refers, significantly, in light of Ben's above thoughts (and in light of the behavior and beliefs of much of white society in the novel). The narrative itself attempts to make sure that among readers, "[I]t will not be possible for any man [who knows Ben's story] ever to say again: I know nothing about it" (316). The passing on of knowledge is the true mission of Brink's novel. Moreover, the main impact Brink strives to have on the reader can be summarized by referring once again to Miller's ideas in *For Your Own Good*:

All that we can do, as I see it, is to affirm and lend our support to the human objects of manipulation in their attempts to become aware and help them become conscious of their malleability and articulate their feelings so that they will be able to use their own resources to defend themselves against the soul murder that threatens them. (276)

In concluding my discussion of Brink's *A Dry White Season*, I will allow our imaginary friend to ask a question. "This novel is about apartheid," he states. "Of what relevance is it to us now?" First, I would stress that the novel illustrates the price many have paid for the present changes in South Africa to take place. Second, the novel stands as testimony to the nature and the consequences of totalitarianism. Finally, the psychological and sociological themes represented in the novel contain key aspects of knowledge all of us need to know to combat bigotry. Hence, while *A Dry White Season* may now seem ripped from yesterday's headlines, it has timeless insights into the human cost incurred during the march towards freedom.

Notes

1. Andre Brink, *Writing in a State of Siege* (New York: Summit Boods, 1983), 52. All subsequent references to this edition.
2. Brink, *A Dry White Season* (New York: Penguin Books, 1984), 161. All subsequent references to this edition.
3. Peter Lambley, *The Psychology of Apartheid* (Athens, Georgia: University of Georgia Press, 1980), 220.
4. Mel Watkins, "A Novelist's Passionate Indictment," *New York Times Book Review* 23 (1980); 15.
5. I.D. MacCrone, *Race Attitudes in South Africa* (New York: Oxford University Press, 1937), 253.
6. Alice Miller, *For Your Own Good*, (New York: Noonday Press, 1990), 9.
7. John Bradshaw, *Bradshaw On: The Family* (Deerfield Beach, Florida: Health Communications, Inc., 1988), 4.
8. Joseph Richman, "Family Determinants of Suicide Potential," *Identifying Suicide Potential*, ed. Dorothy B. Anderson and Lenora McLean (New York: Behavioral Publication, 1971), 34.
9. Franz Boas, *The Mind of Primitive Man*, (1911; reprint, New York: The Macmillan Company, 1938), 224
10. Ernst Cassirer, *The Myth of the State* (Garden City, New York: Doubleday and Company, Inc., 1955), 355.
11. William Barrett, *Irrational Man: A Study in Existential Philosophy* (Garden City, New York: Doubleday/Anchor Books, 1958), 35.
12. Albert Camus, *The Myth of Sisyphus and Other Essays*, trans. Justin O'Brien (New York: Alfred A. Knopf, Inc., 1965), 11.
13. Brink, "Writing Against Big Brother: Notes on Apocalyptic Fiction in South Africa," *World Literature Today*, Spring 1984: 189.

Chapter 4

Abrahams' *The Path of Thunder* (1948) and Fugard's *Tsotsi* (1980): Cross Currents with African American Literature

Turning our attention to authors' representations of Black characters, one sees clearly the connection between racial conflict and identity. The South African works under discussion in this chapter have either protagonists who redefine their identities (Athol Fugard's *Tsotsi*) or whose identities are at odds with the dominant society (Peter Abrahams' *The Path of Thunder*, which I do not consider, unlike some critics, to be a mere miscegination novel). As stated before, the subject of identity raises a myriad of other issues. In this chapter, these issues will be discussed in comparison with certain themes found in American literature, especially African American literature.

A striking feature of many South African works is how the authors discuss certain topics that are also found in American literature. One could make an interesting comparison, for example, between Nadine Gordimer and the writings of the white southern 'radical' Lillian Smith, including *Killers of the Dream* and *The Winner Names the Age*. One might also contrast how Sarah Gertrude Millin, in *God's Stepchildren*, and James Weldon Johnson, in *Autobiography of an Ex-Colored Man*, have diametrically opposed race theories. My primary subject in this chapter is a comparison of the portrayals of the impact of racial conflict on identity (i.e., the identities of both the oppressed and the oppressor) in Abrahams' *The Path of Thunder* and both W.E.B. DuBois' story "Of the Coming of John" and Langston Hughes's short story "Home"; and a comparison of Fugard's *Tsotsi* and Richard Wright's *Native Son*. Issues raised include what similarities there are between the works of these authors of different continents. Also central to an examination of *The Path of Thunder* is whether Abrahams goes beyond his American counterparts in depicting why the protagonist no longer fits in with his society; in what restrictions of racism the protagonist violates during his return home; and in whether Abrahams proposes a solution to interracial strife in the novel, as some critics have suggested.

Another work that is interesting in comparison with treatments of the impact of racial conflict on identity in African American literature is Athol Fugard's *Tsotsi*. The story of a brutal young thug, whose life suddenly changes to something more meaningful, *Tsotsi* is especially interesting in comparison with Richard Wright's *Native Son* in several regards. How do the authors' treatments of the protagonists differ? What are the essential similarities and differences between the white South African author and the African American writer in handling similar themes? How do Wright and Fugard both use existentialism in their works? These are some of the central issues raised by a comparison of Fugard's and Wright's novels. On considering Fugard and Wright and on examining Abrahams, DuBois and Hughes, therefore, one finds revealed interesting questions on the variations found in similar pieces of literature, principally concerning the impact of race and power on identity. Before going any further, I want to emphasize that this chapter is not a comparison of South African and United States history. Nor do I wish to insinuate that the way in which these two countries have implemented racism is identical. For instance, one marked difference between South Africa, in which law upheld racism, and the United States is that in America *de jure* racism and segregation (especially in the South) was ultimately significantly dismantled by legal decisions in the twentieth century; Brown v. the Board of Education is an excellent example of the Supreme Court's finding that "separate is inherently unequal" concerning such institutions as education. This concept — that "separate is inherently unequal" — is completely incompatible with the laws and philosophies of South Africa when ruled by whites. As George M. Fredrickson points out in *White Supremacy*, for instance:

Abrahams' The Path of Thunder *(1948) and Fugard's* Tsotsi *(1980)*

The most important spatial aspect of white minority rule in twentieth-century South Africa has been the territorial division of the country on the principle of "possessory segregation" as originally mandated by the Native Land Act of 1913. This legislation prohibited Africans from purchasing land outside designated native reserves and even from entering into sharecropping arrangements in the "white" agricultural areas. Its larger implication, made clearer in subsequent legislation, was that the reserves were the only places where Africans could reside except to the extent that the interests and convenience of the whites required them to be elsewhere. African laborers were needed on farms outside the reserves, but their status was to be that of contract wage laborers or labor tenants rather than sharecroppers or "squatters."[1]

Still, while one might think that such legislation flies in the face of United States' legal principles, it is precisely on this point that one finds the great importance of *de facto* segregation and racism (something that will be central as legal changes take place in South Africa). In the novels I discuss, Richard Wright's *Native Son* has as its foundation the *de facto* racism that Blacks have often found in the North, e.g., the ghettoization of Blacks in slums, with buildings often owned my white 'slumlords.' Both similarly and contrastingly, Athol Fugard's *Tsotsi*, which shares several major themes with *Native Son*, as I will analyze later, concentrates on the legalities of apartheid — e.g., the pass laws and Blacks' removal from their land to create white areas — which foster a deterministic pattern and economics deprivation which limit Fugard's characters to an equal degree as *de facto* segregation and racism limit the lives of Richard Wright's characters. Thus, without reducing the two countries as mirror images of each other — George Fredrickson's monumental *White Supremacy* certainly refutes the idea — one certainly can assert that the writers compared in this chapter imagined many similar injustices and tragedies as a result of South African and American racism.

Bringing out the aforementioned comparative literary themes is an important sub-genre of African American literature: the story of a Black man who returns home after being away and of the conflicts that ensue in the racially oppressive environment in which he finds himself. This feature of African American literature can be found in W.E.B. DuBois' "Of the Coming of John," in *The Souls of Black Folk*; Langston Hughes's "Home" and "Father and Son" in *The Ways of White Folks*; and Hughes's play *Mulatto* (another version of his short story "Father and Son"), among other works. This aspect of African American literature, moreover, entails several characteristics. First, the protagonist fails, either consciously or unconsciously, to accept his 'place' as appointed by whites on returning home. Second, the writer emphasizes the gaps between the protagonist and the society (of his home) and why these gaps exist. Also, the authors note what the heroes intellectually 'bring' home with them that sets them apart, which is related to how they have lived while away and how this new knowledge and way of living affect them in their 'old' environment. Furthermore, the works also tell of the white response to the protagonist, which ultimately culminates in what is both a historical and literary characteristic of racist white reactions in racially volatile situations—that is, white violence. When one examines all these characteristics, it is especially interesting that in *The Path of Thunder*, Peter Abrahams also wrote in this sub-genre, and the work entails all of the above characteristics. On all of the above mentioned themes which illuminate both a metamorphosis in a Black individual and the racist reaction to it, sociologist William J. Wilson's *Power, Racism and Privilege*, which is a comparative study of America and South Africa, is revealing. Illuminating the white reaction to Blacks, Wilson quotes Herbert Blumer's important work, "Race Prejudice as a Sense of Group Position":

> A basic understanding of race prejudice must be caught in the process by which groups form images of themselves. This process . . . is fundamentally a collective process. . . . To characterize another racial group is, by opposition, to define one's own group. This is the equivalent of placing the two groups in relation to each other, or defining their position vis-a-vis each other. It is the sense of social position emerging from the collective process of characterization which provides the basis of race prejudice.[2]

Most importantly, and most relevant to the representations of whites in the fiction, Wilson further summarizes Blumer's ideas on the basic feelings constituting prejudice:

> (1) an attitude that the [oppressed] race is inferior, (2) a sense that the [subordinate] race is intrinsically alien and different, (3) a feeling of prior claim to certain rights and privileges, and (4) an apprehensiveness that [the subordinate race] plans to encroach on or challenge the dominant group's prerogatives. . . . [I]t is the fourth

feeling, the apprehensiveness that the subordinate racial group is about to challenge the dominant group's position, that is essential to "race prejudice." This fear is often reflected in the dominant group's hostile cries that the subordinate racial group is "getting out of place." (36)

These ideas all have a fictional correlative in the works under discussion by DuBois, Hughes and Abrahams. Thus, on reading *The Path of Thunder*, one can see that the literary feature of the Black (or 'Colored', in this case) hero who returns home, and all of the resulting features of this type of literature, were easily adaptable to the South African situation. It is important, therefore, to compare how a South African deals with a tradition found earlier in African American literature, and how his concerns are both similar to and different from his American counterpart's concerns.

The influence of DuBois and Hughes on Peter Abrahams is clear. In *Tell Freedom*, Abrahams discusses how important African American literature was in his intellectual development. In this autobiography, Abrahams tells how as a young man he discovered Harlem Renaissance writers while working at the Bantu Men's Social Center. He recalls several passages from the literature, including poetry by Langston Hughes. Though he does not mention at any point *The Ways of White Folks*, he certainly was familiar with and admiring of Hughes. Furthermore, he does discuss the great impact DuBois' *The Souls of Black Folk* had on him, stating that "DuBois might have been writing about my land and my people . . . DuBois had given me the key to the understanding of my world. The Negro is not free."[3] Moreover, Abrahams tells how this last line — quoted from DuBois' book — touched his life:

> "The Negro is not free" . . . I remembered those "Reserved for Europeans Only" signs; I remembered no white boys ever carried bags at the market or ran from the police; I remembered my long walks in the white sections of the city, and the lavatories, and the park benches and the tearoom; . . . I remembered spittle on my face . . . "The Negro is not free." (185)

Considering this deep admiration for DuBois and the personal connection he felt with *The Souls of Black Folk*, Abrahams certainly had read "Of the Coming of John" and it is not surprising that there are parallels between that work and *The Path of Thunder*.

First, it is essential to discuss DuBois' work. Education plays a major role in shaping the protagonist's identity in DuBois' semi-autobiographical "Of the Coming of John." In the eyes of the people of his hometown, John plays a role similar to Hickey in O'Neill's *The Ice Man Cometh* — he is to be the source of revitalizing the community (in this case, by establishing and teaching in a new school). Yet, education also makes John have an irreconcilable gap with the racial structures of his home town, in the sense that his education, as much as it excites the Blacks when they think of his return, causes consternation and disapproval among the whites. This split is shown as DuBois writes:

> The white folk of Altamaha voted John a goodboy — fine plough-hand, good in the rice fields, handy everywhere, and always good-natured and respectful. But they shook their heads when his mother wanted to send him off to school. "It'll spoil him, — ruin him," they said: and they talked as though they knew. But full half of the black folk followed him to the station.[4]

For emphasis, DuBois reiterates that whites, in particular the white racist Judge, feel that education "will spoil" John (365). Certainly, John returns home a more serious and perceptive person than he was when he left—one who will not merely accept his 'place.' To the Judge, this is a sign of John's 'spoiling.' To DuBois, however, it is clearly a sign of John's deepening maturity.

What 'unfits' John for his hometown on his return? After being away, in school and travelling for seven years, John returns a somber and pensive man. As with the returns of Roy in "Home" and Lanny in *The Path of Thunder*, some of the people of John's hometown who greet him notice the differences immediately: "The people were distinctly bewildered. This silent, cold man — was this John? Where was his smile and hearty hand-grasp? 'peared kind o' down in the mouf,' said the Methodist preacher thoughtfully. 'Seemed mostus stuck-up,' complained a Baptist sister." (371) This gap that some of the people feel exists between themselves and John has resulted from his education, work and travel. Something of a ne'er do well initially in college, John sobers into a knowledge of the racial conditions of America in general and his hometown in particular. As DuBois writes:

> [W]e who watched him felt four more years of change, which almost transformed the tall grave man who bowed to us commencement

morning. . . . He looked now for the first time sharply about him, and wondered he had seen so little before. He grew slowly to feel almost for the first time the Veil that lay between him and the white world; he first noticed the oppression that had not seemed oppression before, differences that erstwhile seemed natural, restraints and slights that in his boyhood days had gone unnoticed or been greeted with a laugh. He felt angry now when men do not call him "Mister," he clenched his hands at the "Jim Crow" cars, and chafed at the color-line that hemmed in him and his. A tinge of sarcasm crept into his speech, and a vague bitterness into his life. . . . Daily he found himself shrinking from the choked and narrow life of his native town. And yet he always planned to go back to Altamaha,—always planned to work there. (367)

This passage makes clear both John's consciousness of race and how it has deepened over time. Moreover, this passage seems to foreshadow John's feeling of having a mission on returning home. As DuBois makes evident, John's intention is to "settle the Negro problem there" (370), even if it means his death at the hands of whites — "[I]f I perish, I perish" (370) — unfortunately, a forecast of things to come.

In addition, after his return home, John is so unsuited to accept his 'place' that he even unconsciously violates it. Knocking unconsciously at the white Judge's front door,

He had schooled himself to be respectful to the Judge, and then he blundered into his front door. And all the time he had meant right,— and yet, and yet, somehow he found it so hard and strange to fit in his old surroundings again, to find his place in the world about him. (373)

Thus, one sees that the idea of a more free, more fair way of life is so ingrained in John's mind, he cannot even consciously stop himself from widening the gap between himself and his surroundings.

Another important topic in all three works is that the role of racist whites is central in their reacting against the Black protagonists who have a strengthened identity on their returning home. White reaction in all three works is almost uniformly negative to the protagonist, who no longer accepts a racist-decided Black "place" in society. In "Of the Coming of John," John at times both consciously and unconsciously violates the idea of "place," thereby gaining white racist antipathy. All of the negative white reactions to John foreshadow a pattern of which Hughes and Abrahams also write. These writers were making fictional portrayals of a societal problem. The white idea of Blacks' spoiling by increased education and culture are all evidence that, as Wilson states in *Power, Racism and Privilege*, "racial caste systems are instances of social stratification" (4). Moreover, Williams emphasizes that "Class or caste membership develops from historical contact in which groups possessing a power advantage have been able to place themselves in superior positions by solidifying a social structure that features a racial stratification system" (7). Wilson's ideas illuminate why a feature of racism is the internalization of a superior position in the caste system not only by whites of high status but even by those who would be considered 'poor white trash.' Thus, this idealized image of one's status (the individual correlative of the group's status) spans the spectrum of different classes of whites. And this unity is racist whites' feelings of hostility — a psychological mob reaction —certainly based, in part, on white fears both of independent Blacks and of independent Blacks who will threaten the hierarchy of whites' and Blacks' respective 'places.'

Already mentioned is the hostility towards John's being educated in the first place. Here, Wilson's and Blumer's comments on white apprehension of losing their superiority if Blacks fail to maintain an inferior position are clearly dramatized. To the whites of the town, as long as he can do manual labor, John is a 'good' Black. But educated, John is "That damn nigger...plum full o' fool notions" (371). Furthermore, when John has to pay a visit to the Judge and inadvertently knocks at the front door, the Judge's own racism causes him to be angry. Most importantly, however, are the Judge's pronouncements during this visit on how he sees his relationship with Blacks in general and John in particular. The Judge states:

> You know I am a friend to your people . . . but you and I both know, John, that in this country the Negro must remain subordinate, and can never expect to be the equal of white men. In their place, your people can be honest and respectful. . . . But when they want to reverse nature, and rule white men, and marry white women, and sit in my parlor, then, by god! We'll hold them under if we have to lynch every nigger in the land. (373)

In this passage, one is reminded not only of Wilson and Blumer but of Peter Abrahams' comments about white South Africans in an essay in *Return to Goli*. Abrahams states:

Abrahams' The Path of Thunder *(1948) and Fugard's* Tsotsi *(1980)* 115

> The white saw the facts as [he thought] they were. . . . He had defeated this Black savage. . . . He was the superior White man. God had made him so. It was God's will that he should occupy such a position. Nothing that happened could change this. This was something fixed.[5]

Also, the Judge certainly means his statement as a warning to John not to get 'uppity' (it is a significant detail that the Judge fails to ask John to sit during his visit) or to try 'too much' to improve his community. The threat of violence is also important, both as a literary and historical tradition, that the story — in fact, also "Home" and *Path of Thunder* — ends with the killing of the protagonist by whites, for certainly one of the whites in "Of the Coming of John" would have "the coiling twisted rope" (377) to avenge the Judge's son's death at John's hands in defense of his sister, whom the white man was attacking. White violence, then, plays a central role in the tales of educated Blacks returning home. It is the epitome of white racists' reaction to a strong Black identity which threatens to lessen their power; that is, to refuse to allow this identity to exist. Perhaps most frightening is the fact that white violence is — amazingly — merely part of a continuum in the hateful logic of racism. Again, Wilson's work provides an important analysis. Wilson states that racism has "a normative quality" (34). In other words, racism produces certain societal or group norms indicating the way that "dominant members ought to relate to or treat minority members" (34). Thus, individual racism translates into collective racist behaviors. Furthermore, as Williams explains:

> The more dominant-group members identify with their group position, the greater is the likelihood that they will strive to perpetuate their position. It is out of this process that group interests are defined and special norms are developed in turn to protect these interests. (42)

This analysis sheds light on why writers in America and South Africa have focused on how changes in Black identity which threaten whites' real and/or imagined status are met with a white protectionist stance— a stance which has murder as it ultimate conclusion.

Hughes's "Home" also carries a powerful theme similar to DuBois' story. According to Arnold Rampasad's *The Life of Langston Hughes*, on reading "Home," literary agent Maxim Lieber told Hughes, "I can imagine how shocked every bourgeois editor in town would be" by the story.[6] A story entailing racial violence, it bears similarities to DuBois' tale. As does John, Roy, a musician who has lived in Europe, also experiences a gap between himself and his hometown in the South. His sophistication provokes a reaction in his small hometown of Hopkinsville which reveals white antipathy to a cultured and sophisticated Black. As a group of whites sees Roy disembark from the train, Hughes writes:

> "An uppity nigger," said the white loafer when they saw him standing, slim and elegant on the station platform . . . surrounded by his bags with the bright stickers. Roy had got off a Pullman—something unusual for a Negro in those parts.[7]

In addition, his childhood playmate greets Roy by calling him "boy" (35). Moreover, when Roy goes to play the violin for Miss Reese's class in the white high school, the school children merely think of him as a "dressed-up nigger...[who] played a lot of funny pieces" (43). Thus, Roy is primarily an object of disrespect for whites. In essence, these whites' sense of their identities, which rest on a false sense of superiority, are threatened by the presence of a Black man who is clearly more educated and cultured than they. In response, they stigmatize Roy's identity, attributing negative qualities to him which exist solely in their own insecure minds. That their reactions are attacking ones stress that Hughes, like DuBois, felt that white racists will try not to allow Blacks to develop identities which threaten white superiority — to the point of employing verbal violence, which is often the direct predecessor to physical violence.

Of course, the final incident in the story epitomizes white racist creation of a stigmatized identity for a Black man which is completely incorrect in its paranoia regarding Blacks. As Roy talks to Miss Reese, the white music teacher, a movie crowded with whites lets out, and he is hit by a white man. Hughes then writes: "[T]he crowd, passing by and seeing, objected to a Negro talking to a white woman — insulting a white woman — attacking a WHITE woman — RAPING A WHITE WOMAN" (47). Tellingly, Roy's old white playmate spits in his face. As happens in Abrahams' *The Path of Thunder*, therefore, a male-female interracial interaction is the excuse for the murder of the male protagonist.

Also, as Roy is being beaten, it is clear that the white crowd wants to knock him down a peg, to strip him of his culture and sophistication: "They trampled on his hat and cane and gloves as a dozen men tried to get to him to pick him up — so someone else should have the pleasure of knocking him down again. They struggled over the privilege of knocking him down" (47). White violence, therefore, Hughes suggests, is prompted by irrational hate, anger and an insecure need to assert threatened 'superiority' in the face of a Black identity which causes such whites' to feel their self-image of superiority to Blacks is threatened. Such whites' fears of inferiority are submerged by their displacing their inferior status onto the Black who points out — by his very identity — their ignorance and sterility. Thus, the murder of a Black man is actually the whites' defense mechanism to fight for their idealized self-image and, therefore, against a Black person who even unintentionally calls this image and status into question. As in "Home" and the "Of the Coming of John," the protagonist in Peter Abrahams' *The Path of Thunder* is 'welcomed' back to his hometown by meeting with the racist attitude of whites. Just as Roy in "Home" appears to be too well dressed for the liking of whites who first see him, so, too, is Lanny, who is 'Colored.' Also, it is clear that in all three works, the heroes' rude awakening by whites has to do with their having been away so long that they have forgotten — and later reject — that they are supposed to have a 'place' and to act and look the part the 'place' requires. This fact obviously causes whites to sometimes react violently. The veracity of this statement is immediately evident as Lanny gets off the train at Stilleveld, his home. Having lived in Cape Town, Lanny assumes he can be assertive with whites. For example, he tells the white ticket collector, in polite conversation, that he is returning home after seven years (the same number of years John was away in DuBois' story). The man merely gives him a cold glare, showing his resentment for Lanny's alleged familiarity. This white hostility towards Lanny continues as he goes to a coffee stall. One man (jealously) says of Lanny, "It looks like a ape in a better Sunday suit that I have."[8] He also "contempt[uously]" (12) refers to 'Coloreds' as "bastard[s]" (12). It is important to note Lanny's reactions during this scene. As do Roy in "Home" and John in DuBois' story, Lanny retains his dignity in the face of racism, thinking of the white men at the coffee stall, "[T]his is South Africa. . . . At least they won't frighten this colored . . . hurt me, yes, but frighten me, no" (13). Moreover, as one of men at the stall tauntingly asks Lanny if he has "any fancy titles" (13), Lanny is again assertive in stating that he has two degrees. This reply causes him to be hit in the mouth. Furthermore, noticing Lanny's fountain pen, one of the white men shows more bitter hostility. These, incidents, along with Lanny's being summoned by the important white man Gert

Villier so that Gert can decide if he approves of Lanny's plans for a school, all show the irrational degree to which racist whites protect their sense of power and superiority over people they oppress.

Another important topic is that as in DuBois' and Hughes's stories, it is immediately evident that Lanny's identity is changed to the extent that he no longer 'fits in' with his hometown. First, as with DuBois' John and Hughes's Roy, Lanny's education and his dealing with whites as equals in Cape Town mark him as being different from those in his poor, rural town of Stilleveld. The gap between Lanny and his hometown is immediately evident after his arrival with his mother's thoughts:

> Could this be my son. . . . If it was, then time did strange things to people. Changed them. Made them different from what they had been. But here [Stilleveld] everything was the same. The other children who had grown up with him were still the same. . . . there was nothing different, nothing new about them. Only her Lanny was different (21).

Also, Lanny simultaneously feels discomfort at being home and dissatisfaction at the relative lack of progress of his people. Lanny's change while being away, then, has created a gap between him and his hometown.

Moreover, Lanny's conflict with the powerful white Gert over starting a school also indicates an essential aspect of his Lanny's identity — his lack of acceptance of a 'place' for himself in life. This rejection of inferiorization is made evident in an encounter which recalls John's encounter with the judge in DuBois' work. Gert Villier, the big white '*baas*' of Stilleveld, is angry that Lanny would think of starting a school without consulting the whites. Furthermore, noting Lanny's assertiveness, Gert attempts to berate Lanny:

> You are proud. You feel as good as any man . . . you have forgotten your place! . . . We don't like that sort of spirit here, Mister Swartz. We like things the way they have always been. The colored people are satisfied. They are happy as they are. They understand us and we understand them. Remember that! We don't like things the way they are run in Cape Town; we don't want anything changed here, do you understand? I want to warn you now, Swartz. . . . If you make one wrong step, Swartz, you will get more trouble than is good for any living man. We do not like independent bastards here, Mister Swartz (63).

Gert concludes this speech with a clear threat. And following his leaving the meeting with Gert, Lanny is beaten up. Abrahams, therefore, like DuBois and Hughes, quickly introduces the idea that the assertion of equality will be met by white violence — a point he reiterates with the cataclysmic ending of the book with the deaths of Lanny and his white love, Sarie — Gert's adoptive relative.

Especially important in comparing the protagonists of three works is noting their reactions to whites' hostility towards them. As with John and Roy, Lanny's desire to remain dignified, for instance, is evident in his encounter with the white men at the coffee stall. Plus, as stated earlier, Lanny, like the other two protagonists, merely by being who he is — an educated man — meets with white hostility. He also — as do John and Roy — denies inferiority, by his mere experiences and existence, and defies any stereotypical racist notions of a Black or 'Colored' person's 'place' in a racist society. Lanny seems to be pondering these ideas as Abrahams writes after Lanny's being hit by the man at the coffee stall:

> South Africa, Lanny thought, this is South Africa, and this man in front of him resented him because he was educated and showed independence. If he had been humble the man probably would have been kind to him, smiled and sent him away. [As John in DuBois' story was liked by whites for manual labor.] This was still the old struggle for conquest. The history of his country. This man in front of him had to dominate him, he was fearful in case he did not. This was the history of South Africa in stark, brutal reality. (13)

Yet Lanny, like DuBois' John, is committed to educating his people and broadening their horizons so they will not think or act like human beings who are inferior to whites. Until his love for the white Sarie causes him and her to decide to leave the country, these are his commitments. Thus, education is central both to the interracial conflict and to the rejection of one's 'place.'

In spite of the many similarities, there is a major way in which *The Path of Thunder* differs from DuBois' and Hughes's works. One of the most interesting aspects of *The Path of Thunder* is Abrahams' treatment of love and how it is connected to the relationship between racial conflict and identity. Because Abrahams is thought of as a liberal humanist, it is often argued by critics that in the novel, he is arguing that love grants a couple the ability to transcend the racial issue — at least, certainly in the couple's private thoughts about each other and, perhaps, in a more global way. Thus, Abrahams is *not* writing the novel because interracial love stories are "obligatory"[9] as Michael Wade says, for South African authors; nor is the book 'sentimental' for treating the theme of interracial love and having a deterministic ending as Wade also charges (59-60). Neither is the novel a "failure"[10] as Kolawole Ogungbesan states in *The Writing of Peter Abrahams*, because according to him an author can only deal with interracial love by "follow[ing] the government's example, tak[ing] sex out of the bedroom and put[ting] it on the pages of the newspapers" (53). In fact, Abrahams' book does a vast amount more (and other) than these charges give it credit for. The point of view that Abrahams is a sentimental idealist might result from reading the end of his earlier novel *Mine Boy* (out of context) and taking it to be Abrahams' total vision, as he often raises the issue of whether people of different races can live in harmony. In *Mine Boy*, Abrahams writes of the protagonist's, Xuma's, thoughts:

> He felt light and free and gay. People were people. Not white and black people. Ordinary people. And one could understand a white person as well as a black person. And be sorry for white as well as black. There were no white people. Only people. The vision carried him along. He could see himself and Eliza and Paddy and Paddy's woman all sitting at a little table in one of those little tea places in the heart of Johannesburg and drinking tea and laughing and talking. And around them would be other people all happy and without colour. And everywhere in the land it was so. . . . People were happy. And oh the laughter! . . . If only it were so.[11]

Certainly, Abrahams was of two minds concerning the topic of interracial harmony and how it can be achieved. On the one hand, he felt true interracial love could be a radical act (which is echoed in Mako's thoughts in *The Path of Thunder*). On the other hand, in *Tell Freedom* Abrahams also states: "Perhaps life had a meaning that transcended race and colour. If it had, I could not find it in South Africa" (304). His mind, therefore, was in debate about the issues of interracial harmony. And, in fact, *The Path of Thunder* reflects this debate, and is certainly not idealistic in its treatment of love. Clearly, some of the most intriguing issues for the serious reader of the novel is how Abrahams develops the debate over whether love can make a strong political statement; whether the couple in love can find that love transcends the racism of society; or, whether, in fact, interracial love awakens those racists in society to destroy what is considered in a racist society to be highly objectionable, if not intolerable. And is this last factor, in comparison to "Home" and in contrast to "Of the Coming of John," the final factor in the protagonist's destruction? Each of these issues must be dealt with in order to deepen one's understanding of *The Path of Thunder*.

Lanny and Sarie's love is supposedly "man's attempt to overcome obstacles," according to O.R. Dathorne.[12] Though this may be the case, it is clear that even on a one-to-one level Lanny and Sarie *don't* "overcome" even the obstacle of their own racial thinking towards each other. In fact, it is especially important to look at the book in a way critics have neglected — as Abrahams' *debate* about whether the interracial love of Lanny and Sarie can overcome or transcend the ways the thoughts of a racist society would both influence their thinking and mar their romance *or* whether such a love is so aberrant in such a society corrupted by racism that it is a love which will be unfulfilled by the couple and destroyed by the racist society.

Many aspects of the novel lead to the interpretation of it as a *debate* over whether Lanny and Sarie's love transcends their own racist-conditioned thoughts or reveal and perhaps heighten them (both in the couple and in society). For instance, as Lanny looks at Sarie and thinks of his former 'Colored' girlfriend Celia, his thoughts go back and forth:

> [T]he girl a few yards away from him was a white girl and this was the country whose laws, written and unwritten, said in effect: "There shall be no equality between black and white in church and state." Remember that Lanny Swartz, remember that, he told himself. But his eyes stole to where Sarie stood and there was a jump of joy in his heart. (149)

Abrahams continues,

> Think of Celia, he told himself . . . [S]he is your kind. With her there would be no trouble. Half-caste and half-caste belong. Black and white don't. It's unnatural. Think of Celia. . . . But Sarie was close by . . . deep in his mind, eating into his flesh and torturing his brain (149-50).

Lanny's circular thinking shows not only how people are trained to think racially ("like belongs with like") but how he simultaneously knows that a relationship with Sarie will bring trouble from others and how he and Sarie would be going against one of the foundations of a racist, segregated society. Though the passage ends, it is clear that Lanny cannot really rest on one interpretation of what he *should* do, though it is clear that he finds Sarie irresistible.

A few aspects of the book reinforce that Abrahams is using his characters to debate the role of interracial love in South African society. For example, in a passage which conveys Sarie's thoughts, Abrahams writes:

> She would help him [Lanny] remove the dry tightness form his heart. She would do it because it made her happy and he would be happy too. . . . But above all she would do it because she couldn't help herself. Because he was a man and she was a woman. It wasn't her fault that he was born colored or that she was born white. They had no choice in the matter. They were just born. Nobody asked them. And so they would live and love without asking anybody. It wasn't anybody's business. They didn't want to love. They just loved. It happened. They hadn't said a word about it. There was no need to. Nobody would harm him. (168)

These thoughts, Abrahams makes clear, are truly naive — for as shown elsewhere, her adoptive uncle Gert, with whom Sarie has a strained relationship, has the power to disrupt Lanny's plans to start a school should he decide to do so. Moreover, the story of the romance between the 'Colored' Mad Sam and the dead Sarie shows that love, in this novel, does not conquer hate but, in fact, provokes it. Furthermore, the catastrophic ending of the book with the killings of Lanny and Sarie by whites points out how naive the feeling of safety is at the end of the quotation above. Abrahams, therefore, is not arguing in *The Path of Thunder* that love can overcome the 'obstacle' of hate or of society. In fact, Sarie herself later implicitly realizes the naivete of her earlier ideas when Abrahams writes,

> [S]he did not want him [Lanny] to be afraid. There was nothing to be afraid of. He was a colored and she was white. But she didn't feel different, not with him. He was a man and she was a woman. A boy and a girl. And suddenly a frightful thought half-crept into her mind — what would Gert do if he knew? — but she choked it down, vigorously. No one would know. (159)

In this passage, Abrahams makes clear that he is writing a debate on interracial love by making Sarie's thoughts somewhat circular — she can only feel that her and Lanny's love is safe by denial of reality, which is represented by her knowledge of Lanny's fear and by her thoughts of Gert, which she quickly represses. Thus, it seems, denial and repression of the South African reality which surround the characters are the only way they (or, I should say Sarie, in particular) can protect an illusion of transcendence of obstacles. Considering Lanny and Sarie's relationship, one should also remember Abrahams words in *Tell Freedom*. He states:

> Real friendship, friendship that had the creative force of building up wider areas of understanding, was impossible between black and white in our country. The precondition, freedom of association, did not exist. Those whites who associated openly with blacks were fore-doomed to . . . disaster. (256)

Yet another passage shows how the characters' sometimes repressed thoughts dictate that Abrahams is, throughout, debating the efficacy of love in overcoming the 'obstacle' of racism. After initially becoming attracted to Sarie, Lanny

> was acutely conscious that he was on the highveld and that Sarie Villier was a white girl and that he had felt more at ease walking with her than he had been for a long time. He took this uneasy awareness to bed with him. It haunted his sleep and made it restless and full of horrifying dreams. (127)

This vacillation from feeling safe to feeling in danger is also echoed in Sarie's thoughts. But the most important aspect of this passage is that it shows Abrahams' use of foreshadowing, for the "horrifying dreams" caused by Lanny's relationship with Sarie are realized by their cataclysmic deaths at the end of the novel.

Another aspect of the novel that undermines the idea that Abrahams is both a sentimentalist and a believer in the power of love to help a couple at least transcend their own racism are Sarie's views on race — even as the subject is related to Lanny. It is clear that Sarie can only 'transcend' race if she *denies* its existence in Lanny. It is important to her that he be different from other "Coloreds" — and *not* one of 'them.'

Sarie's race-centered views are evident after she becomes attracted to Lanny as, she claims, just another human being and not as a 'Colored' man. Though this claim may seem the liberal humanist's idea of thinking non-racially, Sarie's self-proclaimed lack of bigotry does not extend very far. In fact, it does not even extend to Lanny's sister, Mabel, whom, one would assume, she sees daily as both work in the Villier house. (Sarie, as her father was adopted by Gert's father, is considered a poor relation and thus works as the housekeeper.) Despite seeing Mabel regularly, Sarie still views her first and last as a racial entity. As Abrahams writes:

> Sarie studied her [Mabel] carefully. This was Lanny Swartz's sister. But there was nothing of Lanny Swartz about her . . . Nothing. This was a colored girl. She behaved like a colored girl. Like all colored people Sarie had ever known. . . . Sarie smiled. A colored girl. Like all the others. Nervous and respectful. Only her brother was different. Didn't behave like a colored person. (101-2)

She doesn't stop to realize that some of that nervousness comes from Mabel's consciousness of Sarie's staring at her which makes her "trembl[e]" (102) and act "nervously" (102). Moreover, the lines, "Sarie smiled. A colored girl. Like all the others" can only be interpreted as if Sarie is smiling in self-satisfied smugness, looking down on this 'mere' "colored girl" — the sister of the man she loves. By looking down on Mabel, it seems implicitly as if Sarie is giving herself assurance of her own race-tinted outlook, and 'redeeming' her attraction to Lanny, for he is not 'Colored' to her. She can only transcend racism, it seems, by stripping 'Coloreds' of their membership in any race. As Dathorne states, "Sarie comes to a . . . naive and ridiculous conclusion when she confesses that Lanny's sister, who works for her family, is 'a colored person' but Lanny is 'just a person'" (140). In any case, she remains a racist — a 'benign' one, perhaps, compared to the brutality of Gert, but a racist nonetheless.

Most important in examining whether Sarie is, in fact, a bigot are her attitudes towards Lanny concerning her love for him and her view towards his race. Sarie constantly reiterates that she thinks of Lanny only as "a person" devoid of race — even over his objections. For example, Sarie states that unlike other 'Coloreds' he does not seem afraid of whites for he looks people in the eye and is assertive, which makes him unlike "the others" — 'Coloreds,' that is. Importantly, instead of taking this as notice of his 'humanity,' Lanny states, "I'm not different. . . . I was born here, I'm one of them. The only difference is that I've had chances they've never had. I've been able to see and do and learn things that are foreign to them" (121). Still, instead of taking Lanny's word that he is *both* 'Colored' and 'a person,' Sarie dismisses his response by stating that she still feels he is unlike any other 'Coloreds' she's met, which results in her thinking that Lanny is "not like a colored person. You are just a person" (121). In response to this naive assertion, Lanny tries to explain to Sarie that 'Coloreds' are all 'persons' whose behavior, instead of being innate 'Colored' responses as Sarie seems to think, is conditioned by the environment. As Lanny says, in response to Sarie's assertion that he is not like 'Colored' people, "Colored people only behave as they do because the white people force them to do so. If they are left alone and not bullied and given a chance to live and develop like human beings you won't tell me I'm different from them. Even you won't feel different from them. If only they had a chance to be human beings" (121). Thus, it becomes clear in this passage that Sarie and Lanny have differing views on people's humanity — to her it hinges on whether race is overlooked or obliterated by her mental or perceptual machinations. Yet, here, Lanny indicates that society reduces people to behaving in what are perceived as racially stereotypical ways, and given a chance to go beyond these societal restrictions people could be perceived both as part of a race and part of the human race, which is something that Sarie can neither conceptualize nor accept even when Lanny tells it to her. It is clear then that Sarie is *not* a character who can transcend the "obstacle" of her own racialism, let alone society's. Thus, one comes to doubt what Dathorne says about Abrahams' being "solidly on the side of idealism" and speaking out for it (144). In fact, it seems that in Lanny and Sarie's relationship, Abrahams is, again, debating how one can realize another's humanity and what ways of trying to do this are misguided. In this regard, one must remember that though Abrahams may have a humanist bent, he is also the same man who wrote in his autobiography that he had never been aware of a meaning for life in South Africa that was devoid of racial corruption. Consequently, if Abrahams is an idealist in *The Path of Thunder* it is of a realistic sort, that, as he has Lanny state, looks to the future for a transcendence of racism.

Lanny's debating on love and humanity are especially important to analyze. I refer to Lanny's debate as Abrahams has his character have no chance to come to rest in his feelings. Instead, opposing ideas compete in his mind concerning love, race, and transcendence.

Abrahams shows the complexity of the competing thoughts in Lanny's mind as he ponders his relationship with Sarie. First, he is mindful of Sarie's race even as he thinks of his love for her (something

Sarie fails to be able to do regarding Lanny). Although "he was thinking of Sarie Villier who was a white girl" (134), he still feels that they understand each other to a rare degree. Abrahams continues to present Lanny's debate with himself as he writes that because of their racial difference, only trouble could result from their love, especially regarding his plans to open a school for 'Coloreds,' which Gert would disrupt. Furthermore, Abrahams sums up Lanny's feelings about race in a continuation of the passage quoted above when he writes:

> He wanted to do things for his people, it was true, but he also wanted to be happy. . . . He didn't hate the whites. Only in short spells, when they did him any harm, did he feel bitter. But it passed and he didn't want to fight anybody. . . . Perhaps because he was colored. How did Mako describe it? Living between two worlds. And last night Sarie Villier had been beside him and he hadn't felt like an outsider, like one living between two worlds. He had felt at home with her. "But nothing can come of it, " he said without feeling. (135)

Still, Lanny does at times feel that his relationship with Sarie can make him forget their racial differences (164). Hence, instead of being static in his views of race, love, and transcendence, unlike Sarie, Lanny is engaged in debate with himself. This aspect of the book is especially important, for one sees that Abrahams is not writing a story marred by "sentimentality" (52) as Wade charges is characteristic of Abrahams' works. For Abrahams is not merely writing a tale of love as an antidote to racism; rather, he is showing how arduous it is to overcome racism — one's own and society's — and how difficult it is to overcome racial "obstacles" in oneself and others.

Finally, there is an important point tied between *The Path of Thunder* again to "Of the Coming of John" and "Home." The major example of white power protecting itself comes at the end of the book, not only with Lanny's and Sarie's deaths at the hands of racist whites, but also with the distortion of the facts of the killings in the newspapers. The paper, supplied with the story by one of Gert's henchmen, states that Lanny "had run amok" (279) and killed both Gert and Sarie, thus absolving the whites of these deaths. Abrahams' work, consequently, like Hughes's and DuBois' stories, ends with the final assertion of white power — murder. Moreover, as stated earlier, as in the other stories (especially DuBois'), the protagonist's education plays a large role in threatening whites. This fact is emphasized by the final line of

The Path of Thunder, from the news story: "The story ended with a strong protest against educating black people" (279) — as if education provokes destruction of whites by Blacks. Nevertheless, white violence is the 'final solution' when each of the three protagonists inadvertently elicits a response of envy and hatred by whites. Moreover, when one examines the end, especially the deaths of Lanny and the Afrikaners, Sarie and the racist Gert, it is necessary to remember Abrahams' words from *Return to Goli*: white South Africans'

> whole history — particularly that of the Afrikaans speaking section — has forced on them the need to adapt a mystique of race and colour that supplies moral sanction and self-justification for all their dealings with their black fellow-countrymen. Today they cling with religious fanaticism to this mystique of colour. And it is this mystique of colour that is the real threat to the peace of South Africa today. Inherent in it is the germ of violence and much bloodshed. But even more important than that, it carries the undertones of deep tragedy for the Afrikaans-speaking Whites. (168-69)

What Abrahams emphasizes is that all races will be negatively affected by the logical conclusions of racist white views, which entail death not only for Blacks — but Afrikaners as well.

Some critics have had trouble with the themes and the ending of *The Path of Thunder*. According to O.R. Dathorne in *African Literature in the Twentieth Century*,

> Lanny and Sarie's love is supposedly man's attempt to overcome obstacles, and through this love, Abrahams wishes to say, there is hope for all 'coloreds.' The novel ends, however, with their murder. This time the prescriptive model of interracial love and the laws of hate do not work; they have not been modeled into a novel but make up only a sketchy story with a melodramatic ending and long, semiphilosophical utterances. (141)

Dathorne overemphasizes Abrahams' belief in the healing power of love; and he misses the significance of how Lanny and Sarie's love is tied to their violent end. One also must remember Abrahams' words in *Tell Freedom* when grappling with *The Path of Thunder* and its ending. As Abrahams writes: "The racialism of our land did not hurt only those who were not white. Basically, it hurt all of us, black and white alike. I would have to remember that, always" (258). Yet, Dathorne is not alone in criticizing the book's themes and ending.

Wade, in *Peter Abrahams*, finds fault with *The Path of Thunder*'s ending, stating that it shows that Abrahams suffers from sentimentality. Wade states:

> If we define sentimentality as an aberration from literary realism, characterized by the preference for unlikely symmetries in relationships and events in a form which is unsympathetic to this kind of symmetry, leading to a degradation in the characters and feeling portrayed, it becomes clear that it is a phenomenon to be associated with 'closed-ended' works, those in which a predetermined ending is foisted on the characters from the start. (59-60)

It is not, however, sentimentality which is behind Abrahams' ending. Rather, it is the fact that Abrahams is trying to reflect one of the ways in which South African *society* was 'determined' — with the prohibition of interracial sexual relations which was in effect since 1927 (until recently), according to Wade's own book on Abrahams (51); with the gradual stripping of 'Coloreds' of rights, pushing them nearer Black status than white, which was prevalent roughly during the decade preceding and during the writing of Abrahams' book; and with the fact that intolerant societies very often smash those who go against their mores. Abrahams may have chosen an especially dramatic way to raise these issues — for example, showing the defeat and distortion of the reputation of the hero at the hands of racists — having him, if fact, lynched is nothing if not brutally frank in showing the logical conclusion to which racists with an immoral sense of power and invulnerability will protect themselves at all costs. Furthermore, Abrahams shows that those in power may use it brutally to keep away those who may 'taint' their status. Most importantly, however, Abrahams' writing of the story of Lanny and Sarie, their love, their deaths, and the lies in the newspaper concerning Lanny's final acts all prefigure the words of Martin Luther King's "Letter from Birmingham Jail" when on thinks of the destructive racists who kill them. As King writes: "Lamentably, it is an historical fact that privileged groups seldom give up their privileges voluntarily. Individuals may see the light and give up their unjust posture; but . . . groups tend to be more immoral than individuals."[13] Lanny may strive to be such an individual; and as such he is irrevocably on a dangerous course with much of white South African society.

Moving to our next topic, many similar issues are raised in *Tsotsi* by Athol Fugard and *Native Son* by Richard Wright. At times, there are comparisons, such as the importance of crime to the protagonist. At other times, the authors raise similar ideas and take them in different directions. Though there is no evidence that *Native Son* was an influence on Fugard's novel, exploring the similarities and contrasts in the novels broadens one's understanding of both works.

The protagonist's self-perception is important in both books. In *Native Son*, Wright explores self-hatred and rejection of identity that can be a consequence of being successfully inferiorized. In this novel, Wright also portrays the self-loathing and the hostility towards other Blacks that is a consequence of his protagonist's powerlessness. In *Native Son*, one obvious factor that presents an "inferiorized" portrait of Blacks to the protagonist Bigger and that affects Bigger's self-perception and his relationships is the media. As Wright points out in "How Bigger Was Born," the media condition Bigger to find things desirable that are unattainable to him and that make him feel that Blacks' lives are worthless.[14] For instance, perhaps one factor that prepares Bigger to be attracted to Mary Dalton, the daughter of his rich, white employer, is indicated by the presence of pictures of Jean Harlow, Ginger Rogers, and Janet Gaynor in the room he is given at the Daltons'. These photographs emphasize the promotion of white film idols to Blacks, as well as to whites, thus making them alluring to someone like Bigger. That Bigger has been so conditioned by the media that he looks down on the life to which he and other Blacks have been "consigned"[15] (to borrow the word of a similar character in *The Long Dream*) and finds the life of the whites whom he has seen depicted in films more alluring is emphasized when he is at the movies. After he sees the film which deals with white characters:

> He was filled with a sense of excitement about his new job. . . . Was he going to work for people like you saw in the movies? . . . He looked and saw *Trader Horn* unfold and saw pictures of naked black men and women whirling in wild dances and heard drums beating and then gradually the African scene changed and was replaced by images in his own mind of white men and women dressed in black and white clothes, laughing, talking, drinking, and dancing. Those were smart people; they knew how to get hold of money, millions of it. . . . He remembered hearing somebody tell a story of a Negro chauffeur who had married a rich white girl and the girl's family had shipped the couple out of the country and had supplied them with money.(35-6)

Bigger's lack of interest in the film about Blacks and the fantasies inspired by the other film show that, as Wright states in "How Bigger Was Born," Bigger is both alienated from Black culture and desirous of the lifestyle available to whites that he sees depicted in films and other media (xiii).

The extent of Bigger's inferiorization is shown in his feelings of shame and self-hatred. When he first goes to the Daltons' home, for example, he feels uneasy, for

> He was sitting in a white home; . . . strange objects challenged him; and he was feeling angry and uncomfortable. . . . [Mr. Dalton] was gazing at him with an amused smile that made him conscious of every square inch of skin on his black body. (47)

Another incident reveals Bigger's extreme self-consciousness, and simultaneous hatred and envy of whites. During his night chauffeuring Mary and her boyfriend Jan, Bigger thinks that

> they made him feel his black skin by just standing there and looking at him . . . he was something he hated. . . . he felt that this white man, having helped to put him down, having helped to deform him, held him up now to look at him and be amused. At that moment he felt toward Mary and Jan a cold, dumb, inarticulate hate. . . . If he were white, if he were like them, it would have been different. But he was black. (67-69)

Bigger's self-hatred and alienation from his family are consequences of his belief in the inferiority of both himself and other Blacks, a belief which is intensified by his comparison of himself and his family to Jan and the Daltons. When he returns home after killing Mary, for example, he compares his family's home to the Daltons', and his self-determination with his family's weakness:

> He hated this room and all the people in it, including himself. Why did he and his folks have to live like this? What had they ever done? Maybe they had to live this way precisely because none of them in all their lives had ever done anything, right or wrong, that mattered much. (100)

Also, when Bigger looks at his brother, Buddy, he

> saw him in the light of Jan. Buddy was soft and vague; his eyes were defenseless. . . . Buddy's clothes hung loosely compared with

the way Jan's hung. . . . Looking at Buddy and thinking of Jan and Mr. Dalton, he saw in Buddy a certain stillness, an isolation, meaninglessness. (103)

Bigger also thinks, "How different [his sister] Vera was from Mary! . . . she seemed to be shrinking from life in every gesture she made" (104). Thus, Wright emphasizes that the protagonist's comparison of Blacks to the way that he has seen whites live has "spoiled his own [world] for him" (270).

The primary reason for Bigger's alienation from other Blacks is evident when one realizes that to Bigger, self-worth is determined by one's having power. Bigger thinks:

> There were moments when a feeling and longing for solidarity with other blacks would take hold of him. He would dream of making a stand against the white force, but that dream would fade when he looked at the other black people near him. . . . As he rode, looking at the black people on the sidewalks, he felt the one way to end fear and shame was to make all those black people act together, rule them, tell them what to do, and make them do it. . . . But he felt that such would never happen to him and his black people, and he hated them, and wanted to wave his hand and blot them out. (109)

Thus, Bigger remains alienated from Blacks, forever barred from the whites' world, with his flashes of feeling self-determination as his only consolation.

Flight from identity also plays a major role in *Tsotsi*, though for different and similar reasons than in *Native Son*. As states Geoffrey Hughes, "[W]hat shows Fugard to be a major writer and makes this novel such an astonishing triumph is his creative imagination and range of sympathy which takes us fearlessly into the skull, the reflexes and thought patterns of his characters."[16]

Fugard explores Tsotsi's mentality, making clear that Tsotsi is always trying to force himself not to remember his painful past — a past that included the break-up of his family and his status as a homeless boy. Moreover, as in *Native Son*, questions related to his identity make Tsotsi victimize other Blacks. He is also dependent upon a life of crime to stifle memories. As Fugard writes,

> Tsotsi hated questions for a profound but simple reason. He didn't know the answers . . . neither his name nor his age, nor any of the other answers that men assemble and shape into the semblance of a

life. His memory went back vaguely to a group of young boys scavenging the townships for scraps needed to keep alive. Before that a few vague, moody memories, a police chase and finding himself alone. . . . [H]is not knowing himself had a deeper meaning than his name and his age. His own eyes in front of a mirror had not been able to put together the eyes, and the nose, and the mouth and the chin, and make a man with meaning. His own features in his own eyes had been as meaningless as a handful of stones picked up at random in the street outside his room.[17]

Consequently, when Boston, Tsotsi's fellow gang-member, starts questioning him about his identity, he (Boston) meets with Tsotsi's fury and violence. Lack of self-awareness therefore, keeps Tsotsi in a routine — in his case, the routine is a life of crime. And in writing of these subjects, Fugard, says Geoffrey Hughes, "Tackles the . . . concern[s] . . . of identity" (Gray, 105).

As with Bigger, crime provides a purpose in Tsotsi's life. Ironically, for much of the book, for Tsotsi, life's meaning is in its very meaninglessness and ugliness. Fugard writes, for example:

Tsotsi feared nothingness. He feared it because he believed in it. Even more than that he knew with all the certainty of his being that behind the facade of life lurked nothing. Under men's prayers he had heard the deep silence of it; behind man's beauty he had seen it faceless and waiting; inside man himself beyond the lights of his loves and his hopes, there too was nothing. The problem of his life was to maintain himself, to affirm his existence in the face of this nullity. He achieved this through pain and fear, and through death. He knew no other way. When Gumboot [the gang's murder victim] died, and in those last few seconds before death had looked with hate and then fear at the young man who had chosen him, that moment Tsotsi had known he was alive. It was as simple as that. (29)

Crime, therefore, affirms to Tsotsi that the meaninglessness of his existence is not futile and not without its moments of power. These facts help explain why Tsotsi needs to feel and see his knife, as Bigger needs to see and feel his gun. Fugard indicates that Tsotsi gains self-affirmation through crime — in fact, his only self-affirmation. He can escape his feelings of 'nobodiness' in the gang, for he is someone of stature to his fellow gang members. His stature within the gang allows him to be 'somebody' who can walk "down the street with a purpose" (8) as they head towards their next crimes. Thus, although Tsotsi's attitude, thoughts, and his crimes indicate his belief in life's ugliness, he affirms his existence by committing crimes which, ironically, both ostensibly deliver him from and affirm him in his belief of the nothingness of existence.

Concerning Tsotsi's identity, it is especially important for him to break the ugly barricade with which he covers reality. As Fugard writes in his notebooks, Tsotsi possesses "nihilism, anarchy. Hate."[18] Fugard continues, in his notebooks, "Nothing is precious. Nothing is worth keeping. Destruction....Beauty to be defaced or made ugly. The puppies born dead. Life ugly" (11). In this regard, the baby Tsotsi is given to take care of by a woman is essential. As Hughes writes, "Tsotsi's becoming a father figure leads to his sparing one victim and trying to heal another. Such a change is logical in Fugard's moral scheme, in which the Tsotsi gang are initiated into their lives of crime largely by accident and thus can be saved by accident" (105). The baby, for example, triggers Tsotsi's awareness of himself by disrupting the set routine of his life, and causes Tsotsi to have mixed feelings about memories of his past being awakened. As Fugard states:

> [I]t seemed almost as if there might have been a beginning before the bluegum trees, but regardless of where or when, he had started doing things that did not fit in the pattern of his life. There was no doubt about this. The pattern was too simple, too clear, woven as it had been by his own hands, using his knife like a shuttle to carry the red thread of death and interlace it with others stained in equally somber hues. The baby did not belong and certainly none of the actions that had been forced on him as a result by its presence. . . . It was . . . destructive tearing open the simple hand-worked fabric in which he had wrapped his existence. (40-41)

His memories of the past and consequently of his identity are thus awakened. Importantly, noting Tsotsi's change, Fugard writes, "But he had never been curious. Now he was" (42). In addition, he loses the ability to repress his memories, as is shown in the first meeting of the gang after Tsotsi takes in the baby (49). Moreover, Fugard writes of Tsotsi's new feelings about the gang: "He had never been conscious of them like this before. In fact, it had only rarely happened that he had been conscious of them at all, as the people with whom he lived and had to lead" (49). Importantly, Tsotsi loses his will to decisively initiate a criminal activity, as the other gang members expect from him. Consequently, one sees that Tsotsi's burgeoning self-awareness inhibits his ability to be a criminal (something that fails to happen to Bigger, as his murder of his girlfriend Bessie shows). One then sees the relevance of what Fugard wrote in his notebooks about *Tsotsi*: "Tsotsi — progressions an admission of an even deeper dimension to his living. Tsotsi — a freedom (1) to choose his victim. (2) Not to have a victim" (15).

Existentialism also plays an important part in both works. As Don Maclennan writes of Fugard, "The human problem of how to exist, how to find a meaning in this absurd existence"[19] is central to Fugard's character development in all his works. And, indeed, Fugard acknowledges his influence by Beckett and Camus; Wright, on the other hand, was intuitively existential in *Native Son*, as he did not become interested in the philosophy until the late 1940s. Still, both authors deal with such existential topics as freedom and responsibility, awareness of one's identity and of the existence which surrounds one and self-creation.

The highlight of Wright's use of existentialism comes with Bigger's feelings that "He had murdered and had created a new life for himself" (101). After killing Mary, Bigger, for the first time in his life, feels he had options, which is why he accepts his crime as murder. As Wright states, "though he had killed by accident, not once did he feel the need to tell himself that it had been an accident. . . . And in a certain sense he knew the girl's death had not been accidental. He had killed many times before, only on those other times there has been no handy victim or circumstance to make visible or dramatic his will to kill. . . . the hidden meaning of his life . . . had spill out" (101). Moreover, Bigger feels "elation" (102) as no one, in their blindness towards his identity, would suspect him of such a crime. This gives Bigger a feeling of having choices, as being self-creating. Bigger's 'nothingness,' then, can be transformed by him into a life of vengeance against whites. Thus, his resultant extortion plot shows that he, as does Tsotsi, sees crimes as an essential aspect of his self-definition.

Regarding existentialism in *Tsotsi*, Fugard explores such issues as self-identity and self-creation, although differently from Wright. In *Tsotsi*, diametrically opposed to *Native Son*, it is not crime which ultimately gives meaning to the protagonist's life but the opposite. In fact, as Camus states in *The Myth of Sisyphus*, people often cover over reality with a facade. Crime is, in fact, the facade that covers Tsotsi's own life from him, rather than being a revelatory experience, as in Camus *The Stranger* and in Wright's *Native Son*. Self-creation for Tsotsi comes from his exploring his memories and identity — not from avoiding facing these things by his "pattern" of crime. Hence, the ways in which the protagonists in Wright's and Fugard's novels explore the creation of their identity may be different; yet they both, in opposite ways, involve crimes.

Freedom and responsibility are another important aspect of existentialism. One finds this especially relevant in the writings of Camus and Jean Paul Sartre. In Camus' *Caligula*, for example, the title character uses his freedom to kill, torture and humiliate others. By the end of the play, he discovers that his freedom was incorrectly used. It was a totally reckless use of freedom. Also, in Sartre's *The Flies*, Orestes states that one must use one's freedom in a way that is responsible to others, and not to act dangerously and capriciously towards others. In *Native Son*, however, Bigger seems closer to the pre-enlightened Caligula, feeling that crime is the primary mode of self-creation. Tsotsi, on the other hand, is portrayed as ultimately believing in responsibility, refusing to make the disabled Morris his victim and taking care of the baby. Thus, again, Wright and Fugard share similar issues but develop them in contrasting ways.

In *Caligula*, Caligula states, "Men die; and they are not happy."[20] Wright and Fugard both fill their books with mortality. The deaths of the protagonists culminate this trend. In *Native Son*, this is preceded by the deaths of Mary and Bessie; in *Tsotsi*, it is preceded by the image of the dog with dead puppies; Gumboot's murder; and the baby's death. Both authors, therefore, emphasize the finitude of life. As Fugard states, "all living, all survival, is grounded in pain...it's really a theme that has gone through all my work" (Gray, 125). The pain of life and the inherent pain of mortality are especially heightened in *Tsotsi*.

Choice (which is central in existentialism) also plays an important role in both books. In *Native Son*, Bigger feels he has options concerning what to do and how to manipulate others for his own ends after he kills Mary. In *Tsotsi*, freedom of choice is essential as well. For much of the book, routine is of the utmost importance to Tsotsi — that is, until after he is given the baby and for the first time is confronted by the *choice* of whether to commit a crime. First, however, one sees how Fugard emphasizes the need for sameness in Tsotsi's life. One major example is Tsotsi's rules of behavior. His first rule is to think always only of the present moment, and never to disturb memories of the past. (This repression is clearly a reaction to the painfulness of the pass raid which broke up his family, and growing up an orphan — memories Tsotsi finds of the utmost importance to suppress.) Importantly, the second rule, writes Fugard, "was never to disturb his inward darkness with the light of a thought about himself or the attempt at a memory" (27). The third rule is that "Tsotsi tolerated no questions....questions sounded the vast depths of his darkness, making it a tangible reality" (29). These rules all impose a rigid pattern to Tsotsi's life, making repression and sameness, rather than choice and spontaneity, his operative mode.

Other passages show that the need for sameness and routine keeps the characters in a life of crime while choice ultimately does not. Regarding the gang members, "Time always posed the same question: What can I do with it? Your only escape from this predicament lay in a gang because it had a leader and he decided what to do" (46). And, indeed, when Tsotsi first chooses to make the poor, Black, disabled Morris his victim, he sees it both in terms of his natural routine and his free will. Fugard writes: "What happened next [his following Morris] was as natural in the pattern of his life as waking and sleeping were in those of other men. I'll take you, you bastard, he thought. Tonight I'll take you. His choice was made" (68). At first, it seems this clearly is not the creative choice as Wright perceives Bigger's crimes in *Native Son*. Yet, in both works, the authors give their characters existential aspects, especially regarding freedom and choice within a naturalistic framework. Thus, Bigger's killing Mary is both, as lawyer Max argues, simultaneously an "act of creation" (366) and an act of destiny (something Bigger's life prepared him to do); and Tsotsi's following Morris is an act of choice and something which fits in with the routine of his life. The quality of Tsotsi's choice seems far different — even redemptive — as he chooses not to make Morris his victim. It seems that Fugard is implying that choice involves consciousness, and lack of consciousness of one's actions and identity equals routine and sameness. Also, Tsotsi repeats three times: "I don't have to" (78). It is also at this point that Tsotsi resolves to find out more about his past. Consequently, it seems that in *Tsotsi*, Fugard is tying together moral choice with creation, in contrast to Wright's connecting crime and self-creativity.

As in the case in Fugard's play *Boesman and Lena* and in Wright's *Native Son*, in *Tsotsi* Fugard provides a view of the protagonists' psychology as well as maintaining the naturalistic aspects of the work. In addition, both of these factors reinforce the social protest aspects of the works. In *Tsotsi*, Fugard writes of situations that are relevant to the Black South African condition. Most important are the passages pertaining to the "slum clearance" (8) which forced removals of Blacks

Abrahams' The Path of Thunder· *(1948) and Fugard's* Tsotsi *(1980)*   137

from their homes. The so-called slum clearance is relevant not only because of Black removals but because it is being done for the benefit of whites and for the "impatient white suburb" (39). Blacks, therefore, are forced to face the fact that the death of the township is at hand. Moreover, the "impatient" white suburb is the reason for the decision to step up the demolition, which, most importantly, is responsible for the destruction of the ruins in which Tsotsi keeps the baby, resulting in both of their deaths. Thus, as is true of Mr. Dalton's owning slum property in *Native Son* and thereby keeping Blacks in relative high rent slum housing, in *Tsotsi*, whites' plans for housing removals also affect Blacks to a great — and negative — degree.

There are other aspects of *Tsotsi* which make it, like *Native Son*, a work of social protest. For instance, the fact that Tsotsi's victim, Gumboot, must leave his family behind in order to hold a job is a situation which has been relevant to the reality of South Africa. Also, Tsotsi's fellow gang member, Boston, first goes into a life of crime because of the pass laws which make him ineligible for a pass. Furthermore, as stated earlier, Tsotsi lost his family as a result of a pass raid when he was a little boy. Most poignant is the story of Morris, who lost his legs in a mining accident. Morris thinks, "It is for your [whites'] gold that I had to dig. That is what destroyed me. You are walking on stolen legs" (61). The Black South African condition under white rule, therefore, is of great concern to Fugard in *Tsotsi*.

Another important topic in *Native Son* and *Tsotsi* is the role of women. In *Black Feminist Criticism*, Barbara Christian states, "In Richard Wright's major works, such as *Native Son* or *The Outsider*, black women are seldom seen except in the role of slightly outlined mama or as a victim.[21] Trudier Harris also comments on Wright's limited depictions of Black women:

> When we think of Richard Wright, the portrait of black womanhood that immediately comes to mind is that of Bessie Mears, the drunk, victimized, desperate young woman in *Native Son* who is killed by Bigger Thomas and whose body serves as a piece of evidence in the case concerning Mary Dalton.[22]

These statements raise an issue that goes beyond the question of whether Wright portrays stereotypical Black female characters. Rather, they prompt examination of Wright's vision of women's identity in general — both Black and white — in his fiction.

A revealing aspect of Wright's vision is in his first major work, *Uncle Tom's Children*, which introduced one of his themes: the woman who is a threatening force to Blacks. In "Big Boy Leaves Home," this "force" is embodied by the white woman who stumbles upon the naked Black boys who have been swimming. Her screams set in motion a chain of events that results, ultimately, in the deaths of three of the boys and Big Boy's flight from town to escape lynching. In *Native Son* and *The Long Dream*, Wright again explores the power of white women in a racist society to radically alter or to destroy Black men's lives. What is most interesting, however, is that Wright's depiction of the power of women goes far beyond this theme. In his novels, Wright portrays two major ways in which he feels women can control men. Perhaps the more obvious of the two is the threat presented by a woman's independence. In addition, Wright shows how a man can feel that a woman's dependence can be a form of control over his existence. Among Wright's novels, *Native Son* reveals the complexity of his vision of the power of women.

In *Native Son*, Wright emphasizes, and much has been written about, how Mary Dalton's relationship with Bigger intensifies his sense of impotence by inadvertently making him intensely aware of his feelings of inferiority in relation to whites. It is also especially interesting to examine how the other women in Bigger's life, especially his mother and girlfriend, Bessie, threaten his independence.

Bigger's mother is a character type that Wright reiterates in such works as *The Outsider* and *The Long Dream*: the mother who attempts psychologically to dominate her son. Bigger's mother repeatedly denigrates him, calling him "the biggest fool I ever saw" (11) and "the no-countest man I ever seen in all my life" (15). She also attempts to prey on his conscience by contrasting her supposed familial devotion with his apathy: "All I ever do is try to make a home for you children and you don't care. . . . If you get that job [with the Daltons] . . . I can fix you up a nice place for you children. You could be comfortable and not have to live like pigs" (13). Clearly, Bigger's mother's pressure on him to act as provider causes hostility: "Bigger hated his family because he knew that they were suffering and that he was powerless to help them" (13). Thus, in *Native Son*, the mother causes her son to be estranged from her.

Additionally, Wright stresses the manipulative nature of the women whom Bigger encounters. When Mrs. Thomas visits Bigger in jail, for example, she pressures him to promise her that he will pray. Not only is Bigger pressured by his mother but also by Mrs. Dalton. When he first comes to work for the Daltons, Mrs. Dalton implies that she thinks he should continue his education. This prompts Bigger to compare her to his mother: "He felt that his mother wanted him to do the things she wanted him to do, and he felt that Mrs. Dalton wanted him to do the things she felt he should have wanted to do. But he did not want to go to night school" (62). These women, along with Mary, force upon Bigger their views of how he should behave.

The relationship in which the role of power is most interesting is between Bigger and Bessie. In examining this section of the novel, one might consider Addison Gayle, Jr.'s reservations in *The Way of the New World*:

> . . . the murder of Bessie Mears is the weakest incident in the novel. To murder this woman, of his color and race, means that Bigger severs all ties with the universe, becomes a man completely alone. Further, for a black to murder another is to commit the most heinous of crimes, to substantiate the argument made by Attaway, in *Blood on the Forge*, that the black man who engages in violence becomes so obsessed with hatred and rage that he is incapable of distinguishing between friend and foe, not able to separate the oppressor from the victim. On this level Bigger fails as both rebel and revolutionary.[23]

Yet, if one looks closely at Bigger's feelings about and actions towards Bessie, it becomes evident that instead of her murder being a result of a flaw in Bigger, it is an inevitable consequence of Bigger's perceptions of her identity, his own and his self-defensive desire for control. Indeed, in their relationship, Wright explores a theme which is reiterated in his other novels — the protagonist's need to have power over the woman with whom he is involved. It is ironic that although Bessie inspires Bigger's extortion scheme with her reference to Leopold and Loeb, she becomes a mere pawn in his plan (129). From the outset Bigger perceives Bessie's involvement in the plot in strictly pragmatic terms: "[M]aybe he could use her...Would she act with him, blindly believing his word?....She might come in just handy" (131-132). Furthermore, being in control of Bessie gives Bigger the same sort of thrill he had after accepting responsibility for Mary's death. For example, when he concocts a story about what happened to Mary in order to satisfy Bessie's curiosity about the girl's fate, Bigger "wanted to keep her guessing. He wanted to take as long as possible in order to see that look of complete absorption upon her face. It made him feel alive and gave him a heightened sense of the value of himself" (135). This satisfaction with his power over Bessie is reiterated when Bigger slowly reveals his plans for extortion to her: "[H]e was enjoying her agony, seeing and feeling the worth of himself in her bewildered expression" (142). Furthermore, he feels that her implication in the scheme would complete her subservience to him. He thinks that then Bessie "would be his; her fear of capture and death would bind her to him..."(142).

It is clear, however, even before Bigger implicates Bessie in his crime, that he feels most comfortable with her when he has power over her:

> He felt that there were two Bessies: one a body that he had just had and wanted badly again; the other was in Bessie's face; it asked questions. . . . He wished he could clench his fist and swing his arm and blot out, kill, the Bessie on Bessie's face and leave the other helpless and yielding before him. (133)

Thus, when Bessie becomes burdensome as a result of her qualms about Bigger's crimes, his reaction is similar to that of Wright's other protagonists (e.g., Jake in *Lawd Today* and Cross in *The Outsider*) who feel that their lives are being manipulated by the responsibilities women force them to assume: "If he took her along [when he flees] she would be blaming him for all that had happened; she would be wanting whiskey to help her forget and there would be times when he could not get it for her" (221). Bigger, therefore, concludes that since "He couldn't take her and he couldn't leave her....he would have to kill her. It was his life against hers" (222). Bigger feels he must murder her to preserve his self-determination.

As in other cases in Wright's works, this attempt to maintain one's power results in greater powerlessness. This fact is illustrated after Bigger kills Bessie, throws her down the air shaft, and realizes that the money he had stolen from Mary and had planned to use during his escape is in Bessie's pocket, leaving him only seven cents while he hides from the law. Furthermore, because he can't bear to look at Bessie's dead body, he is unable to get the money from her pocket. Consequently, as a result of Bigger's drive to protect his independence from Bessie, both of them share the roles of victim and victimizer.

Though female characters are less prevalent in *Tsotsi* than in *Native Son*, the role of women is also important in *Tsotsi*. For example, Tsotsi is ready to attack the woman who thrusts the shoebox containing the baby at him. More importantly, however, is the attitude Tsotsi displays towards Miriam. His relationship with her shows that although his finding the baby is a life altering event, he has not lost the distrust and hostility which helped to make him a criminal. First, he has an exploitive attitude towards Miriam. He demands, for instance, that she feed the baby, but doesn't want her to try to do anything to take better care of it, as that would jeopardize his 'ownership' of the baby. In fact, when Miriam says she'd like to take care of the baby because he is not well, Tsotsi "thought of his knife first. I will kill her" (120). Most importantly, Tsotsi returns the baby to the ruins out of fear and distrust, feeling that Miriam might take it. The role of women in the novel, therefore, serves to show that in spite of the meaning the baby gives to Tsotsi's life (e.g., his quitting the gang) he still retains elements of his personality that led to a life of crime, and thus, according to Fugard, Tsotsi's is no total transformation.

Finally, the endings of both works are problematic. *Native Son* ends with Bigger seeming to affirm his crimes: "What I killed for, I am" (391-92). This could mean that he is existentially affirming his acts, proclaiming his self-creation as a result of them. Or, it could have traces of the earlier stated (in the novel) naturalistic meaning of Bigger's actions, that his environment prepared him for nothing more than a criminal existence. In comparison, Tsotsi's death has caused some controversy concerning Fugard's vision in the novel. Dennis Walder, for example, says that Tsotsi dies because "Fugard cannot imagine a continued life him."[24] He continues to say that it seems the ending affirms the idea that "individual action becomes meaningless, an event leading nowhere...life seems to be pointless" (42). This may be an apparent interpretation of the book. But if one remembers that part of the book is social protest, no stronger point could be made than the slum clearance's killing of the main character. Moreover, as stated earlier, Fugard is concerned with man's mortality. The book's ending does not, then, show the futility of life. Instead, it shows the existential ideas of life's finitude and the need to create meaning for one's life in the present, regardless of one's ultimate mortality and of the life-negating nature of apartheid.

By examining the similarities and differences between certain works of American and South African literature, one finds that certain themes recur when issues of race, power and identity are raised in both countries. Also, one sees how the unique visions of each author compared contributes to the originality and power of each work. Most importantly, one also is forced to remember the price Blacks have paid during a history of racism.

Notes

1. George M. Fredrickson, *White Supremacy* (New York: Oxford University Press, 1981), 241.
2. William J. Wilson, *Power, Racism, and Privilege* (New York: The Free Press, 1973), 35.
3. Peter Abrahams, *Tell Freedom* (New York: The Macmillan Company, 1970), 186.
4. W.E.B. DuBois, *The Souls of Black Folk* in *Three Negro Classics*, ed. John Hope Franklin (New York: Avon Books, 1965), 364.
5. Peter Abrahams, *Return to Goli* (London: Faber and Faber, 1963), 175.
6. Arnold Ramparsad, *The Life of Langston Hughes* (New York: Oxford University Press, 1986), 282.
7. Langston Hughes, "Home" in *The Ways of Whitefolks* (New York: Alfred A. Knopf, 1933), 35.
8. Peter Abrahams, *The Path of Thunder* (Chatham, New Jersey: The Chatham Bookseller, 1948), 12.
9. Michael Wade, *Peter Abrahams* (London: Evans Brothers Limited, 1972), 49.
10. Kolawole Ogungbesan, *The Writing of Peter Abrahams* (London: Hodder and Stoughton, 1979), 53.
11. Peter Abrahams, *Mine Boy* (London: Heinemann Educational Books, 1946), 174-75.
12. O.R. Dathorne, *African Literature in the Twentieth Century* (Minneapolis: University of Minnesota Press, 1974), 141.
13. Martin Luther King, Jr. "Letter from Birmingham Jail" in *Why We Can't Wait* (New York: New American Library, 1963), 80.
14. Richard Wright, "How Bigger Was Born," in *Native Son* (New York: Harper and Row, 1940), xiii.
15. Wright, *The Long Dream* (New York, Doubleday, 1958), 220.
16. Geoffrey Hughes, "A Season in Hell: Fugard's *Tsotsi*" in *Athol Fugard*, ed. Stephen Gray, (Johannesburg: McGraw-Hill, 1982), 105.
17. Athol Fugard, *Tsotsi* (Middlesex, England: Penguin Books, 1983), 17-18.
18. Fugard, *Notebooks 1960-1977* (New York: Alfred A. Knopf, 1984), 11.
19. Don Maclennan, "The Palimpsest: Some Observations on Fugard's Plays" in Gray, 218.
20. Albert Camus, *Caligula* in *Caligula and Three Other Plays*, trans. Stuart Gilbert (New York: Alfred A. Knopf, Inc., and Random House, 1958), 8.
21. Barbara Christian, *Black Feminist Criticism* (New York: Pergamon Press, 1985), 45.

22. Trudier Harris, *Black Women in the Fiction of James Baldwin* (Knoxville: University of Tennessee Press, 1985), 206.
23. Addison Gayle, Jr., *The Way of the New World* (Garden City, New York: Anchor Press/Doubleday, 1975), 171.
24. Dennis Walder, *Athol Fugard* (London: Macmillan, 1984), 42.

Chapter 5

Coming of Age: Lynn Freed's *Home Ground* (1986) and Toeckey Jones's *Go Well, Stay Well* (1979)

The impact on identity of racial conflict is an important aspect of "Coming of Age" novels. This topic is especially relevant because people often say the future lies with the children. A stimulating contrast arises if one compares young heroines of Lynn Freed's *Home Ground* and Toeckey Jones's novel for adolescents, *Go Well, Stay Well*. Both books concern the female protagonists' coming of age in South Africa, with racism affecting both of their identities. Though Jones's book is aimed at teenagers, it still raises the same complex issues that are especially interesting in light of Freed's book, which is not. Still, the novels are very dissimilar. Freed's protagonist, Ruth, for example, is one whose growth is ambiguous, leaving the reader ambivalent about the depth of the character's development, identity and consciousness. She also seems to crave recognition by Black men, even as she wants to be distant from them. In addition, Ruth's life has an air of unreality about it, for she seems to want to 'perform' her way through life from the age of eight (as she is when the book begins) to the end of her teens. Jones's protagonist, Candy, on the other hand, is clearly going through a transition from 'innocence to experience,' one in which she grows markedly by the end of the novel. Still, Jones does not merely give Candy a linear development. Instead, the complexity of Jones's book relies in great part on her technique of having complications arise as Candy, the protagonist, attempts to cultivate her friendship with Becky, a Black girl from Soweto. The significance of Candy's having a birthday during the novel (she turns sixteen) is to underscore her development of a consciousness of Blacks, of apartheid, and on a more personal level, of the nature of the girl with whom she is trying to have an interracial friendship. Thus, if one compares Freed's novel with Jones's, one finds that they both raise complicated issues concerning the heroines' thoughts about racial matters and about their own identities, underscoring their social and political transitions.

It is an important point that while Freed's is a complex novel that traces Ruth's adolescence and is aimed most assuredly at the adult reader, Jones's story is part of the genre of the junior novel, about and aimed at adolescent audiences. To those for whom the junior novel may connote simplicity and lack of depth of the portrayals of characters and issues, it should be pointed out that concerns of South African life can appear in works concerning South African adolescents' experience of the inner and outer turmoil of life in the midst of apartheid. One such work is Beverly Naidoo's *Journey to Jo'burg*. In this novel— aimed at nine to twelve year olds — Naidoo portrays the injustice of the pass system; the break-up of a Black family because the mother must work far away from the children; Black rebellion; and the Soweto uprising. On this last point, this junior novel tells the story of the event in terse, powerful prose: "People were screaming, bleeding, falling. More police came in great steel tanks, and more in helicopters, firing from above. A little girl, about eight years old . . . raised her fist, and the next thing she was lying dead."[1] This passage, almost without saying, supports the statements of Jane Yolen in *Writing Books for Children* that readers must know that literature for children and for adolescents "is not all Peter Rabbit. . . . Children's books also embrace realism . . . nitty-gritty, raw, down-to-the-bone realism".[2] This is certainly the case in both Naidoo's novel and Jones's. Moreover, as Dorothy Petit points out in "The Picture of Life in the Adolescent Novel":

> These novels for the adolescent possess the most important qualities of genuine fiction . . . the dimension of all the novels . . . is the individual as he works at the process of finding out who he is in the

societies of present or of the past. . . . The novel shows an individual in society because it is only through our social relationships that we define out relationships and that we define our individuality. (Yolen, 17)

Though Petit's views may seem a bit rigidly overstated, she does make a point which for the significance of this study can be applied to Jones's *Go Well, Stay Well*. Candy certainly develops and discovers her maturing identity through her relations with her Black friend, Becky. At the same time, Candy, becoming increasingly aware of apartheid and how it affects the life of Becky, must question her relationship to a society where whites — herself included — can hide from the reality of the lives of the majority of the country. Moreover, Candy's identity is tested and developed as "an individual in society" because her relationship with Becky forces her to define her identity in terms of what sort of person — indeed, what sort of South African white person — she will be in the face of little support for her interracial friendship. Finally, the novel achieves a purpose that the *Young Adult Services in the Public Library* points out as one of the criteria for a complex novel for young people; to provoke reflection in the reader (Yolen, 23). Thus, *Go Well, Stay Well* should not be overlooked by readers looking for complex fiction on South Africa; in fact, it should be read, among other reasons, by those who are interested in the multifarious literary portrayals of life in South Africa.

Ruth in Lynn Freed's *Home Ground* is greatly removed from Candy in *Go Well, Stay Well*. She, clearly, is a character of greater complexity. When one follows Ruth's childhood and adolescence, Ruth seems not to grow but to be hardened into an older version of herself — controlling; demanding attention; needing to capture others to be her audience. Coming from a family of theater people, "Audience mattered. . . . we needed one to witness the drama of our lives. To stylize the discord. To stand, like the theater itself, between us and the world beyond."[3] 'Performing' her way through life, Ruth lacks serious introspection, and has an inadequate connection that she will recognize to the reality of South Africa — racism, racial unrest, and future of the country as a result of these things — that extends beyond her own little concerns.

Concerning Ruth's identity, one of the striking features of the book is its presentation of some white attitudes, especially Ruth's attitudes towards Blacks. Exhibitionism in front of Blacks seems present in both Ruth and her sister Valerie. For instance, fifteen year old

Valerie runs naked past one of the servants, Rueben, in the hallway. Another sister, Catherine, tries to refute their father's telling them it's unfair to be sexually provocative and expect the servants to ignore such behavior by saying, "Rueben is *hardly* one's vision of lust and passion" (7). Their father tries to answer this by saying that they shouldn't sexually tease a man. It is clear in this passage that Valerie has the attitude in her actions that she will "mak[e] trouble, to create and control a scene" (7). In her 'performance,' the servant has no reality or humanity, nor do her father's opinions. Furthermore, Ruth later shows her own exhibitionism and need to 'create and control a scene' — and the people in it — in her treatment of the Black servants. As the men sit and talk as they are having their hair cut outside, Ruth becomes fixated on the thought of gaining the men's attention. She states, "I wanted to know how close I had to get to come alive for them" (21). In fact, her thoughts of "how close I had to get" could easily be replaced with "how far I had to go." First, she picks up the hair on the ground and throws it up in the air, waiting for it to land on her. Not yet satisfied, her behavior becomes even more grotesque: "I became intoxicated by the power of my own performance" (21). She next imitates the way the men laugh by screaming and baring her teeth. It is increasingly clear that the men not only do not enjoy her exhibitionist performance but are aghast at it. And clearly, Ruth knows that continuing to act this way is offensive to the men, saying, "The joke is over, I knew but I was wild to have it back" (22). Thus, she continues to sadistically inflict her performance on the men:

> They looked in silence. I contorted my mouth into a baboon's style and loped around them. Nothing. Only Lucy [her friend] laughed uncontrollable . . . 'I'm a baboon!' I shouted up to him. He [Sampson] stared down at me soberly. 'You're a baboon!' I shouted, desperate. But he just looked. (22)

Ruth's noticing his clear displeasure only serves to fan the flames for a final perverse attempt to be noticed by the men. Pulling down Sampson's boxer shorts, Ruth shouts, "Come, let's look at his big wee!" (23). The sadistic 'joke' culminates in her next immediate action: "Between his shorts and his left thigh I had reached in and caught hold of a man's penis for the first time. It was exquisitely new to the touch, sensuous, erotic, even then. I shrieked in delight and jumped back. 'Try!' I suggested to Lucy" (23). Sampson's appeal to her to stop — "My manhood, Miss" (23) — is met by Ruth's cruel mimicking: "Men-hoood!

Men-hood!" (23). It is clear in this episode who holds the power in the situation — a perversely narcissistic little girl — a little white girl, it is essential to remember, who feels free to go to the servant's compound in order to subject them to insulting, assaultive humor. (Also, if Sampson seems to tolerate Ruth's behavior too much in the above scene, it may be pointed out that Freed seems to emphasize the power that even a young white could have over a Black person in a society in which racial oppression of Blacks reigned). Moreover, Freed gives evidence of Ruth's need to rid herself of the 'performing'/exhibitionistic side of her personality which was bred into her by her family, as it causes her to want to control her 'audience' — an 'audience' which may be, as Sampson is, abused by her controlling behavior.

Furthermore, Ruth's narcissistic motivations and action bring to mind James Baldwin's ideas about American whites in *The Fire Next Time*:

> White Americans find it as difficult as white people elsewhere to divest themselves of the notion that they are in possession of some intrinsic value. . . . And this assumption . . . is revealed in all kind of striking ways. . . . [T]here is certainly little enough in the white man's public or private life that one should desire to imitate. Therefore, a vast amount of the energy that goes into what we call the Negro problem is produced by the white man's profound desire not to be judged by those who are not white, not to be seen as he is. . . . [The white man has a need] to be released from the tyranny of his mirror.[4]

Baldwin captures, when one applies his thoughts to Ruth's behavior, her compulsive need to continue her 'performance', her discomfort at signs of the men's judging her negatively — or 'seeing her as she is' and the resultant exposure of the "tyranny of [her] mirror," as she hysterically continues her 'jokes' without being able to tolerate looking at how others are being bothered and humiliated by her behavior, for she wants to use her mirror to 'tyrannize' an audience who are members of an oppressed majority. Though on the general level, the entire episode may be metaphorical for white/Black relations in South Africa, on the specific level it reveals how the behavior Baldwin discusses is enacted by a character who possesses the qualities of which he speaks.

An interesting aspect of the book is that in spite of her attitudes and actions towards Blacks as a child, as an adolescent Ruth is supposedly the family's "champion of the underdog," (20) convincing her parents to let a Black servant, Nora, inside the church at her sister's wedding ceremony. Yet she shows discomfort with the servant, John, as she helps with his lessons because, among other things, "If I passed him in the garden he would wave and smile at me like an old friend" (83). Clearly, though she was younger in the earlier incident involving Sampson, she was grotesquely intimate with him but when a Black man shows signs of being attracted to — or merely being familiar with her (as John was initially when she started to feel bothered by him — an almost immediate occurrence) — she no longer controls the scene (until she can get rid of John) and is no longer in power over her audience. (In fact, her ideas that John is not a proper student but one who is both slow and initially interested (before his graphic, sexual come-on to her) in her is only one side of the picture.) One should not only remember Ruth's attitudes towards and dealings with other Blacks but also reflect on an aspect of the book that is implicit in the novel — that Freed is subtly showing possible corrupted sides of Black/white relations in South Africa. In addition, an especially intriguing side of Ruth's character is that she 'plays' at being interested in the situations caused by apartheid, saying, "But this is *their* country. . . . How dare the government just come in and tell them where they can go and what they can do . . . I think they're right to be violent. Why shouldn't Africans be treated just the same as us?" (83-84). Yet it is clear that her fleeting concern for Blacks is sound and fury signifying nothing. Though Valerie's retort that Blacks are only "barely out of the trees" (84) and are "baboons" reiterates her racism, in Ruth's inner thoughts, another aspect of prejudice is revealed as she watches Rueben, who comes to clear the table after the conversation ends: "All I could imagine was Rueben just as he was — servant, solitary, disengaged from real life, with all the dignity he had a shadow of our own. . . . I couldn't see him as a man" (84). Valerie's line after Rueben leaves may seem the height of racism, but she is merely corroborating Ruth's inner thoughts: "Exit baboon" (84). Similarly, neither does Ruth see John's humanity: "He didn't seem human. He never seemed human to me" (87). Thus, this "champion of the underdog" is only role-playing as such. Internally, while her thoughts may not be as harsh as Valerie expresses hers, in the end, Ruth is just as racist.

Another important aspect of the book is Ruth's lack of interest in the South African situation concerning the volatile Black/white relations in the past, the present and the future. As Ruth explains her lack of interest in his history, she thinks,

South African history seemed third rate to me. There were no kings and queens, or walled cities, or wars lasting a hundred years. So what about the Zulus spearing seventy Boers? Or even the Great Trek. How could that compare to the ten causes of the French Revolution? Or the six wives of Henry VIII? (140)

In this passage, Ruth does not merely implicitly lament the teaching of history as she has experienced it, but is, somewhat egotistically, stating that the history is not glamorous enough for her. Moreover, perhaps because of her being so long in 'performance mode,' (as is the rest of her family), she has become alienated from reality. For example, on being told by a guest to her home that "'This is a country had no teeth for me,' [Ruth thinks] [w]e were always hearing that. It was like the Jews and the Messiah" (140-41). Thus, one of the most central aspects of South African life is a subject of complete boredom to her. It seems, if one considers this attitude with her previous attitudes and actions, in a strange conversion, 'performance' is reality and 'real' reality is merely drab and dull.

A later scene that functions as a test for Ruth as to whether she will face and become interested in reality is when she goes to see a talk by an African National Congress speaker, Simon Mngoma. His words are strong:

> What people here may not realize . . . is that we Africans will not be obeying your laws much longer. We will not be "good boys" anymore. You do not hear what I hear in the townships. You do not see what I see on the buses and in the streets where black men live. (191)

Ruth's lack of interest in the reality of South Africa is unsettled by the above word: "I had never heard such threats from a black man or woman. The menace in his innuendo began to unsettle my boredom (191). Yet, almost immediately her ennui returns:

> I wanted to be shocked with all the others. I tried to think of kwashiorkor babies. The distended stomachs, sunken eyes, skinny arms and legs. But I had only seen photographs. And even they didn't hold the horror of the Holocaust chronicles. Starving babies seemed far from me — white girl, Jew. (191)

Yet, does being, in a generic sense, white and Jewish, automatically account for this estrangement from reality? The answer seems to be no. For Ruth is also an individual — one who used to try to play — and only through talk, not action, the "champion of the underdog." One needs to rethink then, the assertion that Ruth comes to be moved by the reality of Black life under apartheid.[5] That she is finally unmoved by Simon's speech reemphasizes the idea she is still uninterested in reality, as opposed to the world of 'performing' as a way to manipulate reality and narcisstically control others by making them the mere reflected audience trapped in her mirror. These ideas are shown in her thoughts immediately after Simon tells her that although whites think Black men want white women, Black men find women of their own race preferable. This triggers a memory from her earlier adolescence; one that is similar to her 'performance' before Sampson and the other Blacks. Dancing with her friend Lucy, she notices a group of Black men in the street below. "'Come', I said to Lucy. 'Let's take off our blouses'" (192). Needy for the men's attention, she bangs on the window, and then continues to take off her pants and underwear. And, as in the earlier incident, as her need to be noticed comes to a point of near hysteria, this time, after having taken her clothes off, "I was wild with my daring, with the audience of black men outside" (192). She continues, "I turned my back on the window and bent over to look at them between my knees (192-93). Significantly, the episode ends with her "prancing around for all the world to see" (193). Immediately, Freed cuts to another scene. In fact, the possible answers for Ruth's behavior show the complexity of Ruth's character. One sees her desire to entrap people in her 'performance'; her need to satisfy her desire for attention; her egotism; her disrespect for her audience, simultaneously with a need be responded to as she wants by them; her intolerance for others' distance from her; and the nature of the mirror in which she is entrapped as she tries to entrap others as vague forms in it. Considering all these ideas, it is not all surprising that she is bored by history and uncaring about the present — even as she lives in one of the most volatile situations — with ominous future portents for all, which is emphasized by Simon — who ultimately succeeded in boring her by discussing the topic which alienates her most — reality.

In Ruth, Freed may be implicitly saying that some whites can so chain themselves to their mirror that to them, seeing the threat of 'no future' is, finally, irrelevant. If only the ability to satisfy one's egotistical desires and flee from reality is prominent, "no future" may be guaranteed for these individuals. And this is the danger of attitudes such as Ruth's.

Coming of Age   153

In Jones's *Go Well, Stay Well*, interracial friendship affects Candy's identity in a way in which Ruth's identity doesn't develop. Clearly, there are many hindrances to development of an interracial friendship. First, there is the initial, inbred, lack of trust by the white girl for the Black girl, Becky. For instance, as Becky tries to help her after she hurts her ankle, Jones writes of Candy's thoughts: "It would have been so much simpler if it had been a white person who had offered help. She didn't know why the girl was doing it. Should she offer to pay her? It was all rather embarrassing.[6] Another reaction Candy has as Becky tries to help her to sit down equally shows Candy's lack of trust for someone Candy initially perceives to be a generic Black person, with all of the shady qualities that entails in Candy's eyes. As Candy's bag slips from her shoulder and Becky reaches for it as it falls, Candy expects Becky — the girl who went out of her way to help her — to steal it.

In addition, Candy's family acts as a hindrance to the budding friendship. Candy had always believed that they had liberal racial attitudes, but she finds they are afraid to let her befriend a Black girl. Though Candy's father lets her mother do most of the talking and acts as if he is ignoring the situation most of the time, it is clear both parents are against the idea for Becky to come to their home (to teach Candy Zulu). First, Candy's mother cites that the neighbors might be offended by a weekly Black visitor. Second, her mother further reveals why she thinks the laws of the land should make white people extra careful about interracial friendship. As she tells Candy, "You know and I know that the laws in this country are ridiculous . . . insane . . . But because of the way things are you can't just do what you like without first considering the possible consequences for other people" (39). Also, when the family is having dinner, Candy's brother Colin taunts her insultingly by asking, "Trying to cultivate coons as comrades like the commies?" (40) He continues, "Inviting coons to tea, indeed. Next you'll be wanting to marry one" (40). Colin goes on to call Candy as "*kaffirsussie*" (40; someone seen as being inappropriately — to racists — close to Blacks. The American equivalent would be 'nigger lover'). When Candy does get her parents to agree to let Becky come to their house, Colin refers to Becky as being 'half of Soweto' (67), showing that he has no tolerance for any Blacks — not even one. (The hypocrisy in this stand is evident as it is revealed that Colin was once involved with a Black girl.) His racist feelings are also emphasized as he runs his hands on Candy's hair and states, "Better watch it . . . It feels like it's staring to go crinkly already" (67). Hence, the family becomes estranged as a result of the main character's helping and befriending a Black — calling to mind Ben du Toit and his family in *A Dry White Season*. In great contrast, however, this book for adolescents, being for a young audience, provides a glimmer of hope that whites might advance from their bigotry. (Colin, for example, follows his girlfriend into Candy's room while Becky visits, and though he maintains an uncomfortable distance, he at least is willing to be in Becky's presence without being insulting.) In any case, Candy's family puts up a barrier between their daughter and her hope to befriend Becky.

It is essential to note how Candy's identity grows as she becomes increasingly involved with Becky. One major aspect of the beneficial impact of Candy's knowing Becky's identity and life is that it makes Candy conscious about how Blacks live. In Becky, Candy is with someone who lives the life of the majority that many whites tried to hide from their consciousness. Moreover, that Candy is being exposed to the reality of Blacks (not merely as servants) results in her, similar to Ben in Brink's *A Dry White Season*, having an existential awakening to the world behind the obstacles whites can make to hide themselves from the Black situation. As Jones writes as Candy's father is driving her home after she first meets Becky:

> They weren't far from home now. Candy looked at the familiar hedgegrows, blinking against the occasional glare from the surface of swimming pools, the tennis courts, the sweeping, neatly edged lawns, half-hidden behind the thick foliage. Suddenly it all seemed unreal: the blue sky, the smart houses gleaming white through the trees, the swimming pool, the tennis courts, the sweeping, neatly edge lawns. "It's like a big green cocoon," Candy thought, "enclosing us all in our cozy, insulated lifestyle." (30)

Candy's consciousness of the unreality of the areas in which she and other whites live has a significant result:

> Now, however, she found herself feeling a lot more curious about Soweto. She was still be terrified to go there, but she felt that if it were possible she would like to visit Becky in her home and see for herself what township life was like. But it wasn't possible. She wasn't to be given an entry permit for a social visit. And she didn't think she would ever be brave enough to sneak into Soweto without one. (31)

It is Becky who overcomes, to a degree, the fragmentation and obstacles facing the races and sparks Candy's growth. Furthermore, later in the book, when hearing about the Soweto uprising Candy strongly wants to go into the township to find out if Becky is all right. This not only shows Candy's growth but also reveals her development as a result of the expansion of her mind, for which Becky is the catalyst.

Yet, before Candy reaches this point of strength, both she and Becky at times act in ways which show their ambivalence towards what is from the outset a potentially close friendship. For example, Candy's father warns her that by giving a Black person her address, because *tsotsis* may find out about it and break into their house, she may have put the whole family in danger. In reaction, Jones writes of Candy's thoughts:

> Candy's heart jolted nervously. Had she done the wrong thing? What if their house were broken into and they were all murdered because of her? Briefly she was gripped by a feeling of terror, imagining herself waking up one night to see a black man climbing through her bedroom window with a knife in his hand. It was an image that haunted her frequently as a child. (32)

Gordimer, among other authors, in *The Lying Days*, notes the myth of the evil, possibly lascivious, violent Black, an image with which whites may be indoctrinated from childhood. One of the best summaries of this mythology is in the African American author Paul Laurence Dunbar's "The Lynching of Jube Benson." To reiterate this passage, a doctor who participated in the lynching of a Black man ponders why he did so:

> Why did I do it? I don't know. A false education I reckon. One false from the beginning. I saw his black face glooming there in the half-light and I could only think of him as a monster. It's tradition. At first I was told that the black man would catch me. Then, when I got over that, they taught me that the devil was black. And when I recovered from the sickness of that belief, here were Jube and his fellows with faces of menacing blackness. There was only one conclusion; this black man stood for all the powers of evil. The result of whose machinations had been gathering in my mind from childhood up.[7]

The "tradition" of bigotry is upheld by some central characters in Jones's book. Candy's parents, who parade as liberals, clearly have some prejudices regarding Blacks, as is shown by her father's envisioning Candy's budding friendship with a young girl as somehow resulting in Blacks' breaking into the house. Furthermore, Candy's mother can barely live up to her 'liberalism' when Candy hurts her ankle. She had stated, "One can draw heart from that, at least. It does seem to show that this dratted government of ours hasn't totally succeeded in destroying all signs of goodwill between the races" (35). Yet, Jones emphasizes Candy's mother's discomfort with the idea of her daughter's having a friendship that will lead to a Black person's visiting their home.

Furthermore, Candy has a troubled passage toward gaining a mature identity. Candy also at times has an ambivalent attitude towards the friendship. Candy, on the one hand, *insists* that Becky make regular visits, in part so that Becky can teach Candy Zulu. On the other hand, for all the family disagreements over this issue, later Candy feels hemmed in by Becky. First, it seems as if the friendship is growing strongly. Then, Candy starts to want to see her white friends — something impossible, given some of her friends' prejudiced attitudes towards Blacks. Her ambivalence causes her to be remorseful for temporarily dropping her friendship with Becky but to continue, for a short period of time, not to see Becky. As Gordimer makes clear in *A World of Strangers* and *Occasion for Loving*, interracial friendships can be hindered by the weight of South African racism and by the desire of the white to return to the 'White City'. Candy makes this retreat. Furthermore, Candy's ambivalence is clearly in part a result of the friendship's being a test of a young white girl's ability to maintain a friendship with a Black person. The testing aspect of the relationship is emphasized strongly by the statement, "The strongest steel has to come through the fire" (61). Jones, therefore, is clearly setting up a 'laboratory experiment,' designed to see whether Candy can overcome her doubts about the friendship in light of her family's and friend's attitudes and her own feelings of being cut off from her white friends. Candy's ambivalence underscores the fact that interracial friendship faces great obstacles in a racist society in which the white has to prove his or her legitimacy as being non-racist.

The pressures of loyalty that plague Candy in her negative feelings towards Becky at times and her desire to return to the 'White City,' with the relative lack of complexity friendships there entail, show the weight she feels she is under. This weight is further made heavy by other issues which cause complications to arise in her friendship with Becky.

Among them are not only Candy's parents' attitudes but also the material inequality of Becky's life as opposed to Candy's relatively opulent lifestyle; and Becky's own attitude towards her and Candy's roles as members of different races. To summarize, a central problem for Becky and Candy is not to have an inferior/superior way of acting towards each other; the second problem is Becky's own indoctrination with race-role stereotypes which she often acts out towards Candy.

When Candy contemplates the inequality of her Becky's greatly contrasting stations in life, Jones writes,

> Candy knew Becky didn't mean to, but she made her feel so guilty. Guilty for being white. But what could she do? How could she help Becky materially, without incurring a need for gratitude and thus spoiling the sense of equality on which their friendship was founded? Suddenly, it just didn't seem possible that she and Becky would be able to continue relating as equals when everything between them was so unequal. (60)

It seems that one of the most striking areas that underscores the inequality of the two girls' stations in life is how they both respond to turning sixteen. To Candy, it is an age of celebration, of being on the brink of burgeoning adulthood and greater independence. Becky, on the other hand, sees it as an age when she will suffer the obstacles, humiliation, and inconveniences of needing to get a pass. The gap between the two girls' paths in life is shown when Jones writes that

> Before meeting Becky, Candy had known that the pass laws were both an inconvenience and an insult to black people. What she had not realized was the virtual power of life and death they held over every individual African. This was something, however, which Becky made her understand all too clearly. (86)

Moreover, even Candy's reaction to hearing the tale of what happened to Becky's best friend — a girl who because of problems with her pass was forced to move away from her parents — is woefully naive, as Becky notes. Writing of Candy's reaction, Jones states, "They can't do that to people" (87). Becky immediately realizes the gap that exists between the two girls — and by extension, the two races. That inequality haunts Candy and Becky is further emphasized when Candy thinks that Becky and other Blacks will not be truly equal until Blacks have the right to vote. Thus, inequality haunts the friendship. Furthermore,

Candy realizes a flaw within herself concerning Becky's having an inferior status to her. Jones states, "But if she wasn't able to accept the idea of a black government, then it was hypocritical for her to talk of wanting Becky to be treated as her equal" (98). These thoughts immediately cause Candy to realize how "damned difficult" (98) an interracial friendship can be, for it forces one to evaluate oneself in light of both personal and political factors. And Candy is only aware that at times she comes up short.

Another aspect of the friendship that is an obstacle is the way in which Becky often forces a negative racialism onto her relationship with Candy. Once when they meet, Becky starts play-acting as if she were an obsequious Black, pleading for work as a wash girl. She continues the 'joke' by calling a drink she is having "[I]nstant picanninny" (50), continuing to explain, "Pour into dehydrated picanninny and hey presto! Instant midnight milk, brand name Becky" (50). These unfunny assaults of humor seem designed to throw the naive Candy off balance. By acting in this way, Becky underscores the fact that she is Black and Candy is white — especially in acting like her (Becky's) idea of a Black woman looking for a job. Yet, perhaps this is also a way used unwittingly by Becky that causes Candy not to be able to escape or transcend their racial differences and knowledge of their radically different stations in life. (These facts are especially interesting in light of Abrahams' writing *The Path of Thunder* on race and the odds against transcendence of racism.) Nevertheless, Becky only succeeds in annoying Candy with such displays as the aforementioned ones, as Candy already is desirous of exploring Becky's way of life. Consequently, Becky's attitudes towards race also hinder the progression of the relationship.

In spite of both girls' rocky road to maturity the relationship deepens in part because of Candy's existential realizations which, as stated earlier, signal a growth in her consciousness and her commitment to the friendship.

In comparison with the earlier passages discussing Candy's consciousness, she later makes great strides in this area. Candy's existential revelation is further developed in the book in her thoughts after she realizes the hostility towards Blacks and the immediate assumption of a "business as usual" attitude by the white passengers as a bus for Blacks causes the whites' bus to have a swerve to avoid it. "Savages!" immediately exclaims one woman, followed by several passengers also expressing their hostility towards Black drivers (62).

Coming of Age 159

Candy's attitude is one of sensitivity to how alienated she feels from such whites and how such whites' racism lets them be able to vehemently denounce Blacks and then merely return to their papers, as if the expressing of such racism is merely part of the status quo. Importantly, Jones makes clear Candy's reaction:

> God! Candy thought. We are all fast asleep, complacently caught up in a dream world behind our locked doors of white privilege. But I can't go on like this she realized suddenly. Not any longer. Meeting Becky had jolted her a fraction awake, and now she couldn't fall into the same, self-satisfied sleep, even if she wanted to. The knowledge frightened her, and yet at the same time, she felt it as a strengthening of her resolve. She would not be put off by her parents' nervousness and the policeman's threatening *Pas op!* She already liked Becky tremendously, and she knew that what she had to draw on, in facing up to whatever might lie ahead. (62)

It is this attitude that propels Candy to want to go to Soweto after hearing of the violence there (in contrast to her earlier thoughts that she couldn't imagine ever going to a Black township). Consequently, Candy's existential realizations, as with Ben du Toit in Brink's novel, force her to have to act to try to aid her friend. Moreover, like Ben, Candy's courage is strengthened by Jones's showing not only the girl's commitment to her friend but also her willingness to take action. Though Candy's boyfriend helps so she doesn't have to make the trip (getting information from someone who lives near Becky), her bravery in wanting to make the trip herself shows the growth not only in her feelings towards her friendship with Becky, but also the strength in deciding to act on her feelings.

Go Well, Stay Well and *Home Ground* each make important contributions to fiction on South Africa. Freed once stated, "I am not interested [as subjects] in the future of our universe, in extraterrestrial beings, in political or criminal intrigue."[8] She certainly, subtly touches on 'the future' of Ruth's life in *Home Ground* by tracing it from childhood to adolescence, and tracing her development — or lack thereof — in a setting where racism is deeply ingrained in the individual and society. Also, the novel is a political one, showing the racial attitudes of its heroine and having, one can assume and as Freed implies, Ruth's behavior towards Blacks to be founded in the racial ignorance of much of her — white — South African society. It is interesting that Freed does not see her book as a political work:

I feel terribly helpless about South Africa. It is a beautiful place, it is home. I'm not a revolutionary, I'm a subversive — not a subversive in the political sense but as a writer. Any writer, to be effective, must have this quality. (*New York Times*, 7)

One might wonder how a writer can be subversive without being political. Certainly, Ruth's treatment of Blacks reflects, at times, her being a product of a society in which Blacks were barely recognized as being fully human. Freed conveys clearly this and other actions as a part of Ruth's character; that is, the stasis of her identity.

In contrast, in *Go Well, Stay Well*, Jones's novel is clearly political, showing in bold letters the effects of racism on society and on the individual. Furthermore, one of the most powerful aspects of the novel is that it is clearly subversive, for it shows the racism that is absorbed into the personalities even of those who, like Candy's mother, think of themselves as liberal. It also shows how racism affects the possibility of interracial friendship and the nature of obstacles to such a relationship — something Nadine Gordimer's *A World of Strangers* deals with in depth. Finally, Jones explores how to be more fully human, whites must break away from deeply ingrained racist ideologies in order to shape their identity as individuals who will not be stymied by white South Africa's history of racism. Thus, both *Go Well, Stay Well* and *Home Ground* explore the difficult issues of how identity is forged by the individual in a racially corrupt society. Finally, both works provoke the reader to see the need for whites and Blacks to work to see beyond oppressive racial mythologies in order to forge new race relations and a new South Africa.

Notes

1. Beverley Naidoo, *Journey to Jo'burg* (New York: J.B. Lippincott, 1985), 46.
2. Jane Yolen, *Writing Books for Children* (Boston: The Writer, Inc., 1973), 88.
3. Lynn Freed, *Home Ground* (New York: Summit Books, 1986), 22. All subsequent references are to this edition.
4. James Baldwin, *The Fire Next Time* (New York: Dell Publishing Co., Inc., 1964), 127-28.
5. *Book List*, "*Home Ground*", 8 (1986), 1661. The review states that Ruth comes to see that the Black servants are forcibly disengaged from real life, separated from their children, dying alone (1661).
6. Toeckey Jones, *Go Well, Stay Well* (New York: Harper and Row, 1979), 9. All subsequent references this edition.
7. Paul Laurence Dunbar, "The Lynching of Jube Benson," in *The Heart of Happy Hollow* (New York: Dodd, Mead and Company, 1904), 236.
8. Janette Turner Hospital, "Exit, Pursued by South Africa," *New York Times Book Review,* 17 August 1986: 7.

Conclusion

The Deep Shadow

At this point instead of ending with a traditional conclusion, I would like to play devil's advocate and ask the author frank and rather brutal questions:

> Why remember?
> Why not forget?
> Isn't apartheid over?
> Why think about the past?

The answer to each of these questions — which is, in essence, one question— is a time-worn and true statement: You won't know where you are going if you don't know where you have been. I raise the aforementioned questions of myself in order to be able to articulate the need to continue to study the literature that responds to the key experience that shaped most of South Africa's history of race relations even while a primarily Black government has taken power. Yet, does this fact in itself mean that discussions and studies of racism and apartheid should be buried, as some might assume apartheid has been? To begin to answer this question, a contrast between two *New York Times* articles from 1994 is fitting. First, the titles of the articles raise intriguing issues: first, from June, 1994, is an article entitled "Apartheid's Reminders Quickly Fade." The second, published half a year later and co-authored by a government minister, is entitled "Apartheid Lives On." The first article is fascinating in its detailing the struggle between the desire for some in South Africa to forget the past and those who feel it is essential to remember. Also intriguing is the writer's perhaps unwitting conveyance of the desire of the media and the world to forget both apartheid and South Africa's ongoing struggle to recover from centuries of oppression. The story opens by referring to "these early days of color-blind democracy"[1] while the author, Amy Waldman, goes on to say that while such things that indicate South Africa's history of racism as now obsolete signs that label public places as for whites or Blacks only may still occasionally be seen, they exist only as relics of the past; a past, and a history, some would find it more comfortable to forget:

> [I]t [such signs] is history that is fast disappearing as the rush to embrace a new order threatens to erase the last physical evidence of South Africa's apartheid past. Public signs that divided entrances for whites and non-whites have vanished or were painted over; hovels in camps once occupied by black laborers have been razed or refurbished, and historians worry that documents and other artifacts of oppression will be lost or destroyed along with the country's collective memory. (A10)

Indeed, Waldman's article provokes one to realize the complicated issues of a desire to forget or erase the "collective memory" of such a painful past in contrast with the reasons for the need to remember. A Black man is quoted as saying that when he showed his children his passbook, he could explain and make alive for them the history that he endured for decades. In addition to this personal, oral history, the article tells of more organized efforts by historians and others to preserve the collective memory of apartheid. Waldman refers to the Natal Museum, which has a collection of the relics of apartheid and quotes a co-curator as saying of Blacks, "We've had middle-aged people say, 'We went through this, and you don't understand what it was. It defined who you were'" (A10). Aside from this collection and a few other planned exhibits, it seems that the trend to forget runs strong (indeed, it is mentioned that Americans, particularly African Americans, make up the strongest market of collectors of apartheid era 'memorabilia'). The statements that reflect the trend among some South Africans to want to forget are intriguing. The co-curator of the

Natal Museum states, for instance, "There's amnesia among whites" (A10). Another man, Hilton Judin, planning to put together an exhibition of relics of apartheid, states that he has encountered an attitude among potential sponsors that "it is too soon to focus on the recent past" (A10). Mr. Judin states, "We're at a stage of reconciliation, and remembering runs contrary to that," as being an unspoken motto of those who what to forget (A10). Yet, Mr. Judin's next statements provide some of the strongest evidence for the need to reflect on South Africa's history of racial oppression. Waldman writes, "He said South Africa seemed to undergo a process of what he called, 'amnesty, amnesia, forgetting,' but noted that the point of preserving history was not to apportion blame. 'We must recognize apartheid as our culture. . . . Even if it's not pleasant, it is the most immediate, and only, culture whites and blacks in this country share. . . . It's a couple of years back, not a big distance, and we're still living in the structures and results of segregation, but now people look at it as if that's just the way it is, rather than the way it was meant [by planners and supporters of apartheid] to be" (A10). Furthermore, more poignant are the statements of a Black City Council Security guard, Khazamula Alson Matebula concerning the possible reasons for some people's desire to forget while believing that the racism of the past must be remembered: "It hurts you in your heart when you see how people lived, not like human beings. . . . Maybe [people] should remember how the situation was in the old times, but it's not nice, not nice" (A10).

In reviewing these statements, I find it interesting that the desire to forget seems associated with a false belief that forgetting the painful past means recovering from it. In fact, healing is reached, in part, through reflection on and understanding of the past. Moreover, to reiterate, you won't know where you are going if you don't know where you've been; a fact clear from many of the statements made above.

"Apartheid Lives On" by Kader Asmal, South Africa's Minister of Water Affairs and Forestry, and Ronald Roberts becomes even more relevant in light of President Mandela's statements in December, 1994 that it could be a generation before many Blacks will be able to live in inhabitable housing. Mandela's statements are haunting in light of statements by the authors of "Apartheid Lives On." The authors make assertions which should be remembered by all interested in progress in South Africa:

The first revolution in South Africa ended the legal disenfranchisement of millions of people. The second must overcome the continuing reality of their economic disfranchisement. The American civil rights movement provides a cautionary tale: tragedy overtakes apparent success if economic rights are not pursued after political rights are won. . . . Decent food, water and a livelihood, equal access to a home and a place in school — these basic needs, no less than the right to vote, should now be a cause not only for eloquent handwringing but also constitutional litigation.[2]

Clearly, we can see that the results of the past must be understood and undone in the present. And reflection on the past is intricately bound to understanding and changing the present and the future. And these tasks are no less the responsibility of the writer, whether novelist or literary critic, than of the politician.

Now I would like to return to an analysis of the novels which are the subject of this study.

The important questions to ask here include what is the trajectory of the South African novels under discussion regarding their depictions of the connection between racial conflict and identity? What aspects of the literature are liberatory myths? And what can we learn from the literature that can be applied to the real, live South African situation?

If we begin with Millin's *God's Stepchildren*, the work is clearly an expression of the author's conflict with people of color and with whites who mingle with them. Millin's conflict is expressed in a number of ways. First, for Millin, there can be no admission that Blacks and people with Black ancestry can be the equal of whites. Second, from Blacks' and so-called 'Coloreds' performances mentally, intellectually, and emotionally, according to Millin, they can never be the equal of whites. Third, those whites who are 'deluded' enough to follow the 'fad' of human equality are mere fools to Millin. The novel, in sum, is an expression of Millin's literary war against anyone who believes in racial equality.

It is also important to look at some of the larger implications of Millin's novel. MacCrone's analysis of racism includes ideas that are certainly applicable to *God's Stepchildren* (especially the part of the novel involving Edith's campaign to prey on Barry.) Furthermore, MacCrone's theories certainly indicate some of the larger importance of Millin's ideas. He writes:

The Deep Shadow

> In his attempt to deal with, and to master, an anxiety whose main sources are subjective, the white man employs the same mechanisms in his treatment of the native as are characteristic of the conventional neurotic. Thus we find displayed in the social attitudes of members of the white group towards the native those very features of aggression and repression, of segregation and isolation, of projection and phobia formation, which represent so many duplications of the defence mechanisms of the neurotic individual. The extra-individual conflicts between the two racial groups are but the intra-individual conflicts within the [white] mind writ large, and until the latter are removed, reduced, or modified, they must continue to exercise their baleful influence upon the race relations and the race contacts of white and black in 'sunny' South Africa.[3]

This passage points out the linkage between dysfunctional (i.e., racist) individuals, groups, and finally how they make up a dysfunctional society, as I discuss in Chapter 3. Hence, one must understand the psychology of racism which has been exhibited in South African society and thus in its literature.

Andre Brink's *A Dry White Season* is also an expression of war — in this case, the war Afrikaners would wage against one of their own if he deviated from mindless support of the racist system. Though this work presents, in the main, a large contrast with *God's Stepchildren*, there is one important link: both works, in different ways, show the extreme hostility one may meet if one believes in human equality and goes against the grain of the status quo. In Millin's work, for example, Andrew Flood was met by the author's — and, in turn, her characters' — deep disapproval and disdain. Similarly, Ben, in Brink's novel, meets with the great opprobrium of those who either staunchly or passively uphold the system under which they live. Thus, in both works, nonconformists are looked upon by those who believe in the racial status quo as being strange and dangerous troublemakers.

Brink's novel not only makes an interesting comparison to Millins'; it also makes a great leap forward in the South African novel. Jonathan's and Gordon's deaths do not merely provide a 'ripped from today's headlines' aura to the book; their deaths are reminders of what such Blacks as Steve Biko and countless others suffered in detention and at the hands of the South African law. Consequently, Brink's novel adds greatly to the literature of racial conflict in raising essential questions concerning life under the brutality of South African racism.

In light of the preceding discussions of Millin's and Brink's novels, the subject of white sterility in the South African novel is especially interesting. For Millin, clearly, 'white is right' — but only those whites who uphold segregation and white supremacy, her novel implies. Gordimer and La Guma, on the other hand, portray in their works the idea that those who upheld the South African system were shallow-minded, and even corrupt, shapers of a society which they either actively or passively attempted to make into a sterile white supremacist haven. Such whites, these authors seem to say, felt they needed such a haven to keep themselves from facing the reality of the country — that they are a small minority in a sea of Blacks and that the only way that such a situation could exist is by a brutal system that is grossly unjust to Blacks. Both Gordimer and La Guma, therefore, expose the corruption underneath the facade of the life that they portray as South Africa under apartheid. Especially important to our discussion of myth and of identity is the fact that these authors are showing that the white personality is corrupted — not made superior — by a system of white supremacy. This is the ultimate irony of the impact of a system of racial superiority on whites.

In contrast to our discussion of the concentration on white sterility in the novels discussed by Gordimer and La Guma, Peter Abrahams' *The Path of Thunder* and Athol Fugard's *Tsotsi* provide graphic depictions of the Black plight. *The Path of Thunder*, for example, shows how racist whites have expressed their conflict with people of color by figuratively raping their lives and characters, if one considers racists' actions against Lanny and Mad Sam, who is "mad" as a result of brutal attack by whites years earlier. Moreover, the whites, as in Brink's much later novel, are brutal in their conflict with non-whites, showing again the impact of racial conflict on white identity. Furthermore, such cruel racism tries to limit the identity of people of color, confronting Lanny with white notions of supremacy. And so, *The Path of Thunder* portrays how racial conflict affects the identities — and the lives — of both whites and non-whites.

Athol Fugard's *Tsotsi* also exposes how the racist system could affect a Black person's identity. Fugard clearly wants the reader to remember that Tsotsi became a *tsotsi* as a result of the system of apartheid, which raped him of his family. And so, his identity has its genesis in the racial situation in South Africa. In addition, one must remember that instead of Tsotsi's being depicted as a villain in his life of crime, Fugard obviously wants the reader to remember the context of Tsotsi's life, in which he comes to feel that life is so worthless that only crime provides meaning. Tsotsi, by the system of apartheid, is stripped of his family, his memory of his identity, and, finally, his life. Thus, the conflict apartheid waged against Blacks who lived under the system is clearly shown as a powerful identity-shaping and life-altering force.

Tsotsi and *The Path of Thunder* may seem to provide an unrelentingly bleak view of the impact of apartheid on Black identities and lives. Yet, both are liberatory mythologies in exposing the inexcusable brutality of South African racism.

The two "Coming of Age" books provide a mixed view. Ruth, in Freed's novel, has an identity in a state of confusion. Part of her wants to believe that she is good-hearted towards Blacks, while at the same time she acts in a very racist and offensive manner towards them. Perhaps Freed is portraying the confusion of whites who want to believe in equality but who have been indoctrinated by a system of white supremacy. Thus, again, South Africa's conflict with Blacks is shown to harm its own white citizen's identities.

Jones's *Go Well, Stay Well* shows the impact of apartheid on both a white and Black girl's identities. The confusion in both girls' identities — their desires to be open and 'equal' but at the same time doing things that undermine this goal — is clearly expressive of a conflict within them brought about by South Africa's conflicts between the races. And though the resolution of the book is hopeful that these conflicts can be overcome, it still is clear that it is a long and difficult process. And so, issues of racial conflict impact negatively upon even those people of good will.

Another form of identity and another liberatory mythology arise in the South African novel as a result of Blacks' willingness to confront racial conflict brought about by racism. This identity — the warrior — takes many forms. Shilling Murile and Mma Tau in La Guma's *Time of the Butcherbird* are two such examples. Another — very different — example is La Guma's Beukes in *In the Fog of the Season's End*. In contrast to Mma Tau's open resistance in the country, Beukes must work covertly in the city to fulfill the work of his dissident network. Finally, an essential aspect of the liberatory mythology the identity of the modern day warrior is that many of them are youths, even children about the ages of five and six. Mbulelo Mzamane's *The Children of Soweto* is a portrayal of the youthful warriors of 1976 — and is also a statement of the persistence of youthful dissidence:

We were the children of the new diaspora, we, the children of Soweto, germinating everywhere we went little new seeds of vengeance, hatred, bitterness, wrath, on the fertile soil of our hearts, watering our cherished seeds with our own blood, sweat and tears and that of our people.[4]

The development of the students' rebellion against being taught in Afrikaans is shown in its genesis in Mzamane's novel. First, the children are politicized even before the policy is implemented by their awareness of the conditions under which they must live. As Mzamane writes, "in our township . . . every passing day brought this toll in human life and saw the untimely death of one brave resident after the other, from the treacherous blades of township *tsotsis* or in the hands of vicious agents of authority" (5-6). Consequently, the children are wiser than their years in being exposed to the brutal aspects of life and knowing of the Nationalist government's complicity in it.

The schoolchildren are also clearly aware of the arrogance involved in the government's policy that they must be taught in Afrikaans. Consequently, they, and some of their teachers, are subversive in teaching and learning in Afrikaans. One teacher, Pakade, possesses, says the narrator, a "satirical mind" (6) and teaches Afrikaans literature in a covertly rebellious manner, causing the students to apply "what we read to assess the attitudes of others [whites] towards us and their own assumptions about themselves" (6). Yet, the students know that while this mild form of subversion is a way of rebelling against the system, more drastic measures are needed.

The schoolchildren's demonstrations and call for a boycott of school are the genesis of their more overt rebellion against the system. Mzamane immediately makes clear that the children may pay a high price for their objections to the racist Nationalist government's educational policy. Police brutality against the students is the authorities' immediate response. As Mzamane writes:

> We came out demonstrating on a cold, wintry morning. But the authorities wouldn't have it. They set police dogs on us. They panel-beat us with police batons. They sprayed us with tear gas. They came out shooting. Army tanks like angry hippos. The contest was too uneven. We retreated in panic, leaving the ground strewn with casualties on both sides. We couldn't match them stone to bullet. But as we retreated, we razed what we could to the ground: their municipality buildings, post offices, beer halls and bottle stores (39-40).

The Deep Shadow

Yet, the children's determination to call for class boycotts even in the face of such a counter-force makes evident that they are not intimidated by the price they must pay for their resistance, including facing arrest and detention.

In fact, Mzamane's novel makes clear the students' desire to resist is, in fact, strengthened by the opposition they face. This strength is shown in the youths' meetings to discuss the state of the country; in their pressure on people who support the government; and in the knowledge they have that they must be prepared to pay the ultimate price — death — for their resistance. This last point is made as the treasurer of the school's student organization states, "Even if they kill me . . . I will not die"(79).

Mzamane's novel is filled with such determination even in the face of jailing and death. For this reason, Mzamane stresses that the primary part of the students' identity is their heroism. As is stated at one of the funerals of one of the students:

> I have felt God reigning over the stand taken by these children of Soweto. I look at these little ones, now departed, as having fallen like true soldiers, our veritable heroes . . . they have set us on the path to freedom, as Moses once set the children of Israel on the road to the Promised Land. Children are proclaiming the gospel of social relevance all over the streets of Soweto. The children are seeking the kingdom on earth of which the prophet Isaiah spoke when he said, "Violence shall no more be heard in thy land, wasting nor destruction within thy borders." And, by God, we shall attain unto that kingdom, victory is ours. Freedom in our life-time! (210).

Consequently, one can see that the schoolchildren's rebellion clearly has relevance to the course of the whole country. And this, Mzamane implies, is the true indication of the youths' heroic nature.

Moreover, the youths' rebellion and sacrifices, Mzamane seems to say, will be clearly justified even to the young people's enemies. Quoting a poem read at the funeral of one of the student leaders, Mzamane writes:

> To those who've caused
> The little ones to weep
> To those who've betrayed their brethren
> To those who've brought about the existence
> of widows, widowers, orphans and refugees . . .
> To those who've brandished handcuffs

Set dogs loose to go to our vitals
Pulled triggers and hurled grenades at the unarmed . . .
Let it not be forgotten
That our anger will endure forever
Our lust for freedom is more lasting than all the gold
In the Witwatersrand . . . (211-12)

Thus, the major aspects of the impact of racial conflict on the students' identities are made evident: determination; bravery; and a desire for justice as well as freedom. All of these qualities are brought out by the students' refusal to shrink from conflict with the system, thus metamorphosing them into youthful warriors.

One central point is this: these and other South African novels being produced by authors under segregation or apartheid can give us a glimpse into the past, present and future of the country. Also, one can apply American author Lillian Smith's statement on the American past to South Africa's distant and recent past, both fictional and real. Smith writes metaphorically thoughts about the American South of the 1940s:

A little white town rimmed with Negroes, making a deep shadow on the whiteness. There it lies, broken in two by one strange idea. Minds broken in two. Hearts broken. Conscience torn from acts. A culture split in a thousand pieces. That is segregation.[5]

This passage could easily be adapted to fit South Africa. The image of the 'little white town' surrounded by the Blacks' shadow can remind one of the majority of Blacks whose presence deeply unsettles many whites. And the fragmentation was not merely physical — removals, the gaps between Blacks' and whites' lifestyles — but also emotional. This fragmentation is a main feature of the books under discussion here. "Hearts broken" — think of Lanny and Sarie in *The Path of Thunder* as well as Mad Sam and the other Sarie. "Minds broken" — think of Ben in *A Dry White Season* who, though he has central revelations as a result of his estrangement from 'the way things are,' still suffers emotional anguish as he becomes increasingly rejected by his family and hounded by the security police. "Conscience torn from acts" — this is clear in, among other things, the whites' attitudes towards the injustice done to Blacks in *Time of the Butcherbird* as well as in perhaps the most blatant example, *A Dry White Season*. All of these points are a result of a "culture split in a thousand pieces".

Thus, when one considers Smith's ideas in light of the South African situation and how segregation and apartheid are reflected in the literature, one can see that such writers as Brink, La Guma, and Gordimer, among others, are grappling in their literature with a system which had the power to fragment the individual as well as society.

"A literature which does not constantly and insistently confront, affront, offend — and thereby explore and test and challenge — the reader and the world, is moribund."[6] All of the works under discussion in this study do 'test and challenge.' From Millin's white supremacist view of 'blood' to La Guma's dismantling of whites in *Time of the Butcherbird*, each work provokes the reader to probe both the unique visions of the authors under study and to gain a greater knowledge of what is revealed about life under a racist regime, especially as racism is related to the question of identity. Truly, as a result of reading South African literature, as Brink writes in *Writing in a State of Siege*, "there remains a chance that [people] may be awakened from sleep in order to learn to face their world anew" (127).

"To face the world anew," now that apartheid is dead, means that its legacies must be redressed — and that includes land reform to return much of the land to the Black majority. Deeply entrenched patterns of apartheid will take generations to disappear without an active overturning of these patterns. It would be disingenuous to pretend otherwise.

The fight against prejudiced and racist attitudes is also a difficult one — one which needs more than changes in laws to implement changes in individuals' attitudes. Pettigrew points out this idea of *Prejudice*:

> To sum up, prejudice, like attitudes in general, can serve three important functions for the individual. It can lend meaning to the world; it can help an individual to adjust socially [e.g., it affirms group membership]; and it can externalize an individual's inner problems — as shown in the research on authoritarianism and frustration-aggression. Yet prejudice, in conjunction with discrimination, can also serve an additional function at the societal level. Typically, prejudice and discrimination together act in concert to protect economic and political interests. Negative group attitudes can arise from competitive fears of marginal and vulnerable groups. More often, they are manipulated to reinforce the interests of those who are already in power.[7]

Another central problem to be resolved is the approach-avoidance conflict which has marked the history of Black-white relations in Africa.

One aspect of this conflict has to be dealt with specifically: the exploitive, white racist feeling towards Blacks that "We want your land and your labor but we don't want you." This exploitive approach-avoidance conflict must be exposed as the neurosis it is and it is up to the psychologically afflicted whites to try to overcome the aforementioned conflict.

One overriding theme has run throughout this book, for it runs throughout each novel and throughout life in both South Africa and America. That is, as Mandela quoted DuBois, "The problem of the twentieth century is the problem of the color-line."[8] Moreover, as life and literature attest, for South Africa, reversing the consequences of "the problem of the twentieth century" will be, the challenge of the twenty-first century.

Notes

1. Amy Waldman, "Apartheid's Reminders Quickly Fade," *The New York Times*, 15 June 1994, A10.
2. Kader Asmal and Ronald Roberts, "Apartheid Lives On," *The New York Times*, 16 October 1994, 19.
3. I.D. MacCrone, *Race Attitudes in South Africa* (New York: Oxford University Press,1937), 301.
4. Mbulelo Mzamane, *The Children of Soweto* (Johannesburg: Ravan Press, 1982),244.
5. Lillian Smith, *Killers of the Dream* (New York: W.W. Norton and Company, 1949), 31.
6. Andre Brink, *Writing in a State of Siege* (New York: Summitt Books, 1983), 126.
7. Thomas F. Pettigrew, "Prejudice" in *Prejudice*, ed. Thomas Pettigrew, et al., Cambridge: Harvard University Press, 1982), 19.
8. W.E.B. DuBois, *The Souls of Black Folk* in *Three Negro Classics*, ed. John Hope Franklin (New York: Avon Books, 1965), 221.

Bibliography

Abrahams, Cecil. *Alex La Guma*. Boston: Twayne, 1985.
Abrahams, Peter. *Mine Boy*. London: Heinemann Educational Books, 1946.
―――. *The Path of Thunder*. Chatham, New Jersey: The Chatham Bookseller, 1948.
―――. *Return to Goli*. London: Faber and Faber, 1963.
―――. *Tell Freedom*. New York: The Macmillan Company, 1970.
―――. *A Wreath for Udomo*. New York: Alfred A. Knopf, 1956.
Adam, Barry D. *The Survival of Domination: Inferiorization and Everyday Life*. New York: Elsevier North-Holland, Inc., 1978.
Asmal, Kader and Roberts, Ronald. "Apartheid Lives on." *New York Times*. 16 October 1994.
Baldwin, James. *The Fire Next Time*. New York: Dell Publishing Co., Inc., 1964.
―――. *Nobody Knows My Name*. New York: Dell Publishing Co., Inc., 1964.
Barnett, Ursula A. *Vision of Order: A Study of Black South African Literature in English* (1914-1980). London: Sinclair Browne, 1983.
Barrett, William. *Irrational Man: A Study in Existential Philosophy*. Garden City, New York: Doubleday/Anchor Books, 1958.
Barzun, Jacques. *Race: A Study in Superstition*. New York: Harper and Row, 1965.
Beier, Ulli, ed. *Introduction of African Literature*. Evanston: Northwestern University Press, 1967.
Bell, Derrick. *Faces at the Bottom of the Well*. New York: Basic Books, 1992.
Boas, Franz. *The Mind of Primitive Man*, New York: The Macmillan Company, 1938.
Book List. "Home Ground.": 8 (1986).
Bradshaw, John. *Bradshaw on : The Family*. Deerfield Beach, Florida: Health Communications, Inc., 1988.
Brink, Andre. *A Dry White Season*. New York: Penguin, 1984.
―――. "Writing Against Big Brother: Notes on Apocalyptic Fiction in South Africa." *World Literature Today*, Spring 1984.
―――. *Writing in a State of Siege*. New York: Summit Books, 1983.
Camus, Albert. *Caligula and Three Other Plays*. Translated by Stuart Gilbert. New York: Alfred A. Knopf, Inc. and Random House, 1958.
―――. *The Myth of Sisyphus and Other Essays*. Translated by Justin O' Brien. New York: Alfred A. Knopf, 1965.
Cassirer, Ernst. *The Myth of the State*. Garden City, New York: Doubleday and Company, Inc., 1955.
Chesnutt, Charles W. *The Marrow of Tradition*. Ann Arbor: University of Michigan Press, 1979.

Children of Apartheid. CBS documentary, 12/5/87.

Christian, Barbara. *Black Feminist Criticism.* New York: Pergamon Press, 1985.

Coetzee, J.M. "Blood, Flaw, Taint, Regeneration: The Case of Sara Gertrude Millin." *English Studies in Africa.* 23 January 1980.

Cotton, Walter Aidan. *The Race Problem in South Africa.* Negro Universities Press, 1969.

Dathorne, O.R. *African Literature in the Twentieth Century.* Minneapolis: University of Minnesota Press, 1974.

Davis, Alexander. *The Native Problem.* New York: Negro Universities Press, 1969.

Dunbar, Paul Laurence. *The Heart of Happy Hollow.* New York: Dodd, Mead and Company, 1904.

Fanon, Franz. *Black Skin, White Masks.* Trans. Charles Lam Markham. New York: Grove Press, 1967.

Franklin, John Hope, ed. *Three Negro Classics.* New York: Avon Books, 1965.

Fredrickson, George M. *White Supremacy.* Oxford: Oxford University Press, 1981.

Freed, Lynn. *Home Ground.* New York: Summit Books, 1986.

Fugard, Athol. *Notebooks 1960-1977.* New York: Alfred A. Knopf, 1984.

———. *Tsotsi.* Middlesex, England: Penguin Books, 1983.

Galton, Francis. *Hereditary Genius.* Cleveland: The World Publishing Company, 1962.

Gayle, Addison, Jr. *Richard Wright: Ordeal of a Native Son.* Garden City, New York: Anchor Press/Doubleday, 1980.

———. *The Way of the New World.* Garden City, New York: Anchor Press/ Doubleday, 1975.

Gordimer, Nadine. *The Essential Gesture.* Edited by Stephen Clingman. New York: Alfred A. Knopf, 1988.

———. *The Late Bourgeois World.* New York: Penguin Books, 1966.

———. *Occasion for Loving.* London: Virago Press, 1958.

———. *A World of Strangers.* New York: Penguin, 1958.

Gray, Stephen, ed. *Athol Fugard.* Johannesburg: McGraw-Hill, 1982.

Hakutani, Yoshinuki, ed. *Critical Essays on Richard Wright.* Boston: J.K. Hall and Co., 1982.

Harris, Trudier. *Black Women in the Fiction of James Baldwin.* Knoxville: University of Tennessee Press, 1985.

Harrison, David. *The White Tribe of Africa.* Berkeley: University of California Press, 1981.

Heywood, Christopher. *Nadine Gordimer.* Windsor, Berkshire, England: Profile Books LTD., 1983.

———. *Papers on African Literature.* Sheffield: Department of English Literature, University of Sheffield, 1976.

Hoernle, R.F.A. *South African Native Policy and the Liberal Spirit.* New York: Negro Universities Press, 1969.
Horney, Karen. *Our Inner Conflicts.* New York: W.W. Norton, 1945.
Hospital, Janette Turner. "Exit, Pursued by South Africa." *New York Times Book Review.* 17 August 1986.
Hughes, Langston. *The Ways of Whitefolks.* Alfred A. Knopf, 1933.
Jan Mohammed, Abdul R. *Manichean Aesthetics.* Amherst: University of Massachusetts Press, 1983.
Jones, Toeckey. *Go Well, Stay Well.* New York: Harper and Row, 1979.
King, Martin Luther. *Why We Can't Wait.* New York: New American Library, 1963.
La Guma, Alex. *Time of the Butcherbird.* London: Heinemann Educational Books, 1979.
Lambley, Peter. *The Psychology of Apartheid.* Athens, Georgia: University of Georgia Press, 1980.
Lelyveld, Joseph. *Move Your Shadow.* New York: Penguin Books, 1986.
MacCrone, I.D. *Race Attitudes in South Africa.* New York: Oxford University Press, 1937.
Marks, Shula and Trapido, Stanley, eds. *The Politics of Race, Class, and Nationalism in Twentieth Century South Africa.* New York: Longman, Inc., 1987.
Memmi, Albert. *The Colonizer and the Colonized.* Boston: Beacon Press, 1965.
Malinowski, Bronislaw. *Myth in Primitive Psychology.* London: Kegan Paul, Trench, Trubner and Co. Ltd., 1926.
Millin, Sarah Gertrude. *God's Stepchildren.* Johannesburg: AD Donker, 1986.
———. *The South Africans.* New York: Boni and Liveright, 1927.
Miller, Alice. *For Your Own Good.* New York: Noonday Press, 1990.
Molema, S.M. *The Bantu, Past and Present: An Ethnographical and Historical Study of the Native Races of South Africa.* Cape Town: S.C. Stuick, 1973.
Moodie, T. Dunbar. *The Rise of Afrikanerdom.* Berkeley: University of California Press, 1975.
Moore, Gerald. *Twelve African Writers.* London: Hutchinson and Co., 1980.
Morrison, Toni. *Playing in the Dark.* Cambridge: Harvard University Press, 1992.
Mzamane, Mbulelo. *The Children of Soweto.* Johannesburg: Ravan Press, 1982.
Naidoo, Beverley. *Journey to Jo'burg.* New York: J.B. Lippincott, 1985.
Newby, I.A, *Jim Crow's Defense.* Baton Rouge: Louisiana State University Press, 1965.
Ogungbesan, Kolawole. *The Writing of Peter Abrahams.* London: Hodder and Stoughton, 1979.
Omond, Roger. *The Apartheid Handbook.* Middlesex, England: Penguin Books, 1985.

Parker, Kenneth, ed. *The South African Novel in English*. London: Macmillan Press, 1978.

Pettigrew, Thomas F., et al., ed. *Prejudice*. Cambridge: Harvard University Press, 1982.

Ramparsad, Arnold. *The Life of Langston Hughes*. New York: Oxford University Press, 1986.

Ray, David and Farnsworth, Robert M. *Richard Wright: Impressions and Perspectives*. Ann Arbor: University of Michigan Press, 1975.

Reilly, John M., ed. *Richard Wright: The Critical Reception*. New York: Burt Franklin and Company, Inc., 1978.

Richman, Joseph. "Family Determinants in Suicide Potential." *Identifying Suicide Potential*, ed. Dorothy B. Anderson and Lenora McLean. New York: Behavioral Publications, 1971.

Rubin, Martin. *Sarah Gertrude Millin: A South African Life*. Johannesburg: AD Donker, 1977.

Seale, Bobby. Lecture. Ithaca, New York: Cornell University, 1989.

Shneidman, Edwin S. ed. *Essays in Self-Destruction*. New York: Science House, Inc., 1967.

Smith, Robert B. and Harper, Michael S. *Chant of Saints*. Urbana: University of Illinois Press, 1979.

Schweitzer, Albert. *On the Edge of the Primeval Forest*. London: A. and C. Black, Ltd., 1922.

Thompson, Leonard. *The Political Mythology of Apartheid*. New Haven: Yale University Press, 1985.

Tudor, Henry. *Political Myth*. New York: Praeger Publishers, 1972.

Twain, Mark. *Pudd'nhead Wislon*. New York: New American Library, 1980.

Uhlig, Mark A., ed. *Apartheid in Crisis*. New York: Vintage Books, 1986.

Waldman, Amy. "Apartheid's Reminders Quickly Fade." *The New York Times*. 15 June, 1994.

Watkins, Mel. "A Novelist's Passionate Indictment." *New York Times Book Review* 23 (1980).

Wiley, David and Issacman, Allen, eds. *Southern Africa: Society, Economy and Liberation*. East Lansing: Michigan State University, 1981.

Index

Abrahams, Peter,
Mine Boy, 120;
The Path of Thunder, xiv, xvii, 91, 107-8, 110-12, 114-15, 117-28, 158, 168-69, 172;
Return to Goli, 1, 2, 4, 14, 114, 127;
Tell Freedom, 111, 120, 123, 127
Boas, Franz,
The Mind of Primitive Man, 2, 89
Brink, Andre,
A Dry White Season, xvi, xvii, xxviii, xxx, 69-103, 154, 167, 172;
"Writing Against Big Brother," 79-80;
Writing in a State of Siege, 70, 72, 91-2, 96, 101
Cassirer, Ernst,
The Myth of the State, xxiii, xxiv, xxx, 2, 3, 20
Cotton, Walter Aidan,
The Race Problem in South Africa, 26
Davis, Alexander,
The Native Problem, 29
DuBois, W.E.B.,
"Of the Coming of John," xiv, 108-9, 112-19;
The Souls of Black Folk, xiii, xiv, xxvi, 12, 11-16, 174
Fanon, Franz,
Black Skin, White Masks, xiii, xviii, xix, xx, xxvi, 20, 23, 27
Fredrickson, George M.,
White Supremacy, 108-9

Freed, Lynn,
Home Ground, xvii, 145-52, 159-60, 169
Fugard, Athol,
Boesman and Lena, 136;
Notebooks 1960-1977, 133-34;
Tsotsi, xiv, 107-8, 128-29, 131-37, 140-41, 168-69
Gordimer, Nadine,
"Great Problems in the Street," 54;
"A Letter from Johannesburg," 40, 48, 54-55, 64;
Occasion for Loving, 40, 156; *A World of Strangers*, xv, xvi, 39, 40-49, 65, 90, 156, 160, 168
Hughes, Langston,
"Home," xiv, 108-9, 115-17, 119;
The Ways of Whitefolks, xiv, 109, 111
Jones, Toeckey,
Go Well, Stay Well, xvii, 145-47, 153-60, 169
La Guma, Alex,
Time of the Butcherbird, xv, xvi, xvii, xxix, 40-41, 48-65, 169, 172-73
Lambley, Peter,
The Psychology of Apartheid, 55, 71-72, 74, 92, 95, 102
MacCrone, I.D.,
Race Attitudes in South Africa, xiii, xx, xxii, xxiii, xxvii, xxviii, xxix, xxx, 1, 25-27, 30, 75, 166-67
Mandela, Nelson, vii, viii, xiii, xiv, xxv, 174

Memmi, Albert,
The Colonizer and the Colonized,
3, 4, 10-13, 17
Millin, Sarah Gertrude,
God's Stepchildren, ix, xi, xv,
xviii, xxi, xxiii, xxvi, 2-35,
107, 166-67;
The South Africans, 14, 16, 17,
28-29
Miller, Alice,
For Your Own Good, 69, 76-68,
82, 86-88, 92, 95, 103
Moodie, T. Dunbar,
The Rise of Afrikanerdom, xxix,
61, 94
Newby, I.A.,
Jim Crow's Defense, 13, 15, 28,
31
Pettigrew, Thomas F.,
Prejudice, xxvii, 1, 24-25, 173
Schweitzer, Albert,
*On the Edge of the Primeval
Forest*, 8-10
Thompson, Leonard,
*The Political Mythology of
Apartheid*, xx, xxi, xxii, xxiii,
xxv, 94
Wright, Richard,
American Hunger, 50-51, 64;
Lawd Today, 140;
The Long Dream, 129, 138;
The Outsider, 138, 140;
Native Son, xiv, 108-9, 128-32,
134-40;
Uncle Tom's Children, 138